Modern Mandarin Chinese

Modern Mandarin Chinese is a two-year undergraduate course for students with no prior background in Chinese study. Designed to build a strong foundation in both the spoken and written language, it develops all the basic skills such as pronunciation, character writing, word use, and structures, while placing a strong emphasis on the development of communication skills.

Each level of the course consists of a textbook and workbook in simplified characters. A free companion website provides all the audio for the course with a broad range of interactive exercises and additional resources for students' self-study, along with a comprehensive instructor's guide with teaching tips, assessment and homework material, and a full answer key.

Key changes to this new edition:

■ This revised edition of level 2 introduces over 200 characters and over 400 new vocabulary items.

■ Additional exercises in the workbooks and online support the expanded number of words and characters incorporated into the textbooks.

■ New cross-references between the textbooks, workbooks, and companion website facilitate using all the resources in an integrated manner.

■ The website has been redesigned and greatly enhanced.

Retaining its focus on communicative skills and the long-term retention of characters, the text is presented in simplified characters and pinyin with a gradual and phased removal of pinyin as specific characters are introduced and learned. This approach allows students to focus on the pronunciation and meaning of new words before the corresponding characters are introduced, ensuring they are guided and supported towards reading only in characters.

Claudia Ross is Professor Emerita of Chinese at the College of the Holy Cross, Massachusetts, USA. Her publications include *Modern Mandarin Chinese Grammar: A Practical Guide* (2014), co-authored with Jing-heng Sheng Ma; *Outline of Chinese Grammar* (2004); and *Traditional Chinese Tales: A Course in Intermediate Chinese* (2001).

Baozhang He is Associate Professor Emeritus of Chinese at the College of the Holy Cross, Massachusetts, USA. His publications include *Difficult Grammar Knots Unravelled* (2015), co-authored with Nansong Huang and Wenzi Hu and *Elementary Chinese* (2006), co-authored with Pei-Chia Chen.

Pei-Chia Chen is Lecturer and Academic Coordinator of the Chinese program at UC San Diego, USA. Her publications include *Elementary Chinese* (2006), co-authored with Baozhang He.

Meng Yeh is Teaching Professor in the Center for Languages and Intercultural Communication at Rice University, USA. Her publications include *Chaoyue: Advancing in Chinese* (2010) and *Communicating in Chinese: An Interactive Approach to Beginning Chinese, Student Lab Workbook* (1999).

Praise for the first edition

"I am deeply impressed by the pedagogical considerations that Prof. Ross and her team put into the project. The approaches to teaching Mandarin Chinese in this series reflected the authors' rich knowledge of Chinese grammar and their vast experience in teaching the language. The materials developed are pedagogically well conceived and equally well supported by theories of language learning/teaching. A truly innovative and delightful addition to the Chinese teaching field."

Cecilia Chang, *Associate Professor of Chinese and Chair of the Asian Studies Department at Williams College, USA*

"This text offers a refreshing approach to learning Chinese that is lacking in the vast majority of learning materials. Each dialogue is contextualized so learners better understand how the language is used in a variety of communicative situations. Students learn not only what to say, but how to use the right language in a given context based on their role, and when and where the situation occurs. Sentence pyramid exercises provide a stepped approach that allows students to actually rehearse and perform the dialogues.

"The material is presented in manageable units with clear and concise explanations that are understandable to students not familiar with linguistics jargon. Valuable information on the social and cultural implications of the language is also provided.

"This is one of the few textbooks on the market that delays the introduction of Chinese characters. This insightful approach allows learners to gain a foundation in the spoken language before being inundated with characters to which they have little context in which to place them. Furthermore, these materials use an innovative diglot approach to introduce Chinese characters where newly learned characters are incorporated into pinyin texts. This effectively eases students into reading without overburdening them. By the end of the text, dialogues and other materials are presented almost entirely in Chinese characters. This approach provides excellent spiraling and reinforcement of characters learned."

Matthew Christensen, *Brigham Young University, USA*

Modern Mandarin Chinese

The Routledge Course Textbook Level 2

Second edition

Claudia Ross, Baozhang He, Pei-Chia Chen, and Meng Yeh

Routledge
Taylor & Francis Group

LONDON AND NEW YORK

Second edition published 2022
by Routledge
4 Park Square, Milton Park, Abingdon, Oxon, OX14 4RN

and by Routledge
605 Third Avenue, New York, NY 10158

Routledge is an imprint of the Taylor & Francis Group, an informa business

© 2022 Claudia Ross, Baozhang He, Pei-Chia Chen, and Meng Yeh

The right of Claudia Ross, Baozhang He, Pei-Chia Chen, and Meng Yeh to be identified as authors of this work has been asserted by them in accordance with sections 77 and 78 of the Copyright, Designs and Patents Act 1988.

First edition published by Routledge 2012

British Library Cataloguing-in-Publication Data
A catalogue record for this book is available from the British Library

Library of Congress Cataloging-in-Publication Data
Names: Ross, Claudia, author. | He, Baozhang, 1955– author. | Chen, Pei-Chia, author. | Ye, Meng, 1950– author.
Title: Modern Mandarin Chinese : the Routledge course textbook level 2 / Claudia Ross, Baozhang He, Pei-Chia Chen, and Meng Yeh.
Other titles: Routledge course in modern Mandarin Chinese Textbook level 2 : Simplified characters
Description: 2nd edition. | Abingdon, Oxon ; New York, NY : Routledge, 2021. | Includes bibliographical references and index.
Identifiers: LCCN 2020048692 (print) | LCCN 2020048693 (ebook) | ISBN 9781138101135 (paperback) | ISBN 9781315657196 (ebook)
Subjects: LCSH: Chinese language—Textbooks of foreign textbooks—English. | Mandarin dialects.
Classification: LCC PL1129.E5 R678 2021 (print) | LCC PL1129.E5 (ebook) | DDC 495.182/421—dc23
LC record available at https://lccn.loc.gov/2020048692
LC ebook record available at https://lccn.loc.gov/2020048693

ISBN: 978-1-138-10113-5 (pbk)
ISBN: 978-1-315-65719-6 (ebk)

Typeset in Scala
by Apex CoVantage, LLC

Access the companion website: www.routledge.com/cw/ross

Contents

Communication goals

- Talk about selecting classes and discuss your daily and weekly academic schedules.
- Express your interest in activities and things.
- Report what someone said or asked about.
- Narrate an event indicating the beginning, the middle, and the end.

Key structures

- 忙 **zhe** + action *busy doing an action*
- 回来 *return back to a location*
- 有 **time** 没 **VP** *stating how long an action has not occurred*
- **zuì** 后 *finally*
- 不过 *however*
- 只是 *it is only that*
- **bǐjiào AdjV** *relatively AdjV*
- 对 **(NP or VP)** 有兴 **qu** *interested in (NP or VP)*
- 对 **VP** 有帮 **zhù** *helpful in doing VP*

Key structures

- 一 noun *the entire noun*
- number + 次 *number of times*
- huòzhě *perhaps, or*
- The potential form of resultative verbs: V 得 ending, V 不 ending
- 是 . . . 的 *focusing on details of past events*
- chú 了 noun phrase 以外 *besides NP, except for NP*
- 穿 *wear* vs. dài *wear*

LESSON 21 天气和气候变化 *WEATHER AND CLIMATE CHANGE*

Communication goals

- Talk about the weather, seasons, and climate change.
- Make comparisons.

Key structures

- yuè 来 yuè + AdjV *more and more AdjV*
- guā fēng *it is windy,* 下 xuě *it is snowing,* 下 yǔ *it is raining*
- V 不了 *unable to V*
- Stating that things are alike and not alike with 一样
- Asking questions to confirm assumptions: 不是 VP 吗?
- 变 + AdjV *turn AdjV*
- Making comparisons with 比
- Stating differences with 不同
- The suffix 化 *-ify, -ize*
- zhí 得 + VP *worth V-ing*

LESSON 22 DUÀNLIÀN 身体 *WORKING OUT*

Communication goals

- Talk about different forms of indoor and outdoor sports and exercise.
- Compare two entities in terms of their similarities and differences.
- Decline an invitation by presenting an earlier commitment.

Key structures

- 在 X 上 *from the perspective of X, when it comes to X*
- xiāng 同 *similarities and* 不同 *differences*
- 为了 *for the purpose of, in order to*
- gèng + AdjV *even more AdjV*
- lìng 外 *in addition*
- 走进来 *walk in* and other directional expressions
- AdjV 是 AdjV . . . 可是 *it's AdjV all right, but*
- lián NP 都/也 VP *can't even VP*
- A 没有 B 那么/这么 AdjV *A is not as AdjV as B*
- gòu *enough*

- 来自 **NP** *come from NP*
- 到 **dǐ** *after all, finally*

Key structures

- **AdjV** 不得了 *extremely AdjV*
- **VP** 的 **NPs with the main noun omitted**
- **V** 着 **indicating an ongoing or background event**
- **V duration** 的 **object, another way to express duration**
- 一边 **VP**₁ 一边 **VP**₂ **two actions at the same time**
- 从来 **NEG VP** *don't ever VP; have never done VP*
- **The adverbs** 刚刚 *just completed an action,* 刚才 *just a moment ago,* 等到 *when an action is completed*

Acknowledgments

We thank all of the people who have been involved in the development of this course: our editors for their guidance and patience, our families for their ongoing support and their confidence in our work, and the students in intermediate Chinese at the College of the Holy Cross for their patience and feedback as we field tested these revised lessons.

The stroke order charts in this book were produced with eStroke software and are included with the permission of EON Media Limited:

www.eon.com.hk/estroke

Introduction

Modern Mandarin Chinese, the Routledge Course is an innovative two-year course for English-speaking learners of Chinese as a foreign language that guides students to build a strong foundation in Mandarin and prepares them for continued success in the language. The course is designed to address the five goals (the 5 C's) of foreign language learning highlighted by the American Council on the Teaching of Foreign Languages (ACTFL). Each *communication*-focused lesson is grounded in the *cultural* context of China, guiding students to make *comparisons* between language and social customs in the United States and the Chinese-speaking world and providing activities that *connect* their language study to other disciplines and lead them to use Chinese in the wider *community*.

Set in China, the course introduces themes that students encounter in their first experience abroad and prepares them to converse, read, and write in Chinese on everyday topics. The themes in Level 2 include *courses and majors, getting sick and seeing a doctor, weather, sports and exercise, shopping and bargaining,* and *celebrating the Chinese New Year*. This second revised edition incorporates topics and vocabulary of contemporary importance, including climate change, global warming, and internet commerce.

Modern Mandarin Chinese, the Routledge Course includes:

■ Textbook with narratives, dialogues, vocabulary, character lists and stroke order tables, jargon-free explanations of use and structure, *Sentence Pyramids* to illustrate phrase and sentence structure, and Notes on Chinese Culture and language use.

- A comprehensive workbook with extensive communication-focused and skill-focused exercises that target all aspects of each lesson.

- Alphabetically arranged indices for vocabulary and characters.

- A *Student Resources* website with interactive listening practice through *Listening for Information* exercises and *Structure Drills,* audio recordings of narratives, dialogues, vocabulary, and *Sentence Pyramids,* and downloadable character practice sheets.

- A *Teacher Resources* section of the website containing a wealth of communication-based classroom activities, project suggestions, lesson plans, and teaching tips.

Innovative features of *Modern Mandarin Chinese, the Routledge Course*

- Separate introduction of *words* and *characters.* Vocabulary items are presented in pinyin in the lesson in which they are introduced so that students learn the pronunciation and meaning of new words before they learn to read and write them in characters. Character introduction is staggered and selective. Characters are introduced at the second or later occurrence of a vocabulary item in the text, with a focus on the introduction of high-frequency characters. Level 1 introduces approximately 640 words and 250 characters. Level 2 introduces approximately 420 words and 200 characters. Since a single character often serves as a component in many different words, by the end of level 2, the gap between written and spoken vocabulary is small.

- Complete replacement of pinyin by characters. When a character is introduced, it replaces the pinyin form in all subsequent occurrences without additional pinyin support. Students must focus on the character as the primary written form of the Chinese word or syllable.

- Character literacy instruction. Once characters are introduced, workbook exercises guide students to understand the structure of characters and to develop reading and writing strategies.

- Integration of form and function. Structures are introduced to support communication, and *Focus on Literacy* and *Focus on Communication* exercises in the workbook guide students to read, speak, and write for communication.

- "Basic to complex" introduction of grammatical structures. Students build a solid foundation in basic structures before learning more complex variations.

- Recycling. Vocabulary and structures are recycled in successive lessons to facilitate mastery.

Additional features of Level 2

Level 2 begins the transition from the study of colloquial Chinese to that of the formal, written, and spoken language. Features include:

- Presentation of themes in *colloquial* and *formal* contexts. Each lesson includes a dialogue that develops a theme in conversational format and a narrative that develops the same theme in a more formal, written style. This presentation facilitates the *introduction of features of formal, literary language,* including vocabulary, sentence structures, and narrative conventions, and serves as a *transition* to the reading and discussion of formal, written texts in subsequent levels of Chinese language study.

■ Development of written narrative skills in a variety of rhetorical modes: description, narrative, explanation, and persuasion. Lessons introduce features of written narrative including the development of a topic, text cohesion, and parallel structure and use a variety of exercises to guide students to write progressively longer and more complex narratives in a variety of rhetorical modes.

■ Continued focus on an understanding of the structure of characters, including the recognition of radicals and the development of dictionary skills.

■ Continued focus on strengthening listening comprehension skills through longer and more complex spoken passages in the form of speeches, reports, and instructions.

■ Continued focus on the strengthening of oral presentation skills through tasks involving responding to oral messages and summarizing explanations, arguments, and descriptions.

■ Continued focus on the strengthening of interpersonal speaking skills through tasks involving interviews, negotiations, and shared responsibilities.

引言

《*Routledge* 现代汉语课程》是针对母语为英语的学习者编写的一套创新汉语教材。本教材为两年的课程，帮助学生打下坚实的汉语基础并为他们继续在语言学习的成功上做好准备。教材的设计上力求全面反映全美外语教学学会 (ACTFL) 倡导的外语学习的五项目标 (5 C's)。每一课以语言交际为中心，以中国文化为背景，引导学生做中美语言及社会习俗方面的对比，并提供大量的教学活动使学生把语言学习与其他专业知识的学习贯穿起来，以使他们能在更广的范围内使用汉语。

教材的背景是在中国，给学生介绍第一次到中国通常会遇到的情景。第二册教材的情景包括课程与专业、看病、天气、运动与健身、购物与讨价还价、及欢度春节。第二版并适时加入现代人关心的重要课题，如气候变迁、全球暖化与电子商务等相关讨论。

《*Routledge* 现代汉语课程》有简繁体两种版本，内容包括：

- 课本中每一课有叙述、对话、生词、所学的汉字及汉字笔顺表、通俗易懂的用法和结构的介绍、句型扩展、语言常识及中国文化点滴。

- 综合练习本内有大量的针对每课所学内容的信息交际及语言技能的练习。

- 以字母顺序安排的生词、汉字及语法点的索引。

- 学生学习网页：汉字和生词学习卡、可以下载的汉字练习表格、及练习本中的句型操练和听力练习等语音档案。

- 教师资源网页：大量的语言交际的课堂活动、教学建议、课程安排及教学技巧。

《现代汉语课程》的创意性特点：

■ "词"、"字"分开介绍。生词在第一次出现的时候，只以拼音的形式介绍。这样，学生可以先把精力集中在发音、意思及用法上，然后再学汉字。介绍哪些汉字是有步骤有选择的。所介绍的汉字一定在课文的词汇中出现过两次以上，重点介绍使用频率高的汉字。第一册介绍了640个生词，250个汉字。第二册介绍420个生词，200个汉字。因为同一个汉字会在不同的生词中重复出现，到第二册结束的时候，学生所能说的词汇和能写的词汇（汉字）差距是很小的。

■ 汉字全部代替拼音。汉字一经介绍，其拼音形式就不再出现。学生必须学着把注意力集中在汉字上，因为只有汉字才是汉语的词或音节的真正书写形式。

■ 识字教学：针对每课所介绍的汉字，课本和练习本都有相应的练习帮助学生了解汉字的结构，并培养学生阅读和书写的策略。

■ 形式和功能结合：句型结构的介绍是为了便于交际。

■ "由简到难"引进语法结构。学生在充分掌握了简单的语法结构后，再逐步学习较为复杂的结构。

■ 重复。为帮助学生掌握运用，句型和生词在后续几课的课文和练习中尽量重复。

第二册的特点

第二册开始从学习白话的口语过渡到正式的口语和书面语。其特点包括：

■ 在正式和非正式的语境中介绍主题。每课都有对话，以对话的形式发展情景，及一段叙述，同样的情境但以正式的书写的形式呈现。这样的安排易于引进正式的书面语的特征，其中包括词汇、句型、叙述的格式，为学生以后阅读讨论正式书面语起一个过渡的作用。

■ 培养学生叙述不同的情景的语言能力：描写、叙述、解释及说服。课中介绍书写体的特征，包括发挥主题、起承转合、对称结构等，并通过不同的练习引导学生逐步以更长更复杂的段落书写不同情境。

■ 继续加强了解汉字的结构，包括识别偏旁部首、学习使用字典等。

■ 通过更长、更复杂的对话、演说、口头报告及指令等不同的听力材料继续加强听力理解。

■ 通过对口头信息的回答、对解释性文字的总结、辩论及描述继续增强学生的口头表达能力。

■ 通过完成提问、面谈、协商及分派职责等教学任务继续加强学生人际交流的能力。

How to use the resources in this course to learn Chinese

This course consists of a textbook, workbook, and website with a wealth of material designed to help you to learn to speak Mandarin and read and write in Chinese. The following is an overview of the resources, with suggestions to help you do your best work.

Textbook

The textbook presents new material and explanations.

■ Stroke order flow charts show you how to write each new character, stroke by stroke. The *Narrative* and *Dialogue* illustrate the use of words and structures, as well as the cultural conventions of communication associated with each topic.

■ *Use and Structure* notes explain how new structures function and how structures and phrases are used.

■ *Sentence Pyramids* show you how words and phrases are grouped into sentences and help you to understand Chinese word order.

■ *Narrative Structure* explanations show you how to organize information into cohesive essays for different communicative functions.

■ *Language FAQs* and *Notes on Chinese Culture* provide additional information about language use and Chinese culture related to the topic of the lesson.

Workbook

The workbook provides exercises that you can do as homework or in class to practice the words, structures, and themes introduced in each lesson. These include:

■ *Focus on Literacy*

■ *Focus on Structure*

■ *Focus on Communication*

Website

Resources include:

■ *Listening for Information* (*Listening Comprehension*) *exercises*

■ *Structure Drills* to help you strengthen spoken production and oral comprehension of new structures and vocabulary.

■ Audio recordings of vocabulary introduced in each lesson.

■ Audio recordings of the *Sentence Pyramids.*

■ Downloadable *Character Practice Sheets*

■ *Focus on Radicals* files for each lesson, with the characters sorted by radical.

Study Tips

■ Learn vocabulary and characters for each section of the text before your classroom lesson and before you begin working on the workbook exercises. If you don't know the words in a lesson, you can't participate in class and you cannot do the homework. Vocabulary and characters are organized by narrative and dialogue part, making it easier for you to focus on the new words and characters for each section of text. *Regularly review* vocabulary and characters from earlier lessons. Use the resources provided with this course to help you study. Download the character practice sheets from the course website to practice writing characters, and use internet resources that demonstrate dynamic stroke order for characters you are learning. Pay attention to the stroke order presented on the practice sheets so that you learn to write characters correctly. Using the same stroke order each time you write a character helps you to remember the character. Conversely, if you write a character differently each time you write it, your brain will have a hard time remembering it. Listen to the vocabulary audio files on the website to help you review vocabulary. Quiz yourself by using the files as dictation, and aim to write each word you hear with accurate pinyin and tones.

■ Learn the structures. *Focus on Structure* exercises in the workbook are cross-referenced to specific *Use and Structure* notes. Read each *Use and Structure* note before you do each exercise, and follow the model sentences in each note as you complete your work. Work through the *Sentence Pyramids* in the textbook to see how phrases are built up into sentences in Chinese. Use the *Sentence Pyramids* in the textbook and website to test yourself, translating the Chinese column into English and checking your answers, and then translating the English column into Chinese. Listen to the *Sentence Pyramids* on the website and use them as dictation practice, testing your ability to accurately write and interpret what you hear. Work through the *Structure Drills* on the website to practice new structures on your own.

■ Use the *Listening for Information* exercises to develop your listening comprehension skills. Do not expect to understand listening files on your first try. Be prepared to listen to the same passage multiple times in order to train your brain to understand what it hears. Use the pause button as you listen to help you to focus on shorter segments of a longer passage. Help your brain to focus on information by reading the instructions and the answer choices before you listen. The *Structure Drills* provided on the website will also help you to develop your listening skills along with your control of new structures and vocabulary.

■ The *Focus on Communication* exercises will guide you to read and write longer passages in Chinese. The *Focus on Literacy* section of the workbook also includes reading passages that challenge you to read around characters that you do not know, and to make inferences based on the text. While reading, identify the sentence structures in each passage so that you know how words and phrases in the text are related. Identify word boundaries so that you group characters correctly, and look for connecting words that tell you if the text is presenting a sequence, or a description, or an explanation, etc. Before you write, think of what you want to say, and jot down the Chinese structures that you can use to express your meaning. Think of how you want to organize your ideas, and make a list of the connecting words or structures you need for the organization you are planning. After you write, proofread your work to make sure that the characters you have written or typed are correct and are the ones that you intended. When reading or writing, if you cannot remember a character or a vocabulary item, use this as an opportunity to review.

If you spend the time you need to prepare and review, you will have a successful and satisfying Chinese learning experience. Good luck in your studies!

Lesson **17**

Xuǎn
课
Selecting courses

Communication goals
By the end of this lesson, you will be able to:

■ Talk about selecting classes and discuss your daily and weekly academic schedules.
■ Express your interest in activities and things.
■ Report what someone said or asked about.
■ Narrate an event indicating the beginning, the middle, and the end.

Literacy goals
By the end of this lesson, you will be able to:

■ Use connecting words to identify the sequence of events in a narrative.
■ Find characters in a Chinese dictionary using radicals and stroke order.
■ Recognize word families in Chinese.

Key structures
■ 忙 **zhe** + action *busy doing an action*
■ 回来 *return back to a location*
■ 有 **time** 没 **VP** *stating how long an action has not occurred*
■ **zuì** 后 *finally*
■ 不过 *however*

- 只是 *it is only that*
- **bǐjiào** AdjV *relatively AdjV*
- 对 **(NP or VP)** 有兴趣 qu *interested in (NP or VP)*
- 对 **VP**有帮 **zhù** *helpful in doing VP*

Narrative

学校后天就要开学了。 这几天学生们都很忙。 有的忙 zhe xuǎn 课，有的忙zhe买课本。 今天我在学生 cāntīng 看见大为了。他前天刚从美国回来。他说他有三个月没有说中文了，所以他的中文说得很不好。他还说他觉得自己很 **bèn**，三个月没说中文就不会说了。我跟他说，他只是不习惯，过几天，他的中文就会好了。**Zuì** 后他问我学校的书店现在开门不开门。他得去买课本。我说现在才两点钟，一 **dìng** 开。吃了饭以后，我就陪大为去学校的书店买书了。

Narrative vocabulary

				Simplified	Traditional
bèn		*stupid*	adjectival verb	笨	笨
cāntīng		*dining hall, cafeteria*	noun	餐厅	餐廳
guò jǐ tiān	过几天	*after a few days*	conversational expression	过几天	過幾天
huí lai	回来	*come back (to a place), return*	verb	回来	回來
kāi	开	*open*	verb	开	開
kāi mén	开门	*open the door, be open (of a business)*	verb + object	开门	開門
kāi xué	开学	*begin school, school starts*	verb + object	开学	開學

kèběn	课本	*textbook*	noun	课本	課本
mángzhe	忙 zhe	*busy doing something*	adjV + suffix	忙着	忙著
xuǎn		*select*	verb	选	選
xuéshengmen	学生们	*students (plural)*	noun	学生们	學生們
yīdìng	一 dìng	*definitely*	adverb	一定	一定
zhè jǐ tiān	这几天	*these past few days*	noun phrase	这几天	這幾天
zhǐ shì	只是	*it is only that*	adverb phrase	只是	只是
zuì hòu	zuì后	*finally*	adverb phrase	最后	最後

Narrative characters

Character	Pinyin	Meaning/ function	Radical	Phrases	Traditional character
惯	guàn	*habitual**	忄	习惯 xíguàn *be used to, be accustomed to*	慣
陪	péi	*accompany*	阝		陪
所	suǒ	*a place**	戶	所以 suǒyǐ *so, therefore*	所
校	xiào	*school**	木	学校 xuéxiào *school*	校
钟	zhōng	*clock, bell**	钅	一点钟 **yīdiǎn zhōng** *one o'clock* 几点钟? *jǐdiǎn zhōng? what time is it?*	鐘

Dialogue

Part A

国强： 大为，这个学期你 xuǎn 了几门课？

大为： 我一共 xuǎn 了四门，一门中国文 huà，一门音乐，一门 shù 学，还有一门中文课。 你呢？

国强： 我 xuǎn 了经 jì 学，zhèng 治学、wùlǐ、huánjìng guǎnlǐ，和一门英文写作。

大为： 我 yuán 来也想 xuǎn wùlǐ 课，但是 wùlǐ shíyàn 课的时间不 héshì。

国强： 怎么不 héshì？ 你每天都有课吗？

大为： 对，我每天都有课，不过星期五只有一 jié 中文课。我得 lì 用 wùlǐ shíyàn 课的时间在图书馆打工挣钱。

国强： 打工那么 zhòng 要吗？

大为： 我只是想多挣点钱，可以到别的地方去玩儿。

Dialogue Part A Vocabulary

				Simplified	Traditional
bùguò	不过	*but*	conjunction	不过	不過
guǎnlǐ		*management*	noun	管理	管理
héshì		*suitable, appropriate*	adjectival verb	合适	合適
huánjìng		*environment*	noun	环境	環境
huánjìng guǎnlǐ		*environmental management, environmental studies*	noun phrase	环境管理	環境管理
jié		classifier for *class periods*	classifier	节	節
jīngjì	经 jì	*economics*	noun	经济	經濟
lìyòng	lì 用	*use*	verb	利用	利用

mén	门	classifier for *classes*; *door*	classifier noun	门	門
shíyàn		*lab, experiment*	noun	实验	實驗
shùxué	shù 学	*math*	noun	数学	數學
wùlǐ(xué)	wùlǐ (学)	*physics*	noun	物理(学)	物理(學)
wénhuà	文 huà	*culture*	noun	文化	文化
xiězuò	写作	*writing, composition*	noun	写作	寫作
xuéqī	学期	*semester*	noun	学期	學期
yuánlái	yuán 来	*originally*	adverb	原来	原來
zhèngzhì	zhèng 治	*politics*	noun	政治	政治
zhèngzhì xué	zhèng 治 学	*political science*	noun phrase	政治学	政治學
zhòngyào	zhòng 要	*important*	adjectival verb	重要	重要

Dialogue Part A Characters

Character	Pinyin	Meaning/ function	Radical	Phrases	Traditional character
但	dàn	*but*	亻	但是 dànshi *but*	但
方	fāng	*side, direction*	方	地方 dìfang *place*, 方 miàn fāngmiàn *aspect, side*	方
共	gòng	*together**	八	一共 yīgòng *altogether*	共
音	yīn	*sound**	音	音乐 yīnyuè *music*	音
英	yīng	*hero, English**	艹	英文 Yīngwén *English*	英

乐	yuè lè	*music** *happy*	丿	音乐 yīnyuè *music* 快乐 kuàilè *happy*	樂
用	yòng	*use*	用	lì 用 lìyòng *use*, 有用 yǒu yòng *useful*, 用功 yònggōng *hardworking*, 用 kuài 子 yòng kuàizi *use chopsticks*	用
挣	zhèng	*earn*	扌	挣钱 zhèng qián *earn money*	掙

Dialogue

Part B

国强： 听说中国文 huà 课不太难，也很有意思，只是老师 bǐjiào yán。

大为： 我也听说中国文 huà 课的老师有一点 yán。因为我一直对中国文 huà 有兴 qu，所以我早就想 xuǎn 这门课了。在中国生活，多学习一些中国文 huà 很有用，还有，对以后找工作也很有帮 zhù.

国强： 老师 yán 没关系，yán 师 chū 高 tú。再说，你很 cōng 明，也很用功，一 dìng 没问题。

Dialogue Part B Vocabulary

				Simplified	*Traditional*
bāngzhù	帮 zhù	*help*	noun	帮助	幫助
bǐjiào		*relatively, comparatively*	intensifier	比较	比較
cōngming	cōng 明	*smart, intelligent*	adjectival verb	聪明	聰明

guānxi	关系	connection, relationship	noun	关系	關係
xìngqu	兴qu	interest	noun	兴趣	興趣
méi guānxi	没关系	not important	verb phrase	没关系	沒關係
yán		strict	adjectival verb	严	嚴
yán shī chū yán gāo tú	师 chū 高 tú	strict teachers make good students	proverb	严师出高徒	嚴師出高徒
yònggōng	用功	hard working, diligent	adjectival verb	用功	用功
yǒu xìngqu	有兴qu	interested in	verb phrase	有兴趣	有興趣
yǒu yòng	有用	useful	adjectival verb phrase	有用	有用

Dialogue Part B Characters

Character	Pinyin	Meaning/ function	Radical	Phrases	Traditional character
帮	bāng	help	巾	帮助 bāngzhù help	幫
关	guān	close, shut	八	关系 guānxi connection; 没关系 méi guānxi not important	關
活	huó	live	氵	生活 shēnghuó live	活
题	tí	topic*, subject*	页	问题 wèntí problem, question	题

系	xì	*system*	纟/糸	关系 guānxi *connection;* 没关系 méi guānxi *not important*	係
兴	xìng	*prosper**	八	兴 **qu** xìngqu *interest,* 高兴 gāoxìng *happy*	興
因	yīn	*reason**	口	因为 yīnwèi *because*	因
直	zhí	*straight*	目	一直 yīzhí *continuously, directly, direct*	直
作	zuò	*do*	亻	工作 gōngzuò *work* (noun)	作

Days before and after today

the day before yesterday	*yesterday*	*Today*	*tomorrow*	*the day after tomorrow*
前天	昨天	今天	明天	后天

What are you studying?

Accounting 会计学 kuàijì xué	Anthropology 人类学 rénlèi xué	Art 艺术 yìshù	Art History 艺术史 yìshù shǐ	Asian Studies 亚洲研究 Yàzhōu yánjiū	Biology 生物学 shēngwù xué
Biochemistry 生物化学 shēngwù huàxué	Business 商务学 shāngwù xué	Chemical Engineering 化工 huàgōng	Chemistry 化学 huàxué	Civil Engineering 土木 tǔmù	Communications 传播学 chuánbō xué

Computer Science 计算机科学 jìsuànjī kēxué 电脑科学 diànnǎo kēxué	Economics 经济学 jīngjì xué	Education 教育 jiàoyù	Electronic Engineering 电机 diànjī	Engineering 工程学 gōngchéng xué	Geography 地理学 dìlǐ xué
Geology 地质学 dìzhì xué	History 历史 lìshǐ	International Relations 国际关系 guójì guānxì	Law 法学 fǎxué	Linguistics 语言学 yǔyán xué	Literature 文学 wénxué
Math 数学 shùxué	Medicine 医学 yīxué	Music 音乐 yīnyuè	Pharmacy 药学 yàoxué	Philosophy 哲学 zhéxué	Physics 物理学 wùlǐ xué
Political Science 政治学 zhèngzhì xué	Psychology 心理学 xīnlǐ xué	Public Health 公共卫生 gōnggòng wèishēng	Religious Studies 宗教学 zōngjiào xué	Sociology 社会学 shèhuì xué	Theater 戏剧 xìjù

Stroke Order Flow Chart

Character   **Total Strokes**

Narrative

惯	丨	忄	忄	忄	忄	忼	悝	悝	慣	慣	惯				**11**
陪	阝	阝	阝	阵	阵	陪	陪	陪	陪						**10**
所	一	厂	厅	戶	戶	所	所	所							**8**
校	一	十	才	木	术	栌	栌	栌	柼	校					**10**
钟	丿	上	午	钅	钅	钌	钊	钟							**9**

Dialogue A

但	丿	亻	亻	们	伯	但	但								**7**
方	丶	亠	方	方											**4**
共	一	十	艹	共	共	共									**6**
音	丶	二	立	立	立	音	音	音							**9**
英	一	十	艹	艹	苹	苹	英	英							**8**
乐	一	仁	牙	牙	乐										**5**
用	丿	冂	月	月	用										**5**
挣	一	十	才	扩	扩	挣	挣	挣	挣						**9**

Dialogue B

帮	一	二	三	丰	邦	邦	邦	帮	帮						**9**
关	丶	丷	丷	兰	羊	关									**6**
活	丶	冫	氵	汇	汇	汗	汗	活	活						**9**
题	丨	口	日	日	旦	早	是	是	是	是	是	题	题	题	**15**
系	一	乙	玄	玄	系	系	系								**7**
兴	丶	丷	丷	兴	兴	兴									**6**
因	丨	冂	冂	冈	因	因									**6**
直	一	十	十	古	古	直	直	直							**8**
作	丿	亻	亻	作	作	作	作								**7**

Word families

You already know that each Chinese character has its own meaning and pronunciation, and that the pronunciation is one syllable in length. Sometimes a character is a word in itself, but characters also combine with other characters to form new words. For example the character 开 is pronounced kāi, and its basic meaning is to *open* or *turn on*. It occurs in a number of words and phrases that we have already learned: 开始 *begin*, 开车 *drive*, 开门 *open the door*, and 开学 *begin school*. You can see how the basic meaning of 开 kāi, to *open* or *turn on*, contributes to the meaning of the multi-character words in which it occurs. Similarly, the character 学 is pronounced xué and its basic meaning is to *study*. The character 学 occurs in many words and phrases, including 学生 *student*, 学校 *school*, 学期 *semester*, 开学 *begin school*, and 数学 *math*. You can see how the basic meaning of 学 *study* contributes to the words in which it occurs. Words formed by the same character in Chinese are said to belong to the same word family. Knowing that the meanings of the individual characters contribute to the meaning of the new words in which they occur is an important reading skill in Chinese. In this and the following lessons in this book, we will point out word families and will call on you to use this knowledge in various exercises.

Narrative focus: describing a situation

Narratives have a structure, and learning the structure of a Chinese narrative will make it easier for you to read and write narratives, that is, paragraphs and essays, in Chinese. The narrative at the beginning of this lesson describes a situation, a conversation with Dawei. It has the following features:

1. It follows a temporal progression. First, it anchors the situation in time (*just before the start of the semester*). Then, it describes the situation that happened at that time (*a conversation with Dawei*). Finally, it closes the situation by stating an event that follows it (*they went to the bookstore to buy books*).
2. It moves from general to specific. Notice how the essay starts with a description of a broad, general situation (学校后天就要开学了 *the semester is going to begin the day after tomorrow*) to a situation that is specific to the writer (meeting Dawei and having a conversation with him), to a final specific action (going to the bookstore after lunch to buy books).
3. It provides the most detail about the main point of the narrative. We know that this narrative is about a conversation with Dawei because most of the details in the narrative are about that conversation.
4. It uses adverbs and other connecting words to make the structure of the main part of the narrative clear. The connecting words in the main part of the narrative (underlined here) give the conversation a sequential structure:

    他说他有三个月没有说中文了，所以他的中文说得很不好。 他还说他觉得自己很 **bèn**，三个月没说中文就不会说了。 我跟他说，过几天，他的中文就会好。 **Zuì** 后他问我 . . .

Each lesson in this textbook begins with a narrative that provides the context for the following dialogue. Several activities in the workbook and on the companion website will be based on the structure of the textbook narrative. As you read each textbook narrative, pay attention to its structure as well as to its meaning so that you can use the structure in your own essays.

Use and structure

17.1.   学生们 The group plural suffix

The plural suffix 们 is used to indicate the plural form of pronouns (我们 *we, us*, 你们 *you*, 他们 *they, them*). It can sometimes be added to a noun when the noun refers to a group of people.

这几天学生们都很忙。
In the past few days, the students have been very busy.

The group plural suffix 们 can only be used when the plural noun is definite. So, it can be used when referring to *the students* but not *some students*. When the group plural suffix is used, it turns the noun into a collective noun that cannot be enumerated. In other words, group plurals with 们 cannot be preceded by a number plus classifier, and you cannot say:

⊗这三个学生们

The group plural suffix 们 is often used at the beginning of speeches when addressing the audience. For example, the president of the college could begin an address to the student body by saying 学生们 . . .

17.2.   忙 zhe (忙着) + VP *busy doing an action*

To say that someone is busy doing some action, say

Subject 忙 zhe + VP
有的（学生）忙 **zhe xuǎn** 课，有的忙 **zhe** 买课本。
Some (students) are busy selecting classes, some are busy buying textbooks.

忙 **zhe** (忙着) is always followed by a verb or verb phrase.

Zhe (着) is a verb suffix. We will learn how to use it to express other meanings besides *busy doing an action* in later lessons.

> **Practice** ⟩ *Workbook: Focus on Structure 17.1; Focus on Communication 17.4, 17.6, 17.7.*

17.3.   The directional verbs 回来 *come back* and 回去 *go back*

回来 *come back* and 回去 *go back* are **directional verbs**. Directional verbs are formed by a verb of motion followed by either 来 *come* or 去 *go*. In 回来 *come back* and 回去 *go back*, the verb of motion is 回 *return to a place*. 来 *come* and 去 *go* indicate whether the movement occurs *towards* (来) or *away from* (去) the speaker or narrator of the situation. Notice that English and Mandarin differ in the order in which the information is conveyed in the equivalent expressions. In English you say *come back* while in Mandarin you say 回来, literally: *return come*. In English you say *go back* while in Mandarin you say 回去, literally: *return go*. We will learn additional directional verbs in Lesson 22.

Notice that 回来 and 回去 are not followed by the subject's destination. When the expression 回来 is used, the destination that is implied is *here*. When the expression 回去 is used, the destination that is implied is *the place that the subject came from*.

他前天刚从美国回来。
He just came back from America the day before yesterday.
你什么时候回去?
When are you going back?

> **Practice** ▶ *Workbook: Focus on Structure 17.2.*

17.4. Indicating how long an action has *not* occurred: 有 X length of time 没(有) VP

To indicate how long an action has not occurred, say:

Subject 有 **length of time** 没(有) VP
他有三个月没有说中文了。
He hasn't spoken Chinese for three months.
我两天没 **shuì** 觉,因为功课太多了。
I didn't sleep for two days because I had too much course work.

When 了 occurs at the end of the sentence, the sentence means that the action has not occurred all the way up to the moment of speaking:

他有三个月没说中文了。
He hasn't spoken Chinese for three months (including right up to the present time).

Notice that the time phrase occurs in the sentence where the *time when* phrase typically occurs: after the subject and right before the verb phrase.

> **Practice** ▶ *Workbook: Focus on Structure 17.4.*

17.5. Paired connecting words

Mandarin connecting words sometimes occur in pairs. We have learned two sets of paired connecting words: 因为 . . . 所以 *because . . . therefore* (*Use and Structure* note 10.10) and **suī**然(虽然) . . . 可是/但是 *although . . . but* (*Use and Structure* note 16.4). Each connecting word occurs before a clause or VP, and many times, both connecting words can be used.

因为 . . . 所以:
因为我一直对中国文 **huà** 有兴 **qu**,所以我早就想 **xuǎn** 这门课了。

Because I have always been interested in Chinese culture, I have long wanted to take this class.

suī 然(虽然) . . . 可是 and **suī** 然(虽然) . . . 但是 (可是 and 但是 are equivalent in meaning):

Suī 然我 **yuán** 来也想 **xuǎn wùlǐ** 课，但是/可是 **wùlǐ shíyàn** 课的时间不 **héshì**。

Although I originally also wanted to take physics, but the physics lab time wasn't convenient.

Grammatically speaking, the first connecting word can always be omitted. However, when it occurs, the effect is to emphasize the situation that it precedes. Compare these sentences without the first connecting words to the ones above.

我一直对中国文 **huà** 有兴 **qu**，所以我早就想 **xuǎn** 这门课了。

I have always been interested in Chinese culture, so I have long wanted to take this class.

我 **yuán** 来也想 **xuǎn wùlǐ** 课，可是/但是 **wùlǐ shíyàn** 课的时间不 **héshì**。

I originally also wanted to take physics, but the physics lab time wasn't convenient.

Practice   *Workbook: Focus on Communication 17.2, 17.3, 17.6, 17.7.*

17.6.   说 *say* vs. 告诉 *tell, inform*

说 means *say* and 告诉 means *tell* or *inform*, but both verbs can be used to say that someone *tells* or *informs* someone of something.

When 说 is used to say that the speaker informs someone about something, the sentence has the following structure:

Subject <u>跟 indirect object 说</u> (some information)
我<u>跟他说</u>，过几天，他的中文就会好。
I told him that in a few days his Chinese will be okay.

说 cannot be followed by the indirect object, the person who is being informed of something. That is, you cannot say:

⊗ 我说他，过几天，他的中文就会好。

When 告诉 is used, the sentence has the following structure:

Subject <u>告诉 indirect object</u> (some information)
我<u>告诉他</u>这几天学生都很忙。
I told him that for the past few days the students have all been very busy.

That is, 告诉 *must* be followed by the indirect object, the person who is being informed of something.

Practice   *Workbook: Focus on Structure 17.6.*

17.7. zuì 后 (最后) *finally*

Zuì 后 (最后) *finally* is used to introduce the last piece of information in a list or narrative.

Zuì 后他问我学校的书店现在开门不开门。
Finally, he asked me if the school's bookstore was open.

Zuì 后 (最后) is sometimes called a **sentence adverb** because it can occur at the beginning of a sentence. However, it can also occur right before the verb.

他 **zuì** 后问我学校的书店现在开门不开门。
Finally, he asked me if the school's bookstore was open.

> **Practice** ▶ *Workbook: Focus on Communication 17.5.*

17.8. Asking indirect questions: 他问我书店开门不开门 *he asked me if the bookstore was open*

Direct questions are questions that the speaker poses to the listener, for example: *What time is it?* Indirect questions are questions that are introduced as part of reported speech, for example: *He asked me what time it was.* An indirect question is not followed by a question mark.

In Mandarin, you form an indirect question by prefacing the question with:

(Person₁) 问 (Person₂) *(Person₁) asks (Person₂)*
Direct question: 现在几点钟? *What time is it now?*
Indirect question: 他问我现在几点钟。 *He asked me what time it is now.*

Notice that the order of information in indirect questions is the same as the order of information in direct questions.

那个人是谁?
Who is that person?
她问我那个人是谁。
She asked me who that person is.
你现在去哪儿?
Where are you going?
她问我我现在去哪儿。
She asked me where I was going.

Asking indirect yes-no questions

When the indirect question involves a yes-no question, either the verb-not-verb form or the 吗 form of the question can be used. However, the verb-not-verb form is much more common.

Direct question: 她学中文吗?
Does she study Chinese?
Indirect question: 他问我她学不学中文。
He asked me if she studies Chinese.

Remember that when asking about completed actions with 了 or about past experience with 过 the form of the verb-not-verb question is **V** 了 **(object)** 没有 or **V**过 **(object)** 没有:

> 你吃过中国饭没有？
> *Have you eaten Chinese food before?*
> 他问我我吃过中国饭没有。
> *He asked me if I had eaten Chinese food before.*

Unlike English, no special word is used in Mandarin to introduce indirect yes-no questions. Compare the following indirect questions in Mandarin with their English translations. Notice that yes-no indirect questions in English are usually introduced with the word *if* or *whether*. No words corresponding to *if* or *whether* are used in Mandarin in yes-no indirect questions.

> 他问我明天有没有考试。
> *He asked me if (whether) there is a test tomorrow.*
> 我问我的 **tóngwū** 他今天晚上忙不忙。
> *I asked my roommate if he was busy tonight.*

> **Practice** ▶   *Workbook: Focus on Structure 17.4, 17.5.*

17.9.   一门课 and 一jié 课 (一节课)

The classifier 门 is used when talking about the number of *courses* you are taking. If you are taking Chinese, English, history, and economics this semester, you are taking four *courses*, or 四门课.

> Q: 这个学期你 **xuǎn** 了几门课？
> *How many courses did you select this semester? (How many courses are you taking this semester?)*
> A: 我 **xuǎn** 了四门。
> *I selected four. (I'm taking four.)*

The classifier **jié** (节) refers to class periods. If you have five classes on Wednesdays, you have 五 **jié** 课 (五节课)。

> 我每天都有课，不过星期五只有一 **jié** 中文课。
> *I have classes every day. However, on Friday I only have one Chinese class.*

> **Practice** ▶   *Workbook: Focus on Communication 17.3.*

17.10.   不过 *however*

不过 *however* is a conjunction that indicates contrast. It overlaps in meaning with 可是 and 但是 *but*. 可是 and 但是 have a broader meaning than 不过 and can be used to indicate almost any kind of contrast. 不过, like its English equivalent *however*, presents some kind of qualification, introducing some detail that differs from the general situation.

> 我每天都有课，不过星期五只有一 **jié** 中文课。
> *I have classes every day. However, on Friday I only have one Chinese class.*

Practice ▶ *Workbook: Focus on Communication 17.2, 17.6.*

17.11.   只是 *it is only that*

Use 只是 to introduce one piece of information that is an exception to a general situation. 只是 occurs before a sentence or a verb phrase.

我只是想多挣点钱。
It's just that I want to earn a little money.

听说中国文**huà**课不太难，也很有意思，只是老师**bǐjiào yán**。
I've heard it said that the Chinese culture class is not too hard and that it is very interesting. It's just that the teacher is relatively strict.

Practice ▶ *Workbook: Focus on Communication 17.2, 17.3, 17.4, 17.6.*

17.12.   bǐjiào (比较) AdjV *relatively AdjV*

Bǐjiào (比较**)** *relatively* is an intensifier, like 很 *very*, 真 *really*, 非常 *extremely* and 有点 *a little*. Like all intensifiers, **Bǐjiào (**比较**)** occurs right before an adjectival verb and indicates the intensity of the adjectival verb.

我觉得 **shù** 学课**bǐjiào**难。
I think the math class is relatively difficult.

Practice ▶ *Workbook: Focus on Communication 17.3, 17.4, 17.5, 17.6.*

17.13.   有一点 AdjV *a little AdjV* and AdjV 一点 *a little more AdjV*

We learned the intensifier 有一点 *a little* in Lesson 10, and it occurs in the dialogue in this lesson as well:

听说那个老师有一点 **yán**。
I've heard that that teacher is a little strict.

We learned AdjV 一点 *a little more adjectival verb* in Lesson 14 (*Use and Structure* note 14.2).

Pay attention to the difference between <u>有一点 **AdjV**</u> *a little adjectival verb* and <u>**AdjV** 一点</u> *a little more adjectival* verb.

<u>有一点</u> **is an intensifier and precedes and** describes an adjectival verb.

那本书有一点贵。
That book is a little expensive.
我觉得中文有一点难。
I think that Chinese is a little hard.

<u>AdjV 一点</u> implies a comparison.

可以**piányi**一点吗？
Can it be a little cheaper?

<u>**AdjV** 一点</u> is often used when saying how someone should do some action, implying a comparison with the way that the person is doing the action now.

请你写大一点。
Please write a little bigger.
请你说慢一点。
Please speak a little more slowly.

> **Practice**   *Focus on Communication 17.4, 17.6.*

17.14.   (someone) 对 something 有兴 **qu** *(someone) is interested in something*

To say that someone is interested in something, say

(someone) 对 (something) 有兴 **qu**
我一直对中国文 **huà** 有兴 **qu**。
I've always been interested in Chinese culture.

对 is a preposition and 对 <u>(something)</u> is a prepositional phrase meaning *toward (something)*. The expression 对 (something) 有兴 **qu** *be interested in something* literally means *towards (something) have interest*. Remember that adverbs (一直 *continuously*, 也 *also*, 都 *all, both*, 还 *still*, etc.) precede the entire prepositional phrase + verb phrase.

我们都对中国文 **huà** 有兴 **qu**。
We are all interested in Chinese culture.
我妹妹也对中国文 **huà** 有兴 **qu**。
My younger sister is also interested in Chinese culture.

Since the verb in this structure is 有, to say that someone is *not* interested in something, negate 有 with 没 and say:

(someone) 对 (something) 没有兴 **qu**
我对中国文 **huà** 没有兴 **qu**。
I am not interested in Chinese culture.

> **Practice**   *Workbook: Focus on Structure 17.8; Focus on Communication 17.7.*

17.15.   (subject) 对 **VP** 有帮 **zhù** (帮助) *(something) is helpful in doing VP*

To say that something is helpful in doing something, say:

(something) 对 **VP** 有帮 **zhù**
学习一些中国文 **huà** 对以后找工作也很有帮 **zhù**.
Studying a little Chinese culture will be helpful in finding a job later on.

帮 **zhù** (帮助) bāngzhù is a noun and means *help*. The structure **(something)** 对 **VP** 有帮 **zhù** literally means *something – towards doing some action – is helpful*. The action is typically complex such as looking for a job or selecting a major or understanding some concept.

In Lesson 11 we learned that the verb *(to) help* is 帮. To say that someone helps someone to do something, use the same word order as you would in English and say:

(someone) 帮 **(someone) VP**
你可以帮我买一 **píng** 水吗？
Can you help me buy a bottle of water?
谢谢你帮我 **zhǔnbèi** 下个星期的口试。
Thank you for helping me prepare for next week's test.

帮 often implies that someone helps you by doing something *for* you. That is the implied situation in the sentence above: 你可以帮我买一 **píng** 水吗？

> **Practice** ▷ *Workbook: Focus on Communication 17.6, 17.7.*

17.16.   Verb phrase as the subject of the sentence

In Mandarin, a verb phrase may occur as the subject of the sentence. That is the case in this sentence from the Dialogue:

[多学习一些中国文**huà**] 很有用。
[Studying a little more Chinese culture] is very useful.

多学习一些中国文 **huà** *study a little more Chinese culture* is the subject of the sentence.

17.17.   A Chinese proverb: Yán 师 chū 高 tú *Strict teachers produce good students*

Yán 师 **chū** 高 **tú** is a *Chinese proverb*. It literally means *strict teachers produce high disciples*. Notice that 师 is part of the word 老师 that we have already learned. Proverbs and classical sayings often express words in single syllables. This is because they derive from classical Chinese, a literary language, in which many words consist of a single syllable.

Chinese people often use proverbs and classical sayings to sum up situations. Notice that 谢国强 uses it as the "last word" in the part of the conversation about the strict teacher.

国强：　听说中国文 **huà** 课不太难，也很有意思，只是老师 **bǐjiào yán**。
大为：　我也听说中国文 **huà** 课的老师有一点 **yán**。因为我一直对中国文 **huà** 有兴 **qu**，所以我早就想 **xuǎn** 这门课了。在中国生活，多学习一些中国文 **huà** 很有用，还有，对以后找工作也很有帮 **zhù**.
国强：　老师 **yán** 没关系，**yán** 师 **chū** 高 **tú**。

Introduction to dictionary skills

Each lesson of this course includes a *Stroke Order Flow Chart* that highlights the *radical* in each new character and illustrates the order in which the strokes of the character are written. We learned in Volume 1 of this textbook that radicals often provide useful information about the meaning of a character. It is also important to be able to identify a character's radical because the arrangement of characters in Chinese dictionaries is based on radicals. You have to know how to count strokes correctly, because in a Chinese dictionary, all of the characters that share the same radical are arranged according to their number of strokes.

In this lesson you will learn how to find characters in a dictionary. You will practice this skill in the *dictionary skills* exercise in each chapter of the workbook, where you will be asked to find several characters that you have not yet learned.

At the end of this textbook you will find an Index of Radicals for Simplified Characters and an Index of Radicals for Traditional Characters. As you can see, there are 189 radicals for simplified characters and 214 radicals for traditional characters. Radicals are listed in terms of the number of strokes used to write them, and the radicals are always listed in the order presented in the tables.

All Chinese dictionaries have a character index arranged according to radicals. The radicals are presented in the order in which they appear in the table of radicals, and all characters that share the same radical are listed after the radical. Characters with the same radical are organized according to the stroke order of the *remainder*, the part of the character that excludes the radical. For example, the radical for the character 少 is 小. 少 is written with four strokes, the three strokes used to write the radical 小 plus one more stroke. That one stroke is the remainder. In a dictionary, 少 occurs in the list of characters following the radical 小 that have one stroke in the remainder. The radical for the character 那 is 阝. The remainder consists of four strokes and is listed in a dictionary after the radical 阝, in the group of characters that consist of 阝 and a remainder of four strokes.

When looking up a character in a Chinese character dictionary, follow these steps:

Steps	Example		
1. Identify the radical.	功→力	校 →木	思→心
2. Count the number of strokes in the radical.	力→2	木 →4	心→4
3. Find the radical in the list of radicals.	力→S (31)/T (19)	木→S (81)/T (75)	心→S (76)/T (61)
4. Count the remaining strokes in the character (the total number of strokes used in writing the whole character minus the number of strokes used in writing the radical).	功→3	校→6	思→5
5. Find your character on the list of characters associated with the radical. The pronunciation of the character, or a number for the character, will be presented with the character.	gōng	xiào	sī
6. Look up the pronunciation or the number in the body of the dictionary to find the meaning of the character.	gōng *success, achievement*	xiào *school*	sī *thoughts*

■ We have seen in Level 1 of this textbook that a character may contain several combinations of strokes that could serve as its radical. For example, in the character 功, both 工 and 力 are radicals, but only one of them serves as the radical for the character 功. Since there is only one official radical for each character, you may need several tries to identify the official radical of a particular character. Usually, the part of the character that is the radical is on the left, or, in characters arranged vertically, it is at the top. However, some radicals always occur on the right or at the bottom of a character. As you learn more characters, you will gain a better sense of the location of their radicals.

■ Another example is the character 问/問 wèn *to ask.* 问/問 consists of two parts: 门/門 mén *door* and 口 kǒu *mouth*, both of which are radicals. In this character, 口 kǒu is classified as the radical, and the character is found in a Chinese dictionary among other characters whose radical is 口 kǒu.

■ Some radicals occur in several different forms. For example, the *water* radical 水 shuǐ may occur in the form of "three dot water" in characters such as 江 jiāng *river* and 海 hǎi "ocean."

Language FAQs

前天 *the day before yesterday*, 后天 *the day after tomorrow* and the spatial orientation of time expressions

Most languages use some metaphor for talking about time, since time is something that you cannot hold or see. Chinese, like English, uses a spatial metaphor when talking about days. The Chinese word for *the day before yesterday* literally means *the day in front of you* and the Chinese word for *the day after tomorrow* literally means *the day behind you*. Notice how the metaphor works. You know what happened in the past so it is the time in front of your eyes: 前天. You don't know what is going to happen in the future; it is made up of events you cannot see. If the past is right before your eyes, the future is behind you: 后天。

	Past	Present	Future	
前天	昨天	今天	明天	后天
the day before yesterday	*yesterday*	*today*	*tomorrow*	*the day after tomorrow*

Notice that English uses the opposite metaphor in expressions such as *the past is behind you* and *your future is in front of you.*

Narrative in English

School will begin the day after tomorrow. These days the students are all very busy. Some of them are busy selecting classes, and some of them are busy buying textbooks. Today I saw Dawei in the school cafeteria. He just got back from America the day before yesterday. He said he hadn't spoken Chinese for three months, so he speaks Chinese very poorly. He also said that he thought he was very stupid. He hasn't spoken Chinese for three months and now he can't speak it anymore. I told him that it's only that he's not used to (speaking) it. In a few days his Chinese will be fine. Finally, he asked me if the school bookstore was open right now. He had to buy textbooks. I said it was only 2 o'clock right now; it was certainly open. After eating, I accompanied Dawei to the school's bookstore to buy books.

Dialogue in English

Part A

Guoqiang: Dawei, how many classes are you taking this semester?

Dawei: I'm taking four altogether, one course in Chinese culture, one course in music, one course in math, and also one course in Chinese language. What about you?

Guoqiang: I'm taking economics, politics, physics, environmental management, and English composition.

Dawei: I originally also wanted to take physics, but the lab time wasn't convenient.

Guoqiang: How wasn't it convenient? Do you have classes every day?

Dawei: Yes, I have classes every day. However, on Fridays I only have one Chinese class. I have to use the physics lab time to work at the library and earn some money.

Guoqiang: Is working that important?

Dawei: It's just that I want to earn a little more money (so that) I can go to other places and have fun.

Part B

Guoqiang: I've heard that the Chinese culture class is not too hard and that it is interesting. It's just that the teacher is relatively strict.

Dawei: I have also heard that the Chinese culture teacher is a little strict. Because I have always been interested in Chinese culture, I have long wanted to take this class. Living in China, studying a little more Chinese culture is very useful. Also, it will be helpful when looking for a job later on.

Guoqiang: It doesn't matter if the teacher is strict. Strict teachers produce good students. Also, you are very smart and also very hardworking. It certainly won't be a problem.

🎧 Sentence pyramids

The Sentence Pyramids *illustrate the use of each new vocabulary item and structure introduced in the lesson. Use them to help you to learn how to form phrases and sentences in Mandarin. Supply the English translation for the last line where indicated.*

1 开学 就要开学了 后天就要开学了 学校后天就要开学了。	*school begins* *school begins* *school begins the day after tomorrow* _____
2 很忙 学生们都很忙 这几天学生们都很忙。	*very busy* *the students are very busy* *These past few days the students have been very busy.*
3 xuǎn 课 忙 zhe xuǎn 课 学生忙 zhe xuǎn 课。 有的学生忙 zhe xuǎn 课，有的忙 zhe 买课本。	*select classes* *busy selecting classes* *students are busy selecting classes* *Some students are busy selecting classes, some are busy buying textbooks.*
4 回来 刚回来 刚从美国回来 前天刚从美国回来 大为前天刚从美国回来。	*return* *just returned* *just returned from the United States* *just returned from the United States the day before yesterday* _____
5 说中文 没说中文 三个月没说中文 有三个月没说中文 他有三个月没说中文。	*speak Chinese* *didn't speak Chinese* *didn't speak Chinese for three months* *have not spoken Chinese for three months* _____
6 不会说 不会说了 三个月没说中文就不会说了。 他三个月没说中文就不会说了。	*not able to speak* *not able to speak anymore* *haven't spoken Chinese for three months and can't speak (it) anymore* *He hasn't spoken Chinese for three months and he can't speak it anymore.*

7 很 bèn 自己很 bèn 他觉得自己很 bèn	*very stupid* *self is very stupid* *He thinks that he himself is stupid.*
8 他的中文就会好。 他的中文就会好了。 过几天，他的中文就会好了。	*His Chinese will be okay.* *His Chinese will be okay again.* *After a few days, his Chinese will be okay again.*
9 开门 开门不开门 书店现在开门不开门 学校的书店现在开门不开门 他问我学校的书店现在开门不 开门。 Zuì 后他问我学校的书店现在开门 不开门。	*open for business* *open or not* *bookstore now open or not* *the school's bookstore open or not* *He asked me if the school's bookstore is open or not.* *Finally, he asked me if the school's bookstore is open or not.*
10 去学校的书店买书 我陪大为去学校的书店买书了。	*go to the school's bookstore to buy books* *I accompanied Dawei to the school's bookstore to buy books.*
11 几门课？ 你 xuǎn 了几门课？ 这个学期你 xuǎn 了几门课？	*how many classes?* *How many classes did you select?* _____
12 héshì 时间不 héshì Wùlǐ shíyàn 课的时间不 héshì。	*appropriate* *the time is not appropriate/convenient* *The physics lab time is not convenient.*
13 挣点钱 想多挣点钱 我只是想多挣点钱.	*earn a little money* *want to earn a little more money* *I only want to earn a little more money.*
14 yán bǐjiào yán 老师 bǐjiào yán。 只是老师 bǐjiào yán。	*strict* *relatively strict* *The teacher is relatively strict.* _____
15 有兴 qu 对中国文 huà 有兴 qu 我一直对中国文 huà 有兴 qu.	*be interested in* *be interested in Chinese culture* *I have continuously been interested in Chinese culture.*

16	
xuǎn 这门课	*take that class*
想 xuǎn 这门课	*wanted to take that class*
我早就想 xuǎn 这门课了.	*I have long wanted to take that class.*

17	
帮 zhù	*helpful*
很有帮 zhù	*very helpful*
对找工作很有帮 zhù	*very helpful in looking for work*
对以后找工作也很有帮 zhù	*very helpful in looking for work later*
学习一些中国文 huà 对以后找工作也很有帮 zhù.	*Studying a little Chinese culture is very helpful in looking for work later.*

18	
关系	*connection*
没关系	*it doesn't matter*
有一点 yán, 没关系	*Being a little strict doesn't matter*
老师有一点 yán, 没关系。	_____

19	
高 tú	*strong students (high disciples)*
chū 高 tú	*produce strong students*
Yán 师 chū 高 tú.	*Strict teachers produce strong students.*

20	
很用功	*very hardworking*
很 cōng 明，也很用功	*very smart and also very hardworking*
你很 cōng 明，也很用功。	_____

21	
没问 tí	*not a problem*
难一点没问题。	*It's no problem if it is a little difficult.*

Lesson 18

选 zhuānyè
Selecting a major

Communication goals

By the end of this lesson, you will be able to:

- Talk about academic majors and fields of study.
- Compare the way that college students in the US and college students in China select their major.
- Explain at least one difference between the college application process in the US and in China.

Literacy goals

By the end of this lesson, you will be able to:

- Comprehend and compose noun phrases consisting of a noun and a description.
- Employ strategies for reading complex Chinese sentences.

Key structures

- **A 跟 B 有关系** *A and B are connected, A and B have a relationship*
- **VP 的 NP** *describing nouns with verbs*
- 难道。。。吗 *Do you mean to say that . . . ?*
- 一bān (一般) *on the whole, generally*

- ràng (让)
- 最 **AdjV** *the most AdjV*
- 方面 *perspective,* and 在 ___ 方面 *from the perspective of* ___
- quán (全) + NP *the entire NP*
- 在 **VP** 以后 *after VP*
- situation 怎么bàn (怎么办)?   *what can you do about it?*

Narrative

选 **zhuānyè** 是一 **jiàn** 很重要的事 **qing**。选 **zhuānyè** 跟你的爱好、学习和 **jiāng** 来都有关系。如果选一个你喜欢的 **zhuānyè**，你就会有兴趣。因为你有兴趣，就会学得好。因为学习 **chéngjì** 好，当然就容易找工作。如果 **zhuānyè** 选得不好，学生对 **zhuānyè** 没有兴趣，学的时候就会觉得很累、很 **jǐn** 张，所以 **chéngjì** 也不会好。这样，**bìyè** 以后也就很难找合适的工作。**Zhuānyè** 没有好 **huài**，只是你喜欢不喜欢。中国人常说："行行出 **zhuàngyuán**。"

Narrative vocabulary

				Simplified	Traditional
bìyè		*graduate*	verb	毕业	畢業
chéngjì		*grades, academic record*	noun	成绩	成績
háng háng chū zhuàngyuán	行行出 zhuàngyuán	*every field produces a leading expert*	proverb	行行出 状元	行行出狀 元
hǎo huài	好huài	*good or bad*	noun phrase	好坏	好壞
huài		*bad, broken*	adjectival verb	坏	壞
jiàn		*item (classifier for events and clothing)*	classifier	件	件
jiānglái	jiāng来	*in the future*	time word	将来	將來
jǐnzhāng	jǐn张	*nervous, tense*	adjectival verb	紧张	緊張

				Simplified	Traditional
lèi	累	*tired*	adjectival verb	累	累
shìqing	事qing	*situation, thing (abstract)*	noun	事情	事情
zhuānyè		*major (course of study)*	adjectival verb	专业	專業

Narrative characters

Character	Pinyin	Meaning/ function	Radical	Phrases	Traditional character
爱	ài	*love*	爫	爱好 **àihào** *hobby, interests*	愛
出	chū	*produce, exit**	凵	行行出 **zhuàngyuán** hángháng chū zhuàngyuán *every field produces a leading expert,* **yán** 师出高 **tú** yánshī chū gāotú *strict teachers produce good students*	出
定	dìng	*set, establish*	宀	一定 yīdìng *certainly,* **jué** 定 juédìng *decide, determine*	定
合	hé	*combine*	口	合适 **héshì** *suitable, appropriate*	合
累	lèi	*tired*	糸 / 纟	累死了 lèisǐle *tired to death*	累
趣	qu	*interest**	走	兴趣 xìngqu *interest*	趣
选	xuǎn	*select*	辶		選
适	shì	*suitable**	辶	合适 héshì *suitable, appropriate*	適
重	zhòng	*heavy, important**	里	重要 zhòngyào *important*	重

Dialogue

The situation: While walking to the bookstore, Xie Guoqiang and Zhang Dawei continue their conversation about their studies.

Part A

国强： 你的 **zhuānyè** 是什么？

大为： 我还没有选 **zhuānyè** 呢。

国强： 你已经是二年级的学生了，难道还没有 **zhuānyè** 吗？

大为： 美国的大学生一 **bān** 在二年级的时候才选 **zhuānyè**。学校 **ràng** 学生在大学一年级的时候先选一些不同的课，你可以利用这个 机会看你最喜欢哪些课，看你哪方面最强，对什么最有兴趣， 然后再 **jué** 定你的 **zhuānyè**。你呢？你的 **zhuānyè** 是什么？

国强： 我的 **zhuānyè** 是经济。在中国，学生上大学以前 **zhuānyè** 就已经 **jué** 定了。

Dialogue Part A Vocabulary

				Simplified	Traditional
bùtóng	不同	*different*	adjective	不同	不同
fāngmiàn	方面	*aspect, perspective, side*	noun	方面	方面
jīhuì	机会	*opportunity*	noun	机会	機會
juédìng	jué定	*decide*	verb	决定	決定
nándào	难道	*do you mean to say . . . ?*	adverb	难道	難道
qiáng	强	*strong*	adjectival verb	强	強
ràng		*allow*	verb	让	讓
yībān	一bān	*usually, typically*	adverb	一般	一般
zuì	最	*most*	intensifier	最	最

Dialogue Part A Characters

Character	Pinyin	Meaning/ function	Radical	Phrases	Traditional Character
级	jí	*grade, level**	纟/ 纟	一年级 yī niánjí *first year*	級
利	lì	*advantageous, beneficial**	刂	利用 lìyòng *use*	利
同	tóng	*same**	口	同学 tóngxué *classmate,* 同 wū tóngwū *roommate,* 不同 bùtóng *different*	同
济	jì	*benefit**	氵	经济 jīngjì *economics*	濟
最	zuì	*most*	日	最后 zuìhòu *finally*	最

Part B

大为：还没有上大学怎么就能 **jué** 定 **zhuānyè** 呢？

国强：中国的高中生在 **bìyè** 以前 **cānjiā** 高考。高考是一个 **quán** 国的考试。学生在知道考试的分数以后，开始 **shēn** 请大学和 **zhuānyè**。

大为：如果进了大学以后，你不喜欢你的 **zhuānyè**，怎么 **bàn**？

国强：我想不会不喜欢吧。再说，换 **zhuānyè** 是一 **jiàn** 很麻烦的事 **qing**。

Dialogue Part B Vocabulary

				Simplified	Traditional
cānjiā		*attend, participate in* ^{verb}		参加	參加
fēnshù	分数	*grades, points* ^{noun}		分数	分數

				Simplified	Traditional
gāokǎo	高考	*National University Entrance Exam*	proper noun	高考	高考
gāozhōng	高中	*high school, senior high school*	noun	高中	高中
gāozhōngshēng	高中生	*high school student*	noun phrase	高中生	高中生
jìn	进	*enter*	verb	进	進
quán		*entire**	quantifier	全	全
quánguó	quán 国	*nationwide*	noun phrase	全国	全國
shēnqǐng	shēn 请	*apply*	verb	申请	申請
zěnme bàn	怎么 bàn	*what can you do about it?*	question phrase	怎么办	怎麼辦

Dialogue Part B Characters

Character	Pinyin	Meaning/ function	Radical	Phrases	Traditional character
麻	má	*coarse, numb, hemp*	麻	麻烦 máfan *bother, bothersome*	麻
烦	fán	*Annoy*	火	麻烦 máfan *bother, bothersome*	煩
换	huàn	*change, exchange*	扌		換
能		*can, able to (physical ability)*	月		能
数	shù	*number**	攵	分数 fēnshù *grade(s),* 数学 shùxué *math*	數

Stroke Order Flow Chart

Character   **Total Strokes**

Narrative

爱	´	⺍	⺈	爫	爫	严	罗	爱	爱				10
出	⺄	凵	屮	出	出								5
定	丶	⺊	宀	宀	宁	宇	定	定					8
合	ノ	人	公	合	合	合							6
累	丶	冂	囗	田	田	里	畧	罢	累	累			11
趣	一	十	土	丰	丰	走	走	走	起	赵	赳	趄	趣 趣	15
选	ノ	⺊	屮	生	先	先	先	选	选				9
适	´	二	千	千	舌	舌	舌	活	适				9
重	ノ	二	三	舌	盲	盲	重	重	重				9

Dialogue A

级	⺯	⺰	纟	纟	纫	级							6
利	´	二	千	禾	禾	利	利						7
同	丨	冂	冂	冃	同	同							6
济	丶	冫	氵	氵	汸	沪	汝	济	济				9
最	丶	冂	日	旦	旦	旱	昂	昂	昂	昻	最	最	12

Dialogue B

麻	丶	一	广	广	疒	床	床	床	麻	麻			11
烦	丶	丷	少	火	灯	灯	灯	炉	烦	烦			10
换	一	扌	扌	扩	护	护	护	换	换	换			10
能	⺅	厶	竹	台	台	育	育	能	能	能			10
数	丶	丷	丷	半	米	米	娄	娄	娄	数	数	数	13

Use and structure

18.1.   A 跟 B 有关系 *A and B have a connection, A is related to B*

To indicate that something is related to something else, or that two things share something in common, say:

> **A** 跟 **B** 有关系
> *A is related to B.*
> 选 **zhuānyè** 跟你的爱好有关系。
> *Selecting a major is related to your interests.*

A and B can be nouns, noun phrases, or verb phrases. In this sentence from the narrative, B is a list of things.

> 选 **zhuānyè** 跟你的爱好、学习和 **jiāng** 来都有关系。
> *Selecting a major is related to your interests, your studies, and your future.*

To say that A is unrelated to B say:

> **A** 跟 **B** 没(有)关系
> *A is unrelated to B*
> 这 **jiàn** 事 **qíng** 跟你没(有)关系。
> *This situation has nothing to do with you.*

> **Practice** ▶ *Workbook: Focus on Structure 18.1, 18.2, 18.3, 18.14, 18.15; Focus on Communication 18.2, 18.8.*

18.2.   VP 的 NP *describing nouns with verbs*

In Mandarin, all descriptions of a noun occur before the noun in the following structure, in which the *main noun* is the noun that is being described.

[description 的] main noun

We have seen in Level 1 of this course that the description can be a noun, pronoun, or adjectival verb.

> Description is a noun: [张大为的]手机 *Zhang Dawei's cell phone*
> Description is a pronoun: [我的]手机 *my cell phone*
> Description is an adjectival verb: [很贵的]手机 *a very expensive cell phone*

In this lesson, we see that the description can also include a verb.

> [你喜欢的] **zhuānyè** *a major that you like*
> 如果选一个[你喜欢的] **zhuānyè**，你就会有兴趣。
> *If you select <u>a major that you like</u>, you will be interested (in it).*

As you can see from the English translation, English treats descriptions that include a verb differently from other descriptions. In Mandarin, noun description always takes the same form:

[description 的] main noun

When the description includes a verb, the description phrase has the following properties:

- The description phrase always ends with 的.

- The description phrase does not include 了。

- The order of information in the description follows the order of information in a simple sentence:

subject + (time when) + (location) + (prepositional phrase) + verb + object.
[我昨天看的]电 **yǐng** *the movie that I watched yesterday*
[我给她买的]那本书 *the book that I bought for her*

Omitting the main noun when a description phrase occurs

In earlier lessons, we saw that when the description is a pronoun, noun phrase, or adjectival verb, 的 can sometimes be omitted. 的 is never omitted when the description includes a verb. However, the main noun may be omitted if it is understood from context.

你选的课都很难。我选的（课）都很容易。
The courses that you selected are very difficult. The ones that I selected are very easy.

See also *Use and Structure* note 18.13: Describing a noun with more than one description.

> **Practice** ▶ Workbook: *Focus on Structure 18.4, 18.5, 18.6, 18.7, 18.8; Focus on Communication 18.2, 18.6, 18.7.*

18.3.   好 huài (好坏) *good and bad points* and the juxtaposition of opposites

In Chinese, when opposites are presented together, they can often be interpreted as "A and B" or "A or B" even though the Chinese expression does not include *and* or *or*. Context will let you know whether to translate an expression with *and* or *or*.

Zhuānyè 没有好 **huài**，只是你喜欢不喜欢。
There are no good or bad majors, it is only whether you like or don't like them.

18.4.   行行出 zhuàngyuán *every trade produces a leading expert*

行行出 **zhuàngyuán** (行行出状元) *every trade produces a leading expert* is a Chinese proverb. As with the expression **yán** 师出高 **tú** (严师出高徒) in Lesson 17, it is used to sum up a situation and functions to end the discussion about the topic. In the narrative in this lesson, it suggests that if you enjoy a field of study, you have a good chance of excelling in it. Since every field has a leading expert, maybe you will become that expert. For more about this expression, see *Notes on Chinese culture* at the end of the lesson.

18.5.   难道。。。吗?   *do you really mean to say that . . . ?*

难道。。。吗?   *do you really mean to say that . . . ?* expresses surprise at a situation, given the circumstances. In Part A of the dialogue, 国强 uses it to indicate his surprise that 大为 does not have a major even though he is in his second year at college:

你已经是二年级的学生了,难道还没有zhuānyè吗?
You are already a second year student (a sophomore) and you don't have a major yet? (. . . do you really mean you still don't have a major?)
你已经来美国二十年了,难道你还不会开车吗?
You've already been in the US for 20 years, do you mean to say you can't drive?
你这么忙,难道你有时间陪我吗?
You're so busy, do you really have time to go with me?

难道。。。吗?   is a rhetorical question. It does not call for an answer.

> **Practice**   *Workbook: Focus on Structure 18.11; Focus on Communication 18.4.*

18.6.   一bān (一般) *on the whole, generally*

一 **bān** (一般) *on the whole, generally* is an adverb. It occurs at the beginning of a verb phrase, before the verb and any prepositional phrase associated with the verb. It is used when a statement is true for almost all of the subjects. Dawei uses 一 **bān** (一般) to indicate that generally speaking, American students select their major in their second year.

美国的大学生一bān在二年级的时候才选zhuānyè。
American college students generally don't select their majors until their second year.

Here are additional examples with 一 **bān** (一般):

美国人一 **bān** 都会开车。
Americans generally can all drive.
美国大学生一 **bān** 都住学生 **sùshè**。
American college students generally live in student dormitories.
大学生一 **bān** 喜欢上网买东西。
College students generally like to buy things online.
我一 **bān** 早上六点就起 **chuáng** 了,不过 **zhōumò** 会晚一点起 **chuáng**。
I usually get up at 6, but on the weekends I can get up a little later.
学校 **cāntīng** 一 **bān bǐjiào piányi**,但是不一定好吃。
Student cafeterias are generally relatively cheap, but the food is not necessarily tasty.

> **Practice**   *Workbook: Focus on Structure 18.10.*

18.7.   ràng (让) *let someone do something*

Ràng (让) is a verb and means *let* or *make*. To say that someone or something *lets* someone do something, say:

Subject **ràng** (让) someone VP
学校ràng学生在大学一年级的时候先选一些不同的课。
The school lets the students first take several different courses during their first year.
上课的时候，老师不 **ràng** 我们说英文。
When we attend class, the teacher doesn't let us speak English.

> **Practice** > *Workbook: Focus on Structure 18.12; Focus on Communication 18.1.*

18.8.   最 AdjV *the most AdjV*,   最 stative verb: *the most stative verb*

最 *the most* can occur before an adjectival verb or a stative verb. When it occurs before an adjectival verb, the English equivalent may be expressed with *(the) most AdjV* or with *AdjV-est*, depending upon the AdjV:

最好 *best*
最强 *strongest*
最贵 *most expensive*
最用功 *most hardworking*

When it occurs before a stative verb like 喜欢, it is generally expressed as *the most*:

看你最喜欢哪些课
See which classes you like the most.
看你最喜欢哪些课，看你哪方面最强，对什么最有兴趣。
See which classes you like the most, and see where you are strongest, and what you are the most interested in.

最 AdjV is equivalent to the *superlative* form of adjectives in many languages.

> **Practice** > *Workbook: Focus on Communication 18.2, 18.3, 18.4, 18.5, 18.7.*

18.9.   这方面 *this perspective*, 那方面 *that perspective*, 哪方面 *which perspective*, NP 方面 *from the perspective of NP*

方面 means *aspect, perspective,* or *side.* It is used figuratively in the expressions 这方面，那方面, and 哪方面 to talk about looking at a situation from a particular perspective. As this sentence from the narrative illustrates, the word 方面 itself is often not translated into English in these structures.

你先选一些课，看你哪方面最强，再 **jué** 定你的 **zhuānyè**。
First you select a few classes and see which areas you are strongest in (which aspects you are strongest in), and then you select a major.

Here is an example of the use of 这方面 in a sentence.

我不懂中国学生怎么进大学。这方面，你可以问问谢国强。

I don't understand the process of how Chinese students get into college. For this, you can ask Xie Guoqiang.

Here is another example of the use of 哪方面.

哪方面的事 qing 你一定不会告诉父母?

What things would you definitely not tell your parents?

方面 also occurs in the structure **NP** 方面 *as for NP, when it comes to NP*

NP 方面

她在数学方面不太强，但是文 **huà**、经济方面她很有兴趣。

When it comes to math she is not too strong, but she is really interested in culture and economics.

男女朋友方面的事 **qing** 我一 **bān** 不告诉我父母。

Things having to do with girlfriends and boyfriends I generally don't tell my parents about. (I generally don't tell my parents about things having to do with girlfriends and boyfriends.)

买车方面的事 **qing**，你就去问小王吧。

Concerning things having to do with buying a car, you should go speak with Xiao Wang.

The location word 在 *at, on*, may occur before 这方面, 那方面, 哪方面, and NP 方面. When 在 occurs it does not change the meaning of the sentence. It is simply compatible with the use of 方面 to consider a situation from a particular side or perspective.

> **Practice** ▶ *Workbook: Focus on Structure 18.13; Focus on Communication 18.4.*

18.10.　quán (全) *NP the entire NP*

Quán (全) means *complete* or *all* or *entire*. It occurs before a NP, usually a one-syllable noun. **Quán** (全) + NP means *the entire noun*. In the dialogue, it is part of the phrase **quán** 国的考试 *national exam*:

高中生在 **bìyè** 以前 **cānjiā quán** 国的考试。

Before high school students graduate, they participate in (take) a national test.

The structure **quán** (全) + **NP** forms many Mandarin words. Here are words whose component parts we have already learned. You should be able to see how **quán** (全) contributes to the meaning of each word.

quán 家 (全家) *the entire family*
quán 年 (全年) *the entire year*
quán 天 (全天) *the whole day* (not *half the day*)
quán 面 (全面) *comprehensive (all sides)*
quán 数 (全数) *total amount*
quán 文 (全文) *complete text*
quán 中国 (全中国) *all China*

> **Practice** ▶ *Workbook: Focus on Structure 18.14.*

18.11.   在 VP 以后 *after VP*; 在 VP 以前 *before VP*

This structure builds on the structures VP 以后 *after VP* and VP 以前 *before VP* introduced in Level 1 of this course, in Lessons 12 and 15 (*Use and Structure 12.13* and *15.11*). 在 focuses on the point in time before or after something happens. The following are the sentences from Dialogue B that illustrate the use of this structure:

中国的高中生<u>在 **bìyè** 以前</u> **cānjiā quán** 国的考试，考大学。
Chinese high school students, <u>at the time before they graduate</u>, participate in a national test to test into college.
学生在知道考试的分数以后，开始 **shēn** 请大学和 **zhuānyè**。
<u>At the time after</u> (students) <u>know their test scores</u>, they begin to apply for college and a major.

> **Practice** ▶ *Workbook: Focus on Structure 18.14; Focus on Communication 18.2, 18.6.*

18.12.   怎么 **bàn**? (怎么办?) *what can you do about it?*

The expression 怎么 **bàn**? (怎么办?) *what can you do about it?* asks what can be done about a situation that the speaker thinks is problematic. 怎么 **bàn**? can occur by itself, or it can follow a sentence that states the problem. The following example is from Dialogue B:

如果进了大学以后，你不喜欢你的 **zhuānyè**，怎么 **bàn**?
If after you enter college, you don't like your major, what can you do about it?

大为 considers this a problematic situation, but 国强 does not, as he indicates in his reply:

国强：我想不会不喜欢吧。
I think you won't dislike it.

> **Practice** ▶ *Workbook: Focus on Structure 18.14; Focus on Communication 18.2, 18.3.*

18.13.   Describing a noun with more than one description

In Lesson 10 we learned that nouns can be described by more than one description phrase (*Use and Structure 10.19*). Each description phrase occurs before the main noun, followed by a classifier if it involves a number or specifier, and in all other cases by 的. Noun descriptions involving verbs can also occur along with other descriptions to describe a single noun. Here are some examples. Notice that the main noun occurs only once, after the last description phrase.

这三本	**xīn**的	昨天买的	中文书
these three	*new*	*bought yesterday*	*Chinese books*

these three new Chinese books that were bought yesterday

那两个　　　　我刚认识的　　　中国学生
those two　　*I just met*　　*Chinese students*
those two Chinese students who I just met

在图书馆用的　　非常快的　　　电**nǎo**
use at the library　　*extremely fast*　　*computer*
the extremely fast computers that are used at the library

(See also note 18.2, describing nouns with verbs.)

> **Practice**   *Workbook: Focus on Structure 18.9.*

Strategies for reading complex Chinese sentences

Written language tends to use more complex structures than spoken language does, and this course will help you to build strategies for reading and composing texts with complex structures. In this lesson, we focus on reading complex sentences. Complex sentences involve multiple clauses and often more than one grammatical structure. Let's see how to approach a complex sentence selected from the narrative in this lesson.

> 如果选一个你喜欢的 **zhuānyè**，你就会有兴趣。

Do not begin by trying to translate the sentence word for word from left to right. English structures and Mandarin structures do not "match up" word for word, so this strategy will lead to trouble. Instead, begin by identifying the grammatical structure or structures included in the sentence. In this sentence the major structure is:

> 如果 . . . 就 *if . . . (then)*.
> 如果选一个你喜欢的 **zhuānyè**，你就会有兴趣。
> *If* _____ *(then)* _____

The 如果 clause of the sentence includes 的, the marker of noun description, so you should identify the main noun and the description (*Use and Structure* 18.2). The main noun is the noun that immediately follows 的, **zhuānyè** *major*. Temporarily remove the description [你喜欢的] from the first clause, and then translate the clause:

> 如果选一个 **zhuānyè**，_____
> *If you select a major* _____

Now you are ready to add the description back in:

> 如果选一个[你喜欢的] **zhuānyè**，_____
> *If you select a major that you like*

Finally, look for any structure patterns in the 就 part of the sentence. In this sentence, the 就 part of the sentence includes 有兴趣, which means *be interested*.

Are there any characters or words in the sentences that you have learned but cannot remember? Look them up, review them, and then continue reading:

> 如果选一个你喜欢的 **zhuānyè**，你就会有兴趣。
> *If you select a major that you like, you will be interested (in it).*

🎧 Sentence pyramids

Supply the English translation for the last line where indicated.

I 事 qing 很重要的事 qing 一 jiàn 很重要的事 qing 选 zhuānyè 是一 jiàn 很重要的事 qing。	*situation, matter* *very important matter* *a very important matter* *Selecting a major is a very important matter.*
2 关系 有关系 跟你的爱好有关系 选 zhuānyè 跟你的爱好有关系。	*connection* *has connections, is related to* *is related to your interests* *Selecting a major is related to your interests.*
3 关系 有关系 都有关系 跟学习和 jiāng 来都有关系 跟你的爱好、学习和 jiāng 来都有关系。 选 zhuānyè 跟你的爱好、学习和 jiāng 来都有关系。	*connection* *has connections, is related to* *are all related* *are all related to your studies and future* *are all related to your interests, studies, and future* *Selecting a major is connected to your interests, your studies, and your future.*
4 有兴趣 很有兴趣 对她的专业很有兴趣 她对她的专业很有兴趣。	*be interested* *be very interested* *be very interested in her major* *She is very interested in her major.*
5 不会好 你的 chéngjì 也不会好 如果 zhuānyè 选得不好，你的 chéngjì 也不会好。	*won't be good* *your (academic) record won't be good* *If you don't select your major well, your grades won't be good.*
6 累 觉得很累 一定会觉得很累 如果你对你的学习没有兴趣，你一定会觉得很累。	*tired* *feel very tired* *certainly will feel very tired* *If you are not interested in your studies, you will certainly feel very tired.*
7 好 huài Zhuānyè 没有好 huài。	*good or bad; good and bad* *Majors are neither good nor bad.*

8 工作 什么工作? 找什么工作? bìyè 以后想找什么工作? 你 bìyè 以后想找什么工作?	*job* *what job?* *look for what job?* *after graduating plan to look for what job?* *After you graduate, what kind of job do you plan to look for?*
9 重要 很重要 高中的 chéngjì 很重要吗?	*important* *very important* _____
10 jǐn 张 很 jǐn 张 考试以前我很 jǐn 张 Cānjiā 考试以前我都很 jǐn 张。	*nervous* *very nervous* *before taking tests I am very nervous* _____
11 还没有 zhuānyè 难道还没有 zhuānyè吗? 你已经是二年级的学生了，难道还没有 zhuānyè吗?	*still don't have a major* *do you mean to say you still don't have a major?* *You are already a second year student, do you mean to say you still do not have a major?*
12 zhuānyè 才选 zhuānyè 在二年级的时候才选 zhuānyè 一bān在二年级的时候才选 zhuānyè 大学生一bān在二年级的时候才选 zhuānyè 美国的大学生一bān在二年级的时候才选 zhuānyè。	*major* *only then select a major* *in the second year, only then select a major* *generally speaking, in the second year, only then select a major* *College students, generally speaking, select a major in their second year.* _____
13 不同的课 一些不同的课 先选一些不同的课 学生先选一些不同的课 学校 ràng 学生先选一些不同的课。	*different classes* *several different classes* *first select a few different classes* *students first select several different classes* *The school lets the students first select a few different classes.*
14 强 哪方面最强 看你哪方面最强 学校 ràng 学生先选一些不同的课，看哪方面最强.	*strong* *what areas are you strongest in?* *see what areas you are strongest in* *The school lets the students first select a few different classes, to see what areas they are strongest in.*

15 不懂 哪 fāngmiàn 不懂? 你哪 fāngmiàn 不懂?	*not understand* *which aspect not understand?* *What part don't you understand?*
16 jué 定 已经 jué 定了 zhuānyè 就已经 jué 定了 学生上大学以前, zhuānyè 就已经 jué 定了 在中国, 学生上大学以前 zhuānyè 就 已经jué 定了。	*determine* *already determined* *major is already determined* *before students attend college, (their) major* *is already determined* *In China, before students attend college,* *(their) major is already determined.*
17 quán 国的考试 cānjiā quán 国的考试 在 bìyè 以前, cānjiā quán 国的考试 中国的高中生在bìyè以前 cānjiā quán 国的考试。	*national exam* *participate in (take) a national exam* *at the time before they graduate, they take a* *national exam* *Chinese high school students, before they* *graduate, take a national exam.*
18 怎么 bàn? 不喜欢你的 zhuānyè, 怎么 bàn? 如果你不喜欢你的 zhuānyè, 怎么 bàn?	*what can you do about it?* *not like your major, what can you do about it?*

 Notes on Chinese culture

Going to a university and selecting a major

In China, when you apply for admission to a university or college, you also apply for a major. Although the situation is changing in both mainland China and in Taiwan, the procedure is essentially as follows. Students who wish to attend college take a national college entrance exam in the summer after their senior year of high school (June in mainland China, July in Taiwan). After you receive your score, you list the university and major that you wish to be considered for. You are admitted to a specific department at a specific university based on your exam score. Once you enroll, it is difficult to change majors or to change universities. Therefore, as Guoqiang suggests, you might as well not be unhappy with your major or with your college.

What does Zhuàngyuán mean?

Zhuàngyuán was a title conferred to the scholar who scored the highest in the final level of competition in the Imperial Examinations, a series of examinations held during much of China's history up until the beginning of the 20th century. The Imperial Examinations were used to select candidates for civil service. After each exam, a certain number of candidates moved up to the next level of competition. The person who scored the highest in the highest level of competition received the title of Zhuàngyuán. The chances of becoming a Zhuàngyuán were extremely low, but in every final round of the Imperial Examinations, one person would become a Zhuàngyuán. The competition was intense and the chances were low, but someone would rise to the top. The expression 行行出 **Zhuàngyuán** derives from this system. It means that there will always be someone who will rise to the top of every field. If you are talented and work hard, it might be you.

Narrative in English

Selecting a major is an important thing. Selecting a major is related to your interests, studies, and future. If you select a major that you like, you will be interested in it. Because you are interested in it, you will do well in your studies. Because your academic record is good, of course it will be easy to find a job. If a major is not selected well, students will not be interested in their major, they will feel exhausted when they are studying and very tense, so their academic record won't be good. In this way, after graduating it will be hard to find an appropriate job. There are no good or bad majors, only majors that you like and those that you don't. Chinese people often say: "every field has its leading expert."

Dialogue in English

Part A

Guoqiang: What is your major?

Dawei: I don't have a major yet.

Guoqiang: You are already a sophomore, you mean to say you don't have a major yet!

Dawei: Generally speaking, American college students don't select their major until their sophomore year. The school lets students first select several different classes in their first year. You can use this opportunity to see which classes you like, to see where you are strongest, and what you are most interested in. Afterwards you decide your major. What about you? What is your major?

Guoqiang: My major is economics. In China, before students begin college their major is already decided.

Part B

Dawei: If you haven't started college, how can you decide on a major?

Guoqiang: During the time before they graduate, Chinese high school students take a nationwide exam, the "Gao Kao," to test into college. After students know their exam scores, they begin to apply to a college and to a major.

Dawei: After you enter college, if you don't like your major, what can you do?

Guoqiang: I think you won't dislike it. (It's not likely that you won't like it.) In addition, changing your major is a lot of work (a troublesome thing).

Lesson 19

Shōushi
房间
Straightening up the room

Communication goals

By the end of this lesson, you will be able to:

■ Describe the location of objects in a room.
■ Talk about putting things in locations.
■ Talk about doing actions until you reach a conclusion or result.

Literacy goals

By the end of this lesson, you will be able to:

■ Identify resultative verbs in an extended text.
■ Identify a family of words and phrases built with the verb 打.

Key structures

■ number + classifier + 多 *more than number*
■ Resultative verbs
■ AdjV **jí** 了 (极了)
■ 就是 NP/VP *only, it is only NP/NP*

- 难 **guài** . . . ! *no wonder . . . !*
- **yòu** (又) AdjV₁ **yòu** (又) AdjV₂ *both AdjV₁ and AdjV₂*
- **bǎ** (把) + **NP** *take something and do something with it*
- 非 **VP** 不可 *must VP*
- 不 **bì** + **VP** *do not need to VP*
- 放在 **location** *put (something) at a location* and 放回 **location** *return something to a location*
- 出去 *go out* and 出来 *come out*

Narrative

开学已经一个多星期了。 大为和国强今年还是室友。虽然课都选好了，课本也都买到了，但是这几天他们都非常忙，没有时间 **shōushi** 宿舍，所以宿舍 **luànjí** 了。 这个周末，国强和大为想请同学来开晚会。在同学们来以前，他们一定得 **shōushi** 一下宿舍。

Title and narrative vocabulary

				Simplified	Traditional
fángjiān	房间	*room*	noun	房间	房間
jíle	jí 了	*extremely adjectival verb*	intensifier suffix for adjectival verbs	极了	極了
kāi	开	*convene (a meeting), "have" (a party), drive*	verb	开	開
luàn		*chaotic, disorganized, messy*	adjectival verb	乱	亂
luàn jíle		*extremely chaotic, disorganized, messy*	adjectival verb phrase	乱极了	亂極了
shōushi		*straighten up*	verb	收拾	收拾
wǎnhuì	晚会	*party* (literally: *evening meeting*)	noun phrase	晚会	晚會

Title and narrative characters

Character	Pinyin	Meaning/function	Radical	Phrases	Traditional character
房	fáng	room*	户	房间 fángjiān room, 房子 fángzi house	房
末	mò	end*	木	周末 zhōumò weekend	末
舍	shè	house, dwelling*	舌,八	宿舍 sùshè dormitory	舍
室	shì	room*	宀	室友 shìyǒu roommate, jiào 室 jiàoshì classroom	室
宿	sù	lodge, stay overnight*	宀	宿舍 sùshè dormitory	宿
虽	suī	although*	虫	虽然 suīrán although	雖
周	zhōu	week	口	周末 zhōumò weekend	周, 週

Dialogue

The scene: 国强在房间里打电脑，大为在找东西。

Part A

大为： 你看见我的中文书了吗？ 我找了半天也没找到。

国强： 没看见。 我们的屋子太 luàn 了。Zhuō 子上、 yǐ 子上都有书，地上也有书，就是书 jià 上没有书。喝了一半的牛奶、昨天没吃 wán 的饺子都还在 zhuō 子上。Chuān 过的 chènshān、 kù 子都 rēng 在床上。屋子这么 luàn， 难 guài 你不知道你的中文书在什么地方。

Dialogue Part A Vocabulary

				Simplified	Traditional
bàntiān	半天	*a long time* (literally: *half a day*)	idiom, time phrase	半天	半天
chènshān		*shirt*	noun	衬衫	襯衫
chuān		*wear*	verb	穿	穿
dì	地	*earth, ground*	noun	地	地
kùzi	kù子	*pants, trousers, slacks*	noun	裤子	褲子
jiù shì	就是	*only, it is only that*	adverbial phrase	就是	就是
nánguài	难 guài	*no wonder*	adverb	难怪	難怪
rēng		*throw away*	verb	扔	扔
shūjià	书 jià	*bookcase*	noun	书架	書架
wūzi	屋子	*room*	noun	屋子	屋子
yǐzi	yǐ子	*chair*	noun	椅子	椅子
zhǎodào	找到	*find*	resultative verb	找到	找到
zhuōzi	zhuō子	*table*	noun	桌子	桌子

Dialogue Part A Characters

Character	Pinyin	Meaning/function	Radical	Phrases	Traditional character
脑	nǎo	*brain*	月	电脑 diànnǎo *computer*	腦
饺	jiǎo	*dumpling**	饣	饺子 jiǎozi *dumpling*	餃
奶	nǎi	*milk*	女	牛奶 niúnǎi *milk*	奶
屋	wū	*room*	尸	屋子 wūzi *room,* 同屋 tóngwū *roommate*	屋

Dialogue

Part B

大为： 没 cuò！ 我们的宿舍 yòu zāng ， yòu luàn。 在同学们来以前，一
定得 bǎ宿舍 shōushi 好。

国强： 对， 非 shōushi 不可了。 所以你不 bì特别花时间找课本了。 一
shōushi 好， 就会找到。

Dialogue Part B Vocabulary

				Simplified	Traditional
bǎ		*take*, classifier for chairs*	verb classifier	把	把
bù bì	不 bì	*no need to*	modal verb	不必	不必
cuò		*mistake*	verb	错	错
fēi VP bù kě	非 VP 不可	*must V*	literary expression	非 **VP** 不可	非 VP 不可
huā	花	*spend (time), spend (money); flower(s)*	verb; noun	花	花
méi cuò	没 cuò	*you are not mistaken; you are correct*	negation + verb	没错	沒錯
yòu		*both . . . and; again*	adverb	又	又
zāng		*dirty*	adjectival verb	脏	髒

Dialogue Part B Characters

Character	Pinyin	Meaning/ function	Radical	Phrases	Traditional character
特	tè	special*	牛	特别 tèbié *especially, special*	特
花	huā	spend, waste flower	艹	花钱 huā qián *spend money*, 花时间 huā shíjiān *spend time, waste time*	花

Dialogue

Part C

大为：这么 luàn ， 从哪儿开始 shōushi 呢？

国强：你看我们的 yīfu 都在床上。门外边有 xié，门里边也有几 shuāng xié。 我们先 bǎ 这几件 gānjìng 的 yīfu 放在 guì 子里， zāng yīfu， chòu wà 子，一会儿洗 gānjìng，再 bǎ zhuō 子上和地上的书放回书 jià 上。

大为：好，这些做 wán 以后，别忘了 bǎ xié 都 shōu 起来， bǎ 过期的 bào 纸, zázhì rēng 了。 我来 bǎ 地 sǎo gānjìng. 对了，那 shuāng 白色的 球 xié 可以放在门口，我等一下出去要 chuān。

国强：好， 我先 bǎ chuānghu 打开。现在就开始吧。

Dialogue Part C Vocabulary

				Simplified	Traditional
bàozhǐ	bào 纸	*newspaper*	noun	报纸	報紙
chòu		*smelly, stinky*	adjectival verb	臭	臭
chuānghu		*window*	noun	窗户	窗戶
chūqu	出去	*go out*	verb	出去	出去
dǎkāi	打开	*open*	resultative verb (verb + resultative ending)	打开	打開

				Simplified	Traditional
fàng	放	*put, place (something somewhere)*	verb	放	放
gānjìng		*clean*	adjectival verb	干净	乾淨
guìzi	guì子	*dresser*	noun	柜子	櫃子
guòqī	过期	*expire*	verb	过期	過期
qiúxié	球 xié	*sneakers, athletic shoes*	noun	球鞋	球鞋
sǎo		*sweep*	verb	扫	掃
sǎo dì	sǎo 地	*sweep the floor*	verb + object	扫地	掃地
shōu		*collect*	verb	收	收
shōuqǐlái	shōu 起來	*collect, gather, put away*	verb	收起来	收起來
shuāng		*pair*	classifier	双	雙
wàzi	wà子	*socks*	noun	袜子	襪子
wán		*finish, be finished*	verb	完	完
xié(zi)		*shoes*	noun	鞋(子)	鞋(子)
yīfu		*clothing*	noun	衣服	衣服

Dialogue Part C Characters

Character	Pinyin	Meaning/ function	Radical	Phrases	Traditional character
白	bái	*white*	白		白
边	biān	*side**	辶	里边 lǐbian *inside*	邊

Character	Pinyin	Meaning/ function	Radical	Phrases	Traditional character
床	chuáng	*bed*	广	起床 qǐ chuáng *get out of bed*	床
等	děng	*wait, etc.*	竹	等一下 děng yīxià *wait a minute*	等
放	fàng	*put, begin vacation*	攵	放 **jià** fàng jià *begin vacation*	放
件	jiàn	classifier for *clothing, situations*	亻	一件事 qing yī jiàn shìqing *one matter,* 一件 yīfu yī jiàn yīfu *one article of clothing*	件
球	qiú	*ball*	王	球xié qiúxié *sneakers, athletic shoes,* 打球 dǎ qiú *play ball*	球
色	sè	*color**	色	**yán** 色 yánsè *color*	色
忘	wàng	*forget*	心		忘
纸	zhǐ	*paper*	纟	bào纸 bàozhǐ *newspaper*	紙

Clothing words introduced in this lesson with their classifiers

chènshān *shirt*	一件 chènshān *a shirt*
kùzi *slacks, pants, trousers*	一 tiáo kù 子 *a pair of pants*
qiúxié *sneakers, athletic shoes*	一 shuāng qiúxié *a pair of sneakers*
wàzi *socks*	一 shuāng wà 子 *a pair of socks*
xié(zi) *shoes*	一 shuāng xié（子） *a pair of shoes*
yīfu *clothing*	一件 yīfú *an article of clothing*

Stroke Order Flow Chart

Character												Total Strokes

Narrative

房	、	㇆	尸	户	户	庐	庐	房				8
末	一	二	十	才	末							5
舍	丿	人	仝	仐	全	伞	舍	舍				8
室	、	丷	宀	宀	宏	宖	室	室	室			9
宿	、	丷	宀	宀	宀	宿	宿	宿	宿	宿		11
虽	、	口	口	尸	吕	吕	吊	虽	虽			9
周	丿	刀	冃	冃	冃	用	周	周				8

Dialogue A

脑	丿	刀	月	月	月	胪	胪	脑	脑	脑		10
饺	丿	𠂊	饣	饣	饣	饣	饣	饺	饺			9
奶	𡿨	女	女	奶	奶							5
屋	㇆	㇈	尸	尸	屋	居	居	屋	屋			9

Dialogue B

特	丿	𠂉	牛	牛	牜	牡	牲	牲	特	特		10
花	一	十	艹	艹	艻	芲	花					7

Dialogue C

白	丿	𠂉	白	白	白							5
边	㇆	力	力	边	边							5
床	、	二	广	广	庐	床	床					7
等	丿	𠂊	𠂉	𥫗	竺	竹	竺	竿	笙	等	等	12
放	、	二	方	方	方	放	放					8
件	丿	亻	亻	仁	件	件						6
球	一	二	王	王	王	玎	玎	玡	球	球	球	11
色	丿	𠂊	夕	名	刍	色						6
忘	、	二	亡	亡	忘	忘	忘					7
纸	𡿨	纟	纟	纟	纤	纤	纸					7

Word families: 打

In this lesson, we continue to expand the meaning and uses of 打. The basic meaning of 打 is *hit*, and we can see this meaning very clearly in the verb phrase 打球 *play ball* (literally: *hit the ball*). But 打 also occurs in expressions in which it contributes a meaning that expands from the basic meaning of *hit*. Here are the expressions with 打 that we have learned thus far.

打电话   *make a phone call*
打电脑   *use a computer*
打开   *open (open a door, open a window, open a book)*

Use and structure

19.1.   Number + 多 + classifier (+ noun), number + classifier + 多 (+ noun) *more than some number (of nouns)*

To say *more than some number (of nouns)*, use the word 多 in the <u>number + classifier + noun</u> phrase. Depending upon the precise meaning, 多 may occur either right after the number or right after the classifier.

number + 多 + classifier (+ noun) means *a few more than that number*:

十多年   *11 or 12 or so years*
二十多里路   *21 or 22 or so miles*
八十多块钱   *81 or 82 or so dollars*
三 **bǎi** 多個學生   *a little over 300 students*

number + classifier + 多 (+ noun) means *that number and a fraction more, but less than the next highest whole number*:

十年多 *10 years and a little bit (but less than 11 years)*
一 **suì** 多 *a little more than a year old*
一个多星期 *a little more than one week*
九个多钟 **tóu** *more than 9 hours*
五块多钱 *more than 5 dollars (but less than 6)*
开学已经一个多星期了。
It's already been more than a week since we started school.
(... *a few days more than a week, but less than 2 weeks.*)
我的同屋已经睡了九个多钟 **tóu** 了。
My roommate has already been sleeping for more than nine hours.
(... *but less than 10 hours.*)

19.2.   Resultative verbs

Many action verbs refer to *open-ended* actions, that is, actions that can continue for some period of time. Open-ended action verbs include 吃 *eat*, 找 *look for*, 说 *speak*, 看 *look at*, and **shōushi** (收拾) *straighten up, clean up*. In Mandarin, open-ended action verbs can be followed by a suffix that indicates the result or conclusion of an action. The open-ended action + the suffix forms a *resultative verb*. The suffixes that can follow action verbs to indicate a result or conclusion are called *resultative suffixes* or *resultative complements*. Here are examples of resultative verbs from the dialogue from this lesson.

Open-ended action verb	**+ Resultative suffix**	**= Resultative verb**
看 *look at*	+ 见 *see, perceive*	= 看见 *see*
找 *look for*	+ 到 *locate*	= 找到 *find*
shōushi *straighten up*	+ 好 *do to a successful conclusion*	= **shōushi** 好 *successfully finish straightening up (straighten up until it is neat)*
选 **select**	+ 好 *do to a successful conclusion*	= 選好 *finish selecting courses*
做 *do*	+ **wán** *finish*	= 做 **wán** *finish doing*
买 **buy**	+ 到 *arrive at destination*	= 买到 *successfully buy*
sǎo *sweep*	+ **gānjìng** *clean*	= **sǎo gānjìng** *sweep clean*

Resultative verbs are very common in Mandarin, and it is easy to form them. If an open-ended action verb can have the result or conclusion indicated by a particular ending, the ending can follow the verb. For example, any action that can be *finished* can be followed by the suffix **wán** (完) *finish*. Here are some examples:

说 **wán** *finish saying*
看 **wán** *finish looking* or *finish reading*
写 **wán** *finish writing*
听 **wán** *finish listening*
买 **wán** *finish buying*
唱 **wán** *finish singing*
我刚看 **wán** 那本书。   *I just finished reading that book.*

The resultative ending 好 is similar to **wán** (完) in indicating that an action is finished. But **wán** indicates merely that an action is finished. 好 has the additional meaning that the action has reached a successful conclusion in preparation for some next step. If an action has reached a successful conclusion and something is going to follow, you can say Verb + 好. Here are some examples:

说好 *talk until you reach an agreement*
做好 *finish doing something that you had planned to finish*
选好 *succeed in selecting things*
我的课都选好了。

I've finished selecting my classes. (. . . and I am now ready to start the semester.)

The resultative ending 见 is used to indicate that you perceive something, either through looking or listening. Notice the difference in meaning between the open-ended action verbs 看 and 听 and the resultative verbs 看见 and 听见:

看 *look* 看见 *see*
听 *listen* 听见 *hear*
昨天晚上宿舍的外边有人在唱歌。你听见了吗?
Last night someone was singing outside of the dormitory. Did you hear it?

The resultative ending 到 adds the meaning that the action succeeds in locating something. It goes with action verbs that have to do with acquiring things, like 找 *look for* and 买 *shop*. Here are some examples:

找 *look for*   找到 *find*
买 *shop*   买到 *buy*
听 *listen*   听到 *hear* (same meaning as 听见)
看 *look*   看到 *see* (same meaning as 看见)
吃 *eat*   吃到 *get to eat some food that one was looking for or thinking of*
我的课都选好了,课本也都买到了。
I've selected all of my classes and I've bought all of my textbooks.

The resultative ending **gānjìng** *clean* can be used as a resultative ending for any open-ended action that results in something getting clean. Here are examples:

shōushi *straighten up*   **shōushi gānjìng** *straighten up to the point where it is clean*
sǎo *sweep*   **sǎo gānjìng** *sweep clean*
洗 *wash*   洗 **gānjìng** *wash clean*
我来 **bǎ** 地 **sǎo gānjìng**。
I'll sweep the floor clean.

We will learn additional resultative verb endings in later lessons. You can use the endings in this lesson with any actions that have these results or conclusions.

Negating resultative verbs

To say that you did an action but did not achieve a specific result or conclusion, say 没 resultative verb. The resultative verb in each of the following sentences is underlined here.

没 + **resultative verb**
我找了半天也没找到。
I looked a long time but didn't find it.
我没听懂那 shǒu 歌。 (shǒu is the classifier for *songs*)
I didn't understand (by listening to) that song.

To say that you have done an action but have <u>not yet</u> achieved a specified result or conclusion, negate the resultative verb with 还没:

我还没做 <u>**wán**</u> 功课。**(**功课我还没做 <u>**wán**</u>。**)**
I have not yet finished the homework.

Asking yes-no questions with resultative verbs

To ask a yes-no question with a resultative verb, say:

> **resultative verb** 吗?
> 你看见我的书了吗?
> *Have you seen my book?*

or

> **resultative verb** 了没有
> 你做 **wán** 功课了没有? **(or** 你功课做 **wán** 了没有? **)**
> *Have you finished your homework?*

> **Practice** ▶ *Workbook: Focus on Structure 19.2, 19.3, 19.4, 19.5, 19.6; Focus on Communication 19.3.*

19.3.   AdjV jí 了 (极了) *extremely AdjV*

jí 了 (极了) *extremely* is a special kind of intensifier for adjectival verbs. Unlike the other intensifiers that we have learned such as 很 *very*, 真 *really*, 有一点 *a little*, **bǐjiào** *rather*, and 非常 *extremely*, **jí** 了 (极了) directly follows the adjectival verb and creates a new word meaning *extremely AdjV*. In this lesson, we see it as a suffix for **luàn** *messy, chaotic*:

> 他们的宿舍 **luànjí** 了。
> *Their dorm room is extremely messy.*

The suffix **jí** 了 can only occur with adjectival verbs when they are used as the main verb of the sentence.

> 那个女孩子 **piàoliangjí** 了。
> *The girl is extremely beautiful.*

In its English translation, **jí** 了 is equivalent to the intensifier 非常 *extremely*, but AdjV **jí** 了 differs from 非常 **AdjV** in several ways. Most importantly, AdjV **jí** 了 is more restricted than 非常 **AdjV**. 非常 **AdjV** can serve as the predicate of a sentence and as a description for a noun or NP. In contrast, AdjV **jí** 了 can only serve as the predicate of the sentence. It can never be used to modify or describe a noun or NP.

You can say:

> 他们的宿舍非常 **luàn** 。 **or** 他们的宿舍 **luànjí** 了。
> *Their dorm room is extremely messy.*

You can say:

> 非常 **luàn** 的宿舍
> *an extremely messy dorm room*
> 非常 **piányi** 的书
> *an extremely cheap book*

But you cannot say:

⊗ **luànjí** 了的宿舍

⊗ **piányijí** 了的书

In addition, AdjV **jí** 了 is more colloquial than 非常 **AdjV** and does not normally occur in formal speech or writing.

19.4.   半天 *half a day, a long time* and V 了半天也没 *resultative verb*

半天 literally means *half a day*, but its most common function is as an idiom meaning *a long time*.

> 我找了半天。
> *I looked for a long time.*

Since the idiom 半天 indicates the duration of an action, it always follows the verb.

> 我已经等了半天了。
> *I've already been waiting for a long time.*

半天 is often used in the structure:

> (subject) **V** 了 半天 也 (or 都, or 还) 没 *resultative verb*
> *(someone) did something for a long time but didn't reach a conclusion or result*
> 我找了半天也没找到。
> *I looked for a long time but didn't find it.*
> 我看了半天也没看 **wán** 。
> *I read for a long time but didn't finish reading.*
> 我做了半天也没做 **wán** 。
> *I did it for a long time but didn't finish.*

When the action involves an object, state the verb + object first and say:

> **(subject)** [V + object] [V 了] 半天 也 (or 都, or 还）没 **resultative verb**
> 我做功课做了半天还没做 **wán** 。
> *I have been doing homework for a long time and still haven't finished.*

or, state the object before the first verb, and say:

> **(subject)** object V 了 半天 也 (or 都, or 还) 没 **resultative verb**
> 我功课做了半天还没做 **wán** 。
> *I have been doing homework for a long time and still haven't finished.*

> **Practice** ▶ *Workbook: Focus on Structure 19.6; Focus on Communication 19.2*

19.5.   就是 *only, it is only*

The expression 就是 *only, it is only* is used to indicate an exception. It precedes a noun phrase or a verb phrase. When 就是 is used in the sentence, the main verb phrase typically includes negation. 国强 uses the expression when describing the mess in the dorm room:

Zhuō子上、 **yǐ**子上都有书，地上也有书，就是书 **jià** 上没有书。
There are books on the table, the chairs, and the floor. Only the bookcase doesn't have books.

Here are additional examples of this use of 就是.

我的课都选好了，就是还没买书。
I've selected my classes, I just haven't bought the books.
我的课本差不多都买到了，就是中文课的还没买到。
I've bought almost all of my textbooks, it's just the Chinese textbook that I haven't yet bought.
学生都到了，就是老师还没到。
The students have all arrived. Only the teacher has not yet arrived.
中文的听、说都很容易，就是写字 **bǐjiào** 难。
Chinese listening and speaking are easy. (The listening and speaking part of Chinese is easy.) It's only writing that is rather difficult.

> **Practice** ▶ *Workbook: Focus on Structure 19.7; Focus on Communication 19.4.*

19.6.   难 guài (难怪) *no wonder*

难 guài *no wonder* is an adverb and occurs either at the beginning of a sentence or before a verb phrase if the subject is mentioned in the preceding sentence. Like the phrase *no wonder* in English, it indicates that a situation is what can be expected given the circumstances. The circumstances are typically mentioned in a previous remark. In this sentence from Part A of the dialogue, 国强 comments on the messy room as the circumstances that make it impossible for 大为 to find his Chinese book.

屋子这么 **luàn** ，难 guài 你不知道你的中文书在什么地方。
The room is such a mess, no wonder you don't know where your Chinese book is.

Here are additional example sentences with 难 guài.

你这个学期选了六门课，难 guài 每天都很忙。
You are taking six classes this semester, no wonder you are busy every day.
你差不多每天都上网买东西，难 guài 现在没有钱了。
You buy things online practically every day. No wonder you don't have any money!
Āiya, 我早上忘了吃早饭，难 guài 现在这么 **è**!
Oh my, I forgot to eat breakfast this morning. No wonder I'm so hungry!
Yuán 来你昨天没有 **zhǔnbèi**，难 guài 考得这么 **zāogāo** 。
So you didn't prepare yesterday, of course you made such a mess of this test.

> **Practice** ▶ *Workbook: Focus on Structure 19.11; Focus on Communication 19.1.*

19.7.   yòu (又) AdjV₁ yòu (又) AdjV₂ *both AdjV₁ and AdjV₂*

Yòu AdjV₁ **yòu** AdjV₂ (又 AdjV₁ 又 AdjV₂) is used to indicate that some noun is *both AdjV₁* and *AdjV₂*.

> 我们的宿舍 **yòu zāng, yòu luàn**.
> *Our dorm room is both dirty and messy.*

To convey the meaning *both . . . and*, you need to use two instances of **yòu (又)**, one before each adjectival verb. Ordinarily, the adjectival verbs occur without an intensifier.

> 那个饭馆的 **cài yòu piányi yòu** 好吃。
> *The food in that restaurant is both cheap and good.*
> 他的女朋友 **yòu cōng** 明 **yòu piàoliang** 。
> *His girlfriend is both smart and pretty.*

> **Practice**   *Workbook: Focus on Structure 19.9; Focus on Communication 19.2,*
> *19.4, 19.5.*

19.8.   bǎ (把) + NP *take something and do something with it*

The verb **bǎ** (把) is often used when talking about doing something *to* or *with* an object. Sentences with **bǎ** (把) can often be phrased as:

> Subject **bǎ** *(takes) something and does something with it.*
> 一定得 **bǎ**宿舍 **shōushi** 好。
> *We definitely have to take this room and clean it up. (. . . clean up this room.)*

Bǎ is used with the verbs like 放 that refer to putting things some place.

> 我们先 **bǎ** 这几件 **gānjìng** 的 **yīfu** 放在 **guì**子里。
> *Let's first take these clean clothes and put them in the dresser.*

Bǎ can be used with resultative verbs when the action does something to the object. That is, it can be used with resultative verbs when the sentence can be phrased as:

> Subject **bǎ** *(takes) something and does something with it.*
> 我們一定得 **bǎ**宿舍 **shōushi** 好。
> *We have to clean up the dorm room.*
> (*We have to take the dorm room and clean it up.*)
> 我来 **bǎ**地 **sǎo gānjìng**.
> *I'll sweep the floor clean.*
> (*I'll take the floor and sweep it clean.*)

When talking about completed actions, 了 occurs after the resultative verb.

> 大为 **bǎ gānjìng** 的 **yīfu** 放在 **guì**子里了。
> *Dawei put the clean clothing in the dresser.*
> 他们 **bǎ**房间 **shōushi** 好了。
> *They cleaned up the room.*

Negating a sentence with bǎ (把)

When negating **bǎ** sentences, negation occurs before **bǎ**, either right before **bǎ** or before a modal verb (such as 可以 or **yīnggāi**) that occurs before **bǎ**. The form of negation used depends upon whether the sentence refers to a situation in the past or to some situation in the present or future. When talking about a situation in the past, **bǎ** is negated with 没:

> 你怎么没 **bǎ** 地 **sǎo gānjìng**？
> *How come you didn't sweep the floor clean?*

When referring to a situation in the present or future, the form of negation is 不:

> 你不 **yīnggāi bǎ** 你的 **yīfu** 都 **rēng** 在地上。
> *You shouldn't throw your clothes on the floor.*

To tell someone not to do something, say 别 or 不要 + action:

> 别 **bǎ** 你的 **xié** 子放在 **zhuō** 子上。
> *Don't put your shoes on the table.*
> 不要 **bǎ** 你的 **yīfu** 放在地上。
> *Don't put your clothing on the floor.*

> **Practice** ▶ *Workbook: Focus on Structure 19.7, 19.8, 19.11; Focus on Communication 19.2, 19.3, 19.5.*

19.9. 非 VP 不可 *must do the action*

非 VP 不可 *must do the action* is a literary expression that is also used in informal speech.

> 我们的房间太 **luàn** 了。非 **shōushi** 不可。
> *Our room is too messy. We have to clean it.*

非VP 不可 means the same thing as 得 **(děi)** VP or 不能不 VP *you can't **not** do the verb.*

When the object of the verb refers to a specific or definite object (e.g., 选那门中文课 *take that Chinese class*, 看那个电 **yǐng** *watch that movie*), the object is often stated before 非 VP 不可:

> 牛奶已经快过期了，非喝 **wán** 不可。
> *The milk has almost reached its expiration date. We have to drink it up.*
> 那门中文课，我非选不可。如果我不选就不能 **bìyè**。
> *That Chinese class, I have to take (it). If I don't take it, I won't graduate.*
> 那个电 **yǐng** 非常好，你非看不可。
> *That movie is great. You have to see (it).*

> **Practice** ▶ *Workbook: Focus on Structure 19.10, 19.11; Focus on Communication 19.1, 19.5.*

19.10.   不 bì (不必)VP *no need to, don't have to VP*

不 **bì** VP （不必 VP） means *no need to* or *don't have to VP*. It is the opposite of 非VP 不可 or 得 **(děi)** VP. It is equivalent in meaning and use to the expression 不用 introduced in Lesson 16 and is used in informal speech and writing.

你不 bì 找课本了。
You don't have to look for your textbook anymore.

Practice ▸ *Workbook: Focus on Structure 19.10; Focus on Communication 19.2, 19.4.*

19.11. 放在 location *put (something) in a location* and 放回 location *return something to a location*

The verb 放 *(to) put, (to) place* is always followed by the location where an object is put or placed. In this lesson, we see that it can be followed by 在 + location *at a location*, and 回 + location *return to a location*:

我们先 **bǎ** 这几件 **gānjìng** 的 **yīfu** 放在 **guì** 子里 。。。
We'll first put these clean clothes into the dresser . . .
再 **bǎ zhuō** 子上和地上的书放回书 **jià** 上。
then (we'll) take the books that are on the bed and on the floor and put them back into the bookcase.

Practice ▸ *Workbook: Focus on Structure 19.7, 19.11; Focus on Communication 19.1, 19.3.*

19.12. 出去 *go out*, 出来 *come out*, 进去 *go in*, and 进来 *come in*

In Lesson 17 we learned the directional verbs 回来 *come back* and 回去 *go back*. The verb 出 *go out, exit*, and 进 *enter* may also be followed by 来 *come* or 去 *go* (*Use and Structure 17.3*).

出来 means that someone or something is **coming out** of some place **towards** the speaker or some reference point.

我在 **sùshè** 外边等你出来。
I am outside the dorm waiting for you to come out.

出去 means that that someone or something *is* **going out** of some place **away from** the speaker or reference point.

进来 means that someone or something is **entering** some place **towards** the speaker or reference point.

进去 means that someone or something is **entering** some place, **away from** the speaker or reference point.

那 **shuāng** 白色的 球 **xié** 可以放在门口 ， 我等一下出去要 **chuān**.
*You can put that pair of white sneakers at the doorway, I'll wear them when **I go out** in a little while.*
我进来的时候我的室友在 **shōushi** 房间。
*When I **entered**,my roommate was straightening out the room.*

We will learn more about directional verbs in Lesson 22.

Practice ▸ *Focus on Communication 19.1, 19.4.*

🎧 Sentence pyramids

Supply the English translation for the last line where indicated.

1 中文书 我的中文书 看见我的中文书 你看见我的中文书了吗？	*Chinese book(s)* *my Chinese book(s)* *see my Chinese book(s)* _____
2 看见 没看见。	*see* *(I) haven't seen (them).*
3 找到 没找到 我找了半天也没找到。	*find* *didn't find* *I looked for a half a day but didn't find (it).*
4 luàn 太 luàn 了 我们的屋子太 luàn 了。	*messy* *too messy* _____
5 在什么地方? 你的中文书在什么地方? 不知道你的中文书在什么地方 难 guài 你不知道你的中文书在什么地方。 屋子这么 luàn ，难 guài 你不知道你的中文书在什么地方。	*located where?* *where is your Chinese book?* *don't know where your Chinese book is* *No wonder you don't know where your Chinese book is.* *The room is so messy, no wonder you don't know where your Chinese book is.*
6 luàn yòu zāng, yòu luàn 我们的宿舍 yòu zāng ， yòu luàn.	*messy, chaotic* *both dirty and messy* _____
7 shōushi 好 bǎ 宿舍 shōushi 好 我们一定得 bǎ 宿舍 shōushi 好。	*clean (it) up* *take the dorm and clean it up* *We definitely have to take the dorm room and clean it up.*
7 非 shōushi 不可 对，非 shōushi 不可了。	*can't not clean it (must clean it)* _____

8 床上 在床上 yīfu 都在床上 我们的 yīfu 都在床上	*on the bed* *located on the bed* *the clothing is all on the bed* ————————————
9 地上 在地上 你的课本在地上。	*on the floor* *located on the floor* *Your textbook is on the floor.*
10 guì 子 在 guì 子里 放在 guì 子里 bǎ gānjìng 的 yīfu 放在 guì 子里 我们 bǎ 这几件 gānjìng 的 yīfu 放在 guì 子里。	*dresser* *inside the dresser* *put (it) inside the dresser* *take the clean clothes and put them in the dresser* *Let's take these clean clothes and put them in the dresser.*
11 书 jià 地上的书放回书 jià 上 bǎ zhuō 子上的书放回书 jià 上 bǎ zhuō 子上和地上的书放回书 jià 上。	*bookcase* *the books on the floor, put them back in the bookcase* *take the books on the table and put them back in the bookcase* *Take the books on the table and on the floor and put them back in the bookcase.*
12 shōu 起来 bǎ xié 都 shōu 起来 你能不能 bǎ xié 都 shōu 起来?	*organize* *take all the shoes and gather them* *Can you gather all the shoes?*
13 rēng bǎ zázhì rēng 了 bǎ 过期的 zázhì rēng 了	*throw away* *take the magazines and throw them away* *Take the expired magazines and throw them away.*
14 sǎo gānjìng bǎ 地 sǎo gānjìng 我来 bǎ 地 sǎo gānjìng 。	*sweep clean* *take the floor and sweep it clean* *I'll sweep the floor clean.*
15 门口 放在门口 可以放在门口 那 shuāng 球 xié 可以放在门口 那 shuāng 白色的球 xié 可以放在门口。	*doorway* *put them at the doorway* *can put them at the doorway* *These sneakers, you can put them at the doorway.* ————————————

16 打开 bǎ chuānghu 打开 我 bǎ chuānghu 打开。	*open* *take the windows and open them* _____
17 有一点 jiù 就是有一点 jiù 这件 yīfu 很 piàoliang，就是有一点 jiù。	*a little old* *it is just that it is a little old* *This article of clothing is very pretty, it's just that it is a little old.*
18 买东西 出去买东西 你什么时候出去买东西?	*buy things* *go out to buy things* *When are you going out to buy things?*
19 luànjí 了 你的宿舍 luànjí 了。 你的宿舍 luànjí 了，非 shōushi 不可。	*extremely messy* *your dorm is extremely messy* _____

 Notes on Chinese culture

Leave your shoes at the door

Generally speaking, in Chinese culture, you do not wear your shoes in the house. Instead, you leave them at the doorway, usually inside, but sometimes outside of the door to the house. This way, the dirt from the outside does not get tracked into the house. Once you come inside, you wear slippers, and when guests come, you provide slippers for them as well. Be prepared to take off your shoes when you visit Chinese friends.

Narrative in English

It's already been over a week since school started. Dawei and Guoqiang are still roommates this year. Although they've finished selecting their classes and they have bought all of their textbooks, the last few days they have both been extremely busy, and they haven't had time to clean their dorm room, so their dorm room is extremely messy. This weekend, Guoqiang and Dawei want to invite their classmates over for a party. Before their classmates come, they definitely have to clean their dorm room.

Dialogue in English

The scene: Guoqiang is in the room typing; Dawei is looking for something.

Part A

Dawei: Have you seen my Chinese book? I've been looking for it all day and I haven't found it.

Guoqiang: I haven't seen it. Our room is too messy. There are books on the table and the chairs; there are books on the floor. Only the bookcase doesn't have any books. A half-drunk glass of milk and the dumplings we didn't finish eating last night are all on the table. Shirts we've worn and socks are all thrown on the beds. The room is such a mess, no wonder you don't know where your Chinese book is.

Part B

Dawei: You're right! Our dorm room is both dirty and messy. Before our classmates come, we have to clean up the room.

Guoqiang: Right, we have to clean it up. So there's no need for you to spend a lot of time looking for your textbook. As soon as we straighten things up, we'll find it.

Part C

Dawei: It's such a mess, where do we start cleaning?

Guoqiang: Look, our clothes are all on the beds. There are shoes outside the doorway and there are a few pairs of shoes inside of the doorway. Let's first take the clean clothes and put them in the closet. We can wash the dirty clothes and the smelly socks in a little while. Then we can take the books that are on the table and the floor and put them back in the bookcase.

Dawei: Okay, after we finish that, don't forget to gather up all the shoes, and take the expired newspapers and magazines and throw them out. I'll sweep the floor. By the way, that pair of white sneakers you can leave at the doorway; I'll wear them when I go out in a few minutes.

Guoqiang: Okay. First, I'll open the window. Let's get started.

Lesson 20

看 bìng
Getting sick and seeing a doctor

Communication goals

By the end of this lesson, you will be able to:

- Describe and answer questions about the symptoms of an illness.
- Talk about the details of a past event.

Literacy goals

By the end of this lesson, you will be able to:

- Identify characters that share the same shēngpáng (声旁) "phonetic element" and guess the meaning of unfamiliar characters with familiar shēngpáng (声旁).

Key structures

- 一 noun *the entire noun*
- number + 次 *number of times*
- huòzhě *perhaps, or*
- The potential form of resultative verbs: **V** 得 **ending**, **V** 不 **ending**
- 是 . . . 的 *focusing on details of past events*
- **chú** 了 noun phrase 以外 *besides NP, except for NP*
- 穿 *wear* vs. **dài** *wear*

Narrative

大为昨天晚上跟几个朋友到一家饭馆去吃晚饭。从饭馆回来以后，**dù** 子就不 **shū** 服。一 **yè** 上了好几次 **cè** 所。国强一看就知道他 **bìng** 了。国强说这就是中国人说的 "**bìng** 从口 **rù**。" 大为可能是吃得太多了，也可能是不习惯吃 **là** 的，**huòzhě** 是饭菜不干净，把 **dù** 子吃坏了。他决定马上带大为到学校的 **yī** 院去看 **bìng**。

Narrative vocabulary

				Simplified	Traditional
bìng		*illness, sickness; sick*	noun; verb	病	病
bìng cóng kǒu rù	bìng 从口 rù	*disease enters the body through the mouth*	proverb	病从口入	病從口入
cèsuǒ	cè 所	*toilet*	noun	厕所	廁所
cì	次	*classifier for time*	classifier	次	次
dùzi	dù 子	*stomach*	noun	肚子	肚子
hǎojǐcì	好几次	*a good many times, many times*	number phrase	好几次	好幾次
huòzhě		*or*	conjunction	或者	或者
jiā	家	*classifier for restaurants, family*	classifier	家	家
kàn bìng	看 bìng	*see a doctor*	verb + object	看病	看病
kěnéng	可能	*possibly, possible*	adverb, adjectival verb, noun	可能	可能
là		*hot and spicy*	adjectival verb	辣	辣

mǎshàng	马上	*immediately*	adverb	马上	馬上
shàng cèsuǒ	上 cè 所	*go to the toilet*	verb + object	上厕所	上廁所
shūfu	shū 服	*comfortable*	adjectival verb	舒服	舒服
yè		*night**	noun	夜	夜
yī yè	一 yè	*the whole night*	noun phrase	一夜	一夜
yīyuàn	yī 院	*hospital*	noun	医院	醫院

Narrative characters

Character	Pinyin	Meaning/function	Radical	Phrases	Traditional character
把	bǎ	*take**	扌		把
菜	cài	*food, dishes of food*	艹	白菜 báicài *cabbage*	菜
带	dài	*take*	巾		帶
服	fú	*serve, obey, clothing**	月	**shū** 服 shūfú *comfortable*, 衣服 yīfu *clothing*	服
干	gān	*dry*	干	干净 gānjìng *clean*	乾
坏	huài	*bad, broken*	土	好坏 hǎo huài *good (or) bad*	壞
决	jué	*decide**	冫	决定 juédìng *decide*	决
净	jìng	*clean**	冫	干净 gānjìng *clean*	淨
院	yuàn	*courtyard, academy, institute**	阝	电 yǐng 院 diànyǐng yuàn *movie theater*, yī 院 yīyuàn *hospital*	院

Dialogue

Part A

The setting: In the dormitory

国强： 大为，你好像不太 **shū** 服。昨天晚上睡得好吗？

大为： 我 **dù** 子不 **shū** 服，睡不 **zháo**， **yè** 里上了好几次 **cè** 所。早上也吃不下，很想 **tù**.

国强： 怎么会 **lā dù** 子呢？你昨天晚上是在哪儿吃的晚饭？

大为： 我是在一家中国饭馆吃的。

国强： 你是跟谁一起去的？

大为： 我跟 **Màikè** 和他的两个同学一起去的。

国强： 你是什么时候开始觉得 **dù** 子不 **shū** 服的？

大为： 吃了饭以后就开始觉得不 **shū** 服。

国强： 你大 **gài** 生 **bìng** 了。穿好衣服我们就去 **yī** 院吧。

Dialogue Part A Vocabulary

				Simplified	Traditional
dàgài	大 gài	*probably*	adverb	大概	大概
hǎoxiàng	好像	*appear, seem to be*	verb	好像	好像
lā dùzi	lā dù 子	*have diarrhea*	verb + object	拉肚子	拉肚子
shēng bìng	生 bìng	*become sick*	verb + object	生病	生病
shuìzháo	睡 zháo	*fall asleep*	verb + resultative ending	睡着	睡著
shuìbúzháo	睡不 zháo	*unable to fall asleep*	potential form of resultative verb	睡不着	睡不著
yèlǐ	yè 里	*middle of the night*	time phrase	夜里	夜裡
zháo		*reach the intended goal**	resultative ending	着	著

Dialogue Part A Characters

Character	Pinyin	Meaning/ function	Radical	Phrases	Traditional character
穿	chuān	*wear*	穴		穿
睡	shuì	*sleep*	目	睡觉 shuì jiào *sleep,* 睡 zháo shuìzháo *fall asleep*	睡
像	xiàng	*resemble*	亻	好像 hǎoxiàng *appears to be*	像
衣	yī	*clothing**	衣	衣服 yīfu *clothing*	衣

Part B

The setting: In the doctor's office

Yī 生: 你怎么了? 哪儿不 **shū** 服?

大为: 我从昨天晚上开始 **lā dù** 子。 头 **yūn**, 想 **tù**。

Yī 生: **Dù** 子 **téng** 吗?

大为 有一点 **téng**。 觉得很累, 全 **shēn** 没有 **lì** 气。

Yī 生: 发 **shāo** 吗?

大为: 好像不发 **shāo**。

Yī 生: **Késou** 不 **késou**?

大为: 不 **késou**。不流 **bí** 水也不打 **pēntì**。

Yī 生: **Chú** 了 **dù** 子 **téng** 以外, **shēntǐ** 还有哪儿不 **shū** 服?

大为: 我头也 **téng**。

Yī 生: (*Looks at the chart*) 你没发 **shāo**, **yīnggāi** 不是 **gǎnmào**。来, 我看一下你的 **ěrduo** 和 **yǎnjīng**。 . . . 把 **zuǐba** 张开让我看看 **sǎng** 子红不红, 发 **yán** 没有, 看 **shé** 头, 上火不上火。

Dialogue Part B Vocabulary

				Simplified	Traditional
bí shuǐ	bí 水	*snot*	noun phrase	鼻水	鼻水
chúle	chú 了	*except, besides*	preposition	除了	除了
ěrduo		*ear(s)*	noun	耳朵	耳朵

dǎ pēntì	打 pēntì	sneeze	verb + object	打喷嚏	打噴嚏
fā shāo	发 shāo	have fever	verb + object	发烧	發燒
fā yán	发 yán	be inflamed	verb + object	发炎	發炎
gǎnmào		catch a cold; common cold	verb; noun	感冒	感冒
késou		cough	verb	咳嗽	咳嗽
lìqi	lì气	energy	noun	力气	力氣
liú	流	flow	verb	流	流
liú bíshuǐ	流 bí水	have a runny nose	verb + object	流鼻水	流鼻水
quán shēn	全 shēn	entire body	noun phrase	全身	全身
sǎngzi	sǎng 子	throat	noun	嗓子	嗓子
shàng huǒ	上火	be inflamed, have too much heat (see Notes on Chinese Culture)	verb + object	上火	上火
shāo	shāo	cook, simmer fever	verb noun	烧	燒
shétóu	shé头	tongue	noun	舌头	舌頭
shēntǐ		body	noun	身体	身體
téng		painful, hurt	adjectival verb	疼	疼
tóu	头	head	noun	头	頭
tóu téng	头 téng	have a headache	phrase (adjectival verb; subject + verb)	头疼	頭疼
tóu yūn	头 yūn	lightheaded, dizzy	phrase (adjectival verb; subject + verb)	头晕	頭暈
tù		vomit	verb	吐	吐

yǎnjīng		*eye(s)*	noun	眼睛	眼睛
yīshēng	yī生	*doctor*	noun	医生	醫生
yǐwài	以外	*except (for), outside of*	noun	以外	以外
yūn		*dizzy*	adjectival verb	晕	暈
zěnme le?	怎么了?	*what's the matter?*	conversational expression	怎么了	怎麼了
zhāngkāi	张开	*open up*	verb	张开	張開
zuǐba		*mouth*	noun	嘴巴	嘴巴

Dialogue Part B Characters

Character	Pinyin	Meaning/ function	Radical	Phrases	Traditional character
发	fā	*emit*	又	发 shāo fā shāo *have fever*	發
流	liú	*flow*	氵	流行 liúxíng *fashionable, prevalent,* 流 **bí** 水 liú bíshuǐ *have a runny nose*	流
气	qì	*air, spirit*	气	客气 kèqi *polite,* 天气 tiānqì *weather,* **lì** 气 lìqì *strength, energy*	氣
全	quán	*entire*	入	全 shēn quánshēn *entire body,* 全国 quánguó *national*	全
让	ràng	*let, make*	讠		讓
头	tóu	*head*	大	钟头 zhōngtóu *hour,* 头 téng tóu téng *headache,* shé 头 shétóu *tongue*	頭

Part C

Yī 生：你昨天晚上吃什么了？

大 为：我是跟朋友在一家四 chuān 饭馆吃的。吃了很多，还喝了几瓶 pí 酒。

Yī 生：你大 gài 吃了一些不干净的东西。可能你也不习惯吃 là 的，所以 dù 子不shū 服。我给你开一点 yào 。一天吃三次，一次吃两片。很快就会好。下次别喝得太多，也别吃得太 bǎo 。还有，最近天气 biàn 冷了，很多人 gǎnmào 。小心一点，出去的时候 jì 得 dài 口 zhào 。如果过几天还没好， huòzhě 是有别的 zhèngzhuàng， 再回来看我。

大 为：谢谢您。

Dialogue Part C Vocabulary

				Simplified	Traditional
bǎo		*full (from eating)*	adjectival verb	饱	飽
biàn		*become, change into*	verb	变	變
dài		*wear (on the head or upper extremities)*	verb	戴	戴
jìde	jì 得	*remember*	verb	记得	記得
kāi yào	开 yào	*write a prescription*	verb + object	开药	開藥
kǒuzhào	口 zhào	*face mask*	noun phrase	口罩	口罩
piàn	片	*tablet, slice*	classifier	片	片
Sìchuān	四 chuān	*Sichuan*	Chinese province	四川	四川
tiānqì	天气	*weather*	noun	天气	天氣
xiǎoxīn	小心	*careful*	adjectival verb	小心	小心
yào		*medicine*	noun	药	藥
zhèngzhuàng		*symptom*	noun	症状	症狀
zuì jìn	最近	*recently*	adverb	最近	最近

Dialogue Part C Characters

Character	Pinyin	Meaning/function	Radical	Phrases	Traditional character
酒	jiǔ	*alcohol, wine*	酉	**pí** 酒 píjiǔ *beer*, 喝酒 hē jiǔ *drink (alcohol)*	酒
冷	lěng	*cold*	冫		冷
片	piàn	*tablet, slice*	片	**zhào** 片 zhàopiàn *photograph*	片
瓶	píng	*bottle*	瓦	一瓶水 yī píng shuǐ *one bottle of water*	瓶

Symptoms of illness (zhèngzhuàng)

dùzi téng	dù 子 téng	*have a stomachache*
ěrduo téng		*have an earache*
sǎngzi téng	sǎng 子 téng	*have a sore throat*
tóu téng	头 téng	*have a headache*
dǎ pēntì	打 pēntì	*sneeze*
fā shāo	发烧	*have fever*
méi yǒu lìqi	没有 lì 气	*have no energy*
késou		*cough*
lā dùzi	lā dù 子	*have diarrhea*
liú bíshuǐ	流 bí 水	*have a runny nose*
tóu yūn	头 yūn	*be dizzy*

Stroke Order Flow Chart

Character   **Total Strokes**

Narrative

Char	1	2	3	4	5	6	7	8	9	10	11	12	13	Total Strokes
把	一	扌	扌	扣	扣	扣	把							7
菜	一	十	艹	艹	艹	艹	芏	苹	苹	莘	菜			11
带	一	十	世	世	世	世	世	带	带					9
服	丿	月	月	月	肝	肥	服	服						8
干	一	二	干											3
坏	一	十	土	圹	圷	坏	坏							7
决	丶	冫	冫	江	决	决								6
净	丶	冫	冫	汋	冷	净	净	净						8
院	阝	阝	阝	阝	陟	陟	陟	陟	院					9

Dialogue A

Char	1	2	3	4	5	6	7	8	9	10	11	12	13	Total Strokes
穿	丶	宀	宀	宀	灾	空	空	穿	穿					9
睡	丨	刀	月	月	目	盰	盰	盰	盰	睡	睡	睡	睡	13
像	丿	亻	亻	伫	伫	侉	侉	像	像	像	像	像		13
衣	丶	二	广	衤	衣	衣								6

Dialogue B

Char	1	2	3	4	5	6	7	8	9	10	11	12	13	Total Strokes
发	一	少	发	发	发									5
流	丶	冫	氵	汇	汇	泸	法	浐	济	流				10
气	丿	二	气	气										4
全	丿	人	仐	仝	全	全								6
让	丶	讠	计	计	让									5
头	丶	丷	二	头	头									5

Dialogue C

Char	1	2	3	4	5	6	7	8	9	10	11	12	13	Total Strokes
酒	丶	冫	氵	汀	汇	沔	沔	洒	酒					10
冷	丶	冫	冫	从	汄	冷	冷							7
片	丿	丿	尸	片										4
瓶	丶	丷	兰	兰	羊	并	并	瓶	瓶	瓶				10

Use and structure

20.1. 一 **yè** *the whole night,* 一天 *the entire day,* 一年 *the whole year*

一 NP means *the whole NP*. Typically, NP is a time expression, or something that can be measured in terms of its duration, and 一NP means *the entire time* specified by the NP:

一 **yè** 上了好几次 **cè** 所。
Through the entire night he went to the toilet many times.
她一天都没吃饭。
She didn't eat for a whole day.
因为这个 **xīn** 工作，他去年一年去了三次中国。
Because of this new job, last year he went to China three times.
他一星期没来上课。
He didn't come to class the whole week.

The NP in 一 NP need not involve duration, but it must consist of individual parts (e.g., hours in an evening or a day, days in a week, years in a life, etc.). 一 NP indicate that a following VP is true of all of the parts. The expression 一家人 *all of the members of a family* is an example of this.

一家人都想去日本 **lǚyóu**。
All of the members of the family want to go to Japan to travel.

一 NP and 全 NP *compared*

In Lesson 18 we learned the expression 全 NP, which we also translated as *the entire NP* (*Use and Structure* 18.10). Although 一 NP and 全 NP may be translated the same way in English, they are often not identical in use or meaning. As noted earlier, the NP in 一 NP phrases typically refers to time, and 一 NP indicates that a situation is true for the entire time specified by the NP. The NP in 全 **NP** phrases typically refers to a person, place, or thing, and 全 **NP** means the entire person, place, or thing.

我昨天打球打了五个钟头，早上起床以后全 **shēn** 都 **téng**。
I played ball for five hours yesterday. Today after I got up my whole body was sore.
最近天气 **biàn** 冷，我们全家都 **bìng** 了。
The weather recently turned cold. Our whole family is sick.
全校的学生 **bìyè** 以前都得学中文。
All of the students in the school have to study Chinese before they graduate.
她很有名，全中国的人都认识她。
She is very famous. All of the people in China recognize her.

The NP in 一 **NP** phrases may sometimes refer to a person, place, or thing. When it does, 一 **NP** and 全 **NP** are equivalent in meaning.

我们一家人都想去日本 **lǚyóu**。
我们全家人都想去日本 **lǚyóu**。
All of the members of my family want to go to Japan to travel.

Practice ▶ *Workbook: Focus on Structure 20.8.*

20.2. Indicating frequency with 一次 *once* and *time when* with 这次 *this time*

次 is a classifier and means *time(s)*. We have already learned it as part of the expression 请你再说一次 *Please say it again one more time.* 次 is always preceded by a number, or the question word 几, or a specifier such as 这 *this*, or 上 and 下 when they are used to refer to time as in the examples below.

一次 *once*
两次 *twice*
几次? *how many times?*
好几次 *a good number of times (a lot)*
这次 *this time*
上次 *last time*
下次 *next time*

The 次 phrase may indicate either the time when a situation takes place or the frequency of an action, depending upon the word that precedes 次 and the position of the 次 phrase in the sentence.

次 phrases used to indicate *time when*

We have already learned that *time when* phrases occur before the verb phrase:

subject + time when + VP

This is the phrase order to follow for all 次 phrases that indicate the *time when* a situation takes place:

下次别喝得太多, 也别吃得太 **bǎo** 。
Next time don't drink too much, and don't eat until you are too full.
你上次吃得很多。 这次怎么吃得那么少?
Last time you ate a lot. This time why are you eating so little?
一次吃两片 。
One time (each time) eat two tablets.

次 phrases used to indicate the frequency of an action

Frequency expressions occur with action verbs. They are located *after* the verb or the entire VP.

subject + action + frequency

The most common location of the frequency phrase is immediately after the action verb:

昨天晚上我上了好几次 **cè**所 。
Last night I went to the toilet many times.
我坐过两次飞机。
I've ridden on an airplane twice.

If the verb includes an object and the object is specific (for example, *this* noun or *that* noun), number + 次 may follow the verb, or it may follow the verb + object:

我看了三次那个电 **yǐng** 。
or
我看了那个电 **yǐng** 三次。
I saw that movie three times.

If the object is a proper noun, number + 次 may follow the verb, or it may follow the verb + object:

上个月他去了一次北京。
or
上个月他去了北京一次。
Last month he went to Beijing once.

If the object is a pronoun, number + 次 *must* follow the pronoun. It cannot follow the verb:

我每年只看他一次。
I only see him once every year.

Note that when the object is specific, it can also be stated first in the sentence as a *topic*. In this case, the frequency phrase directly follows the verb.

object + subject + verb + 次 phrase
那个电 **yǐng** ，我看了三次。
That movie, I saw (it) three times.

Practice   *Workbook: Focus on Structure 20.1, 20.7, 20.8.*

20.3.   上 cè 所 (上厕所)

上 **cè** 所 can be translated into English as *use the toilet, washroom,* etc. It is a *verb + object* phrase. The verb is 上 *go up, ascend.* As in English, there are many expressions that refer to using the toilet. In this lesson, we see that you can also say 去 **cè** 所, literally: *go to the toilet.*

The verb 上 is used in a number of idiomatic expressions that cannot be translated word for word into English. In earlier lessons, we have learned other idiomatic expressions in which 上 is the verb: 上车 *get in a vehicle* and 上课 *attend class, go to class.*

20.4.   吃 là 的 (吃辣的) *eat hot and spicy food*

吃 **là** 的 (吃辣的) means *eat hot and spicy food.* **Là** 的 (辣的) is a noun description without the following noun that is being described. The full noun phrase, including the noun that is being described, could be **là** 的东西 *hot and spicy things* or **là** 的菜 *hot and spicy dishes,* but a following noun is usually omitted unless you are talking about a specific type of hot and spicy food.

Practice ▸ *Workbook: Focus on Structure 20.7, 20.8.*

20.5. huòzhě (或者) *or, perhaps*

Mandarin has two words that translate as *or* in English, 还是 and **huòzhě (或者)**, and they are distinct in use.

We learned 还是 in Lesson 12 (*Use and Structure* 12.4). It is used when stating alternative choices in questions. 还是 questions often end with 呢。

你想吃中国菜还是吃法国菜呢?
Do you want to eat Chinese food or French food?

Huòzhě occurs in statements, not questions, and is used to state alternatives:

我们可以去 **tiàowǔ huòzhě** 去唱歌。
We can go dancing or we can go singing.
大为可能是吃得太多了, 也可能是不习惯吃 **là** 的, **huòzhě** 是饭菜不干净, 把 **dù** 子吃坏了。
Dawei perhaps by eating too much, (or) it's also possible that he is not used to eating hot and spicy things, or that the food was not clean, (in doing so) he messed up his stomach.

Huòzhě is *not* used in questions.

Practice ▸ *Workbook: Focus on Structure 20.2, 20.7; Focus on Communication 20.1.*

20.6. The potential form of resultative verbs: 睡不 zháo (睡不着) *unable to fall asleep*

In Lesson 19 (*Use and Structure* 19.2), we learned how to form resultative verbs and to use them to indicate the result or conclusion of an action. In this lesson, we learn the **potential form** of resultative verbs. That is, we learn how to say *able to* or *not able to* reach a particular conclusion or result.

Before we see how the potential is formed, we first review resultative verbs. Remember, resultative verbs have two parts. The first part is the verb that indicates the action.

找 *look for*, 写 *write*, 洗 *wash*, etc.

The second part indicates the result or conclusion.

找 + 到 = 找到 *find*
写 + **wán** = 写 wán *finish writing*
听+ 懂 (*understand*) = 听懂 *listen and understand*

To indicate that you are *able to reach the result*, add 得 (pronounced **de**) between the action verb and the resultative ending:

找得到 *able to find*
买得到 *able to purchase*
写得 **wán** *able to finish writing*

听得懂 *able to understand by listening*
那本书在学校的书店买得到。
You will be able to buy that book at the school bookstore (because they will have it).

To indicate that you are *unable to reach the result*, add 不 between the action verb and the resultative ending:

找不到 *unable to find*
写不**wán** *unable to finish writing*
听不懂 *unable to understand by listening*
我听不懂老师的话。
I don't understand what the teacher is saying.

To *ask* whether someone is able to reach some result by doing some action, ask:

Verb 得 resultative ending Verb 不 resultative ending ?
你听得懂听不懂?
Do you understand by listening? (Can you listen and understand?)
这本书今天晚上看得 **wán** 看不 **wán** ?
Can you finish reading that book tonight?

or

Verb 得 **resultative** ending 吗?
你听得懂吗?
Do you understand by listening? (Can you listen and understand?)
这本书今天晚上看得 **wán** 吗?
Can you finish reading that book tonight?

In this lesson we learn the resultative verb 睡 zháo (睡着) *fall asleep*, consisting of the action verb 睡 **shuì** *sleep* and the resultative ending zháo (着) *attain a targeted goal*. To say that you are *able to fall asleep*, say 睡得 **zháo**. To say that you are *unable to fall asleep*, say 睡不**zháo** (睡不着):

我 **dù** 子不 **shū** 服，睡不 **zháo** ， **yè** 里上了好几次 **cè** 所。
My stomach was uncomfortable, I could not fall asleep, and in the middle of the night I went to the toilet many times.

As we learned in Lesson 19, when you follow an action verb with a resultative ending, you make a new verb. If the new verb takes an object, it occurs after the entire resultative verb and never in between the action verb and the resultative ending:

Say this:	*Not this:*
我还没看 **wán** 那本书。 *I still haven't finished reading that book.*	⊗ 我还没看那本书 wán 。

Verb suffixes like 了 and 过 that follow the verb must occur at the end of the entire resultative verb and can never occur between the original action verb and the resultative ending.

Say this:	Not this:
我找到了我的课本。 *I still haven't finished reading that book.*	⊗ 我找了到我的课本

Notice that the resultative verb 睡 zháo *fall asleep*, in basic or potential form, can be followed by the object 觉:

我昨天晚上睡不 **zháo** 觉。
Last night I couldn't fall asleep.

Resultative verbs in the potential form can often be paraphrased with 会 (能) resultative verb or 不会 (不能) resultative verb. (See also *Use and Structure* note 20.7.)

这本书我今天晚上能看 **wán** 。
I am able to finish reading this book tonight.

However, the potential form is more common and often more natural sounding than 会 or 能 + resultative verb. If it is possible to use the potential form of a resultative verb, it is often preferable to do so.

Practice   *Workbook: Focus on Structure 20.3; Focus on Communication 20.3, 20.5.*

20.7.   睡 zháo (睡着) *fall asleep* vs. 睡觉 *sleep*

睡 **zháo** *fall asleep* is a resultative verb. It is formed with an action verb 睡 *sleep* and the resultative ending **zháo**. To say that someone has fallen asleep, say:

他已经睡 **zháo** 了。
He has already fallen asleep.

睡觉 is a verb + object phrase and means *sleep*. To say that someone is sleeping, say:

她在睡觉。
She is sleeping.

To ask someone what time they go to sleep, ask:

你晚上几点钟睡觉?
What time do you go to sleep at night?

Zháo is used as an ending for action verbs in which the action involves reaching some goal. It is often used as an ending for the verbs 找 *look* for and 买 *shop*. With these verbs, verb + **zháo** is equivalent to verb + 到:

找到	找 **zháo**	*find*
买到	买 **zháo**	*succeed in buying*

Practice   *Workbook: Focus on Communication 20.5.*

20.8. Summary of the meanings expressed by resultative verbs

Resultative verbs consist of an action verb (ActV) and a resultative ending and are used to express the following four situations. Note the form of the resultative verb phrase used to express each of the four situations.

- An action occurred and a result or conclusion was reached:

  ActV + resultative ending 了
  我 (已经) 做 **wán** 今天的功课了。
  I've already finished today's homework.

- An action occurred and a result or conclusion was not reached:

  （还) 没 **ActV + resultative ending**
  今天的功课我还没做 **wán** 。
  I haven't finished today's homework yet. (I still haven't finished today's homework.)

- It is possible to reach a particular conclusion or result when performing the action:

  ActV 得 **resultative ending**
  你觉得你做得 **wán** 今天的功课吗?
  Do you think you can finish today's homework?

- It is not possible to reach a particular conclusion or result when performing the action:

  ActV 不 **resultative ending**
  我做不 **wán** 今天的功课。
  I can't finish today's homework.

20.9. Focusing on a detail of a past event 是 . . . 的

We have learned that 了 is used to indicate that an action is complete, and that it can be used to indicate that an action happened. When you know that an action happened but want to emphasize some detail of the action, for example *when* it happened, or *where* it happened, or *who* did the action, or *who* someone did an action *with*, you need to use the 是 . . . 的 structure. In the 是 . . . 的 structure, 是 occurs right in front of the detail that you are focusing on. 的 occurs immediately after the verb, or at the end of the sentence. The sentence does not include 了.

In this sentence, 是 . . . 的 is used to focus on the <u>location</u> of the action:

我是<u>在一家中国饭馆</u>吃的晚饭。
I ate in a Chinese restaurant.

In this sentence, 是 . . . 的 is used to focus on the <u>time when</u> the action occurred:

我是<u>昨天晚上</u>吃的中国饭。
I ate Chinese food last night. (It was last night when I ate Chinese food.)

In this sentence, 是 . . . 的 is used to focus on the <u>people with whom</u> the action occurred:

我是<u>跟小王和他的两个同学</u>一起去的。
I went with Xiao Wang and two of his classmates.

If the object of the verb is a pronoun, 的 must occur at the end of the sentence and cannot occur immediately after the verb.

> 我是在中国认识她的。
> *I met her in China.*

Asking about the details of a past event

You can use the 是 . . . 的 structure to ask about the detail of a past event.

To ask about location, include 是 before the question phrase that asks about location.

> 你昨天晚上是在哪儿吃的晚饭?
> *Where did you eat last night?*

To ask about the time when an action occurred, include 是 before the question phrase that asks about time.

> 你是什么时候开始觉得 **dù** 子不 **shū** 服的?
> *When did you begin to feel that your stomach was uncomfortable?*

To ask about the people with whom an action occurred, include 是 before the phrase that asks about the other participants:

> 你是跟谁一起去的?
> *Who did you go with?*
> 我是跟 Màikè 和他的两个同学一起去的
> *I went with Maike and his two friends.*

是 may sometimes be omitted:

> 你是跟谁一起去的。
> *Who did you go with?*
> 我跟 Màikè 和他的两个同学一起去的。
> *I went with Mike and two of his classmates.*

Comparing the functions of 了 and 是 。。。 的

了 is used to indicate that an action is complete, and typically, that it occurred. 是。。。 的 is used to focus on a detail of an event that your listener knows has already occurred. If your purpose is just to let someone know that some action happened, use 了:

> 我昨天晚上在一家中国饭馆吃饭了。
> *Last night I ate at a Chinese restaurant.*

If your listeners know what you did and you want to tell them the details (when, where, with whom), then you use 是。。。 的. For example, if your roommate knows that you ate out last night but doesn't know what kind of restaurant you ate at, you could say:

> 我昨天晚上是在一家中国饭馆吃饭的。
> *Last night I ate at a CHINESE restaurant.*

20.10.   Chú 了 X 以外 (除了 X 以外) + sentence *besides X, except (for) X*

The structure **chú 了 X 以外** is used to indicate some relationship between **X** and other similar entities. It can be used to say that *besides X* or *including X* some statement is true, or that *except for X*, some statement is true. **X** may be a noun or noun phrase, a verb phrase, or a clause.

Saying *besides X* or *including X*:

When saying *besides X* or *including X*, the sentence that follows **chú 了 X 以外** usually includes the adverb 也 or 还. Notice that in these sentences, **chú 了 X 以外** can be translated into English as *besides X, in addition to X* or *including X*.

X as a noun or noun phrase:

> **Chú** 了茶以外，我也喜欢喝咖啡。
> *Besides tea, I also like to drink coffee.*
> **Chú** 了中国话以外, 我也会说法国话和日本话。
> *Besides Chinese, I can also speak French and Japanese.*

X as a verb phrase:

> **Chú** 了唱歌以外，他也喜欢 **tiào wǔ**。
> *Besides singing, he also likes to dance.*

X as a clause (see also *Use and Structure* note 20.11):

> **Chú** 了 **dù** 子 **téng** 以外，**shēntǐ** 还有哪儿不 **shū** 服?
> *Besides your stomach hurting, what else is bothering you?*

Saying *except for X*

When saying *except for X*, the sentence that follows **chú 了 X 以外** usually includes the adverb 都. It may also include negation:

> **Chú** 了 *X* 以外, **(subject)** 都 **(Neg) VP**

X as a noun or noun phrase:

> **Chú** 了小高以外，我的同学都是美国人。
> *Except for Xiao Gao, my classmates are all Americans.*
> **Chú** 了红 **shāo ròu** 以外，那个饭馆的菜都不好吃。
> *Except for the red-simmered meat, the dishes in that restaurant don't taste good.*
> **Chú** 了饺子以外，别的中国 **cài** 小马都不喜欢吃。
> *Except for dumplings, Xiao Ma doesn't like to eat (other) Chinese dishes.*
> **Chú** 了 **là** 的以外，别的我都可以吃。
> *Except for spicy food, I can eat everything.*

X as a verb phrase:

学中文，**chú** 了写汉字以外，别的我都喜欢。
As for studying Chinese, except for writing Chinese characters, I like everything.
Chú 了流 **bí** 水以外，我没有别的 **zhèngzhuàng** 。
Except for a runny nose, I don't have any other symptoms.
Chú 了当家 **jiào** 以外，我没做过别的工作。
Except for being a tutor, I haven't had any other jobs.

The full pattern includes **chú** 了 *and* 以外, but either **chú** 了 or 以外 may be omitted.

Chú 了茶，他也喜欢喝咖啡。
Besides tea, he also likes to drink coffee.
酒以外，别的我都可以喝。
Except for alcohol, I can drink everything else.

> **Practice** ▶ *Workbook: Focus on Structure 20.6, 20.7; Focus on Communication 20.1, 20.3, 20.5.*

20.11. 我头也 téng *headaches, stomachaches, my head, your stomach*

In English we talk about "having" a headache or a stomachache. In Chinese, you say the body part "hurts":

头 **téng** *headache,* **dù** 子 **téng** *stomachache*
头 **téng** *and* **dù** 子 **téng** are sentences consisting of a subject (头 *head,* **dù**子 *stomach*) and a verb **téng** *ache, hurt.*

When saying that someone's head hurts, or someone's stomach hurts, state the person first and say:

我头 **téng** 。 *My head hurts.*
大为 **dù** 子 **téng** 。 *Dawei's stomach hurts.*

In sentences like these, the person is sometimes called the "topic" of the sentence.

> **Practice** ▶ *Workbook: Focus on Structure 20.7; Focus on Communication 20.1, 20.2, 20.5.*

20.12. 穿 *wear* and dài *wear*

穿 and **dài** both mean *wear,* but they are specialized for different parts of the body.

穿 is used when talking about wearing items on the torso or legs:

穿 **xié** *wear shoes*

Dài is used when talking about wearing items on the head, neck, or arms:

dài 口 **zhào** *wear a face mask.*

We will see more examples of 穿 in Lesson 23 and of both verbs in Lesson 24. See also *Use and Structure 24.7.*

Focus on literacy: look for bùjiàn (部件) that rhyme

In Level 1 of this textbook, we noted that some bùjiàn (部件) *recurring component parts of characters* provide pronunciation cues, indicating that a character rhymes with, or nearly rhymes with, another character sharing that bùjiàn. Bùjiàn that provide rhyme cues are called shēngpáng (声旁) in Chinese. Linguists often refer to them as the "phonetic element" of a character.

Approximately 80% of characters contain a shēngpáng. However, not all shēngpáng provide reliable phonetic cues.

Some shēngpáng, like 方 fāng, are very reliable and indicate the pronunciation of the consonants and vowels of the characters in which they occur (though not necessarily the tone):

方 fāng , 房 fáng , 放 fàng

However, sometimes 方 just indicates the vowel and following consonants:

方 fāng , 旁 páng

元 yuán is another very reliable shēngpáng, and characters that contain it usually rhyme with it (though they do not necessarily have the same tone):

元 yuán, 园 yuán, 远 yuǎn, 院 yuàn

Sometimes, however, 元 indicates a "near rhyme," that is, the character in which it occurs has a pronunciation close to but not the same as yuán:

元 yuán, 玩 wán

In short, you cannot rely on shēngpáng to lead you to the exact pronunciation of characters. However, they are very useful in helping you to recall the pronunciation of characters you have already learned. Therefore, you should pay attention to the bùjiàn of characters as you learn them and see if they contain phonetic elements that occur in characters you have already learned. In the workbook chapter for this and following lessons, we will have you search for characters that share a shēngpáng that reflects a rhyme or near rhyme.

🎧 Sentence pyramids

Supply the English translation for the last line where indicated.

1 cè 所 上 cè 所 上了好几次 cè 所 一 yè 上了好几次 cè 所。	*toilet* *go to the toilet* *went to the toilet many times* *Went to the toilet many times throughout the night.*
2 bìng 了 知道他 bìng 了 一看就知道他 bìng 了 国强一看就知道他 bìng 了。	*sick* *know he is sick* *as soon as (he) looked he knew he was sick* *As soon as Guoqiang looked he knew he was sick.*
3 rù 从口 rù Bìng 从口 rù	*enter* *enter from the mouth* *Illness enters from the mouth.*
4 là 的 吃 là 的 不习惯吃 là 的 他不习惯吃 là 的。	*hot and spicy* *eat hot and spicy (food)* *not used to eating hot and spicy food* _____
5 坏了 吃坏了 他把 dù 子吃坏了。	*bad* *became bad by eating* *He turned his stomach bad by eating. (He ate something and got stomach trouble as a result.)*
6 看 bìng 到 yī 院去看 bìng 到学校的 yī 院去看 bìng 带大为到学校的 yī 院去看 bìng 马上带大为到学校的 yī 院去看 bìng 国强决定马上带大为到学校的 yī 院去看 bìng。	*get examined for an illness (see a doctor)* *go to the hospital to see a doctor* *go to the school's hospital to see a doctor* *take Dawei to the school's hospital* *immediately take Dawei to the school's hospital to see a doctor* *Guoqiang decided to take Dawei immediately to the school's hospital to see a doctor.*
7 shū 服 不太 shū 服 你好像不太 shū 服。	*comfortable* *not too comfortable* *You do not appear to be too comfortable.*

8 睡不 **zháo** 我昨天晚上睡不 **zháo** 。	*unable to sleep* _____
9 是在哪儿吃的晚饭? 你是在哪儿吃的晚饭? 你昨天晚上是在哪儿吃的晚饭?	*where ate dinner?* *Where did you eat dinner?* _____
10 一家中国饭馆 在一家中国饭馆吃的 我是在一家中国饭馆吃的。	*a Chinese restaurant* *ate at a Chinese restaurant* _____
11 跟谁一起去 你跟谁一起去的?	*went with whom?* _____
12 跟 **Màikè** 一起去 跟 **Màikè** 和他的两个同学一起去 (是) 跟 **Màikè** 和他的两个同学一起 去的 我 (是) 跟 **Màikè** 和他的两个同学一 起去的。	*go with Maike* *go with Maike and two of his classmates* *went with Maike and two of his classmates* _____
13 **dù** 子不 **shū** 服 觉得 **dù** 子不 **shū** 服 什么时候开始觉得 **dù** 子不 **shū** 服 你是什么时候开始觉得 **dù** 子不 **shū** 服 的?	*stomach not comfortable* *feel that (your) stomach was uncomfortable* *what time did (you) begin to feel that* *stomach was uncomfortable?* _____
14 怎么了? 你怎么了?	*what's the matter?* *What's the matter with you?*
15 **dù** 子 **téng** **dù** 子有一点 **téng** 我头 **yūn, dù** 子有一点 **téng**。	*stomach hurts* *stomach hurts a little* *My head is dizzy and my stomach hurts a* *little.*
16 **lì** 气 没有 **lì** 气 全 **shēn** 没有 **lì** 气 我觉得很累, 全 **shēn** 没有 **lì** 气。	*energy* *not have energy* *whole body does not have energy* *I feel very tired, my whole body does not* *have energy.*

17	
发 shāo	*have fever*
我不发 shāo	*I don't have fever*
我好像不发 shāo。	*I don't appear to have a fever.*

18	
打 pēntì	*sneeze*
流 bí 水 huòzhě 打 pēntì	*runny nose or sneeze*
我不 késou。也不流 bí 水 huòzhě 打 pēntì.	*I don't have a cough. I also don't have a runny nose and am not sneezing.*

19	
哪儿不 shū 服？	*where are you uncomfortable?*
还有哪儿不 shū 服？	*In addition, where are you uncomfortable?*
Chú 了 dù 子 téng 以外，shēntǐ 还有哪儿不 shū 服？	*Besides a stomachache, what else on your body is uncomfortable?*

20	
yǎnjīng	*eye(s)*
ěrduo 和 yǎnjīng	*ear(s) and eye(s)*
你的 ěrduo 和 yǎnjīng	*your ears and eyes*
我看一下你的 ěrduo 和 yǎnjīng。	*I'll take a look at your ears and eyes.*
来，我看一下你的 ěrduo 和 yǎnjīng。	_____

21	
sǎng 子	*throat*
看看 sǎng 子	*look at your throat*
让我看看 sǎng 子	*let me look at your throat*
把 zuǐba 张开让我看看 sǎng 子。	*Open your mouth, and let me look at your throat.*

22	
不干净的东西	*unclean things*
一些不干净的东西	*a few unclean things*
你大 gài 吃了一些不干净的东西。	*You probably ate some unclean things.*

23	
吃 là 的	*eat spicy food*
不习惯吃 là 的	*not used to eating spicy food*
可能你也不习惯吃 là 的。	_____

24	
开 yào	*write a prescription*
开一点 yào	*write a prescription for a little medicine*
我给你开一点 yào。	_____

25 两片 一次吃两片 一天吃三次，一次吃两片。	*two tablets* *each time take (eat) two tablets* *Take the medicine three times a day, each time take two tablets.*
26 **bǎo** 吃得太 **bǎo** 别吃得太 **bǎo** 下次别喝得太多, 也别吃得太 **bǎo**。	*full* *eat until too full* *don't eat until you are too full* *Next time don't drink too much, and don't stuff yourself.*
27 **gǎnmào** 很多人 **gǎnmào** 天气 **biàn** 冷了，很多人 **gǎnmào** 最近天气 **biàn** 冷了，很多人 **gǎnmào**。	*have a cold* *a lot of people have colds* *The weather turned cold, a lot of people have colds* ————————————————
28 回来看我 再回来看我 有别的 **zhèngzhuàng** 了，再回来看我 如果几天以后没有好， **huòzhě** 是有别的 **zhèngzhuàng** 了，再回来看我。	*return to see me* *return again to see me* *have other symptoms, return to see me* *If you aren't better after a few days, or you have other symptoms, come back to see me.*

 Language FAQs

Expressions associated with illness: 看 bìng, 吃 yào, 头 téng, etc.

In English, you see **a doctor**, **take** medicine, **have** a headache, **are** dizzy, and a doctor **writes** a prescription. In Mandarin, you see **an illness**: 看 **bìng**. (In Mandarin, you can also 看 **yī** 生, but the expression is not as common as 看 **bìng**.) You **eat** medicine: 吃 **yào**. Your head hurts: 头 **téng** or your head is dizzy: 头 **hūn**. In other words, languages sometimes express identical situations in different ways. Be sure to use the Chinese expressions and not translations of the English ones when talking about illness in Mandarin.

Notes on Chinese culture

上火 *be inflamed*, *have excessive heat*, and explanations of illness in traditional Chinese medicine

In traditional Chinese medicine, illnesses are often explained in terms of an imbalance of yin and yang, or the cold and hot energy within a body. 上火 is excessive heat and is considered responsible for things such as fever, sore throats, and other inflammations. One way to address the condition of 上火, *excessive heat*, is to eat foods with cooling properties. There is some disagreement over the properties of individual foods, but it is generally agreed that yin foods, foods with cooling properties, include soy products, mung beans, water, and watery fruit such as watermelon, and that yang foods, foods that provide heat, include spices, ginger, alcohol, chocolate, and red meat.

Sichuan food and the cuisines of China

Every region of China has its own cuisine characterized by particular flavors and ingredients. Sichuan food is famous for its use of spicy red peppers and Sichuan peppercorn. Sichuan food is definitely yang, full of heat. 回 **guō ròu** *twice cooked pork* and **mápó-dòufu** *Mapo Tofu* are two famous Sichuan dishes. Hunan food is also hot and spicy. The food of Beijing and northern China includes wheat products such as noodles, dumplings, and steamed breads, as well as beef and lamb. Shanghai and the surrounding region (Jiangsu) is famous for its seafood, for its use of vinegar and sugar, and for its 红 **shāo** dishes. Guangdong (Cantonese) food uses a broad range of ingredients. Some characteristic flavorings include black beans and oyster sauce. Dim Sum comes from the Cantonese tradition. Guizhou food is known for its use of vinegar and hot peppers, and Fujian is famous for its stews, its use of seafood, and its emphasis on salty, sweet, and sour (vinegary) flavors. Restaurants in China typically specialize in the cuisine of a specific region, and you won't find the same "Chinese food" in different restaurants.

Find a map of China online and identify the regions mentioned in this Culture note.

Narrative in English

Last night Dawei went to a restaurant with several friends to eat dinner. After he came back from the restaurant, his stomach was uncomfortable. He went to the toilet many times throughout the night. As soon as Guoqiang saw him, he knew he was sick. Guoqiang said that this is what Chinese people describe as "illness enters through the mouth." Dawei may have eaten too much, or he might not be used to eating spicy things, or the food wasn't clean, and (in one of these ways) he ate his way to an upset stomach. He decided to take Dawei to the school's clinic to see about his illness.

Dialogue in English

Part A

Guoqiang: Dawei, you don't seem very comfortable. Did you sleep well last night?

Dawei: My stomach is upset. I couldn't sleep, and I went to the bathroom many times last night. This morning I can't eat anything and I feel like throwing up.

Guoqiang: How come you have diarrhea? Where did you eat last night?

Dawei: I ate at a Chinese restaurant.

Guoqiang: Who did you go with?

Dawei: I went with Maike and two of his classmates.

Guoqiang: When did you begin to feel that your stomach was upset?

Dawei: Right after I ate, I began to feel uncomfortable.

Guoqiang: You are probably sick. Put on some clothes and let's go to the hospital.

Part B

The setting: In the doctor's office

Doctor: What's the matter with you? Where are you uncomfortable?

Dawei: I have had diarrhea since last night. I'm dizzy and I feel nauseous.

Doctor: Does your stomach hurt?

Dawei: It hurts a little. I feel very tired. My entire body has no energy.

Doctor: Do you have a fever?

Dawei: I don't seem to have a fever.

Doctor: Are you coughing?

Dawei: I'm not coughing. I also don't have a runny nose and I'm not sneezing.

Doctor: Aside from having a stomachache, where else are you uncomfortable?

Dawei: My head hurts.

Doctor: (*Looks at the chart*) You don't have fever, it's probably not a cold. Come, let me look at your ears and your eyes. . . . Open your mouth, let me see if your throat is red, if you have an inflammation. (Let me) look at your tongue and see if it is inflamed.

Part C

Doctor: What did you eat last night?

Dawei: I ate at a Sichuan restaurant with friends. We ate a lot, and we also drank a few bottles of beer.

Doctor: You probably ate something that wasn't clean. You also may not be used to eating spicy things, so you got a stomachache. I will write you a prescription for some medicine. Take it three times every day, take two pills each time, and you'll get better very soon. Next time don't eat so much and don't stuff yourself. Also, the weather has changed recently and a lot of people are catching colds. Be a little careful. If you aren't better in a few days, or you have other symptoms, come again to see me.

Dawei: Thank you.

Lesson 21

天气和气候
变化
*Weather and
climate change*

Communication goals
By the end of this lesson, you will be able to:

- Talk about the weather, seasons, and climate change.
- Make comparisons.

Literacy goals
By the end of this lesson, you will be able to:

- Write an opinion paragraph.
- Recognize the use of four-character expressions in formal written Chinese.

Key structures
- **yuè** 来 **yuè** + AdjV *more and more AdjV*
- **guā fēng** *it is windy*, 下 **xuě** *it is snowing*, 下 **yǔ** *it is raining*
- **V** 不了 *unable to V*
- Stating that things are alike and not alike with 一样
- Asking questions to confirm assumptions: 不是 VP 吗?
- 变 + AdjV *turn AdjV*
- Making comparisons with 比
- Stating differences with 不同
- The suffix 化 *-ify, -ize*
- **zhí** 得 + VP *worth V-ing*

Narrative

虽然大为在北京已经住了一年多了，可是他还是不习惯北京的天气。北京的 **dōng** 天 **xuě** 下得不多，可是非常冷，**wēndù** 很 **dī**。 夏天又 **mēn** 又热，**yǔ** 下得也很少。最近几年北京的夏天热得 **yuè** 来 **yuè** 早，热的时间也 **yuè** 来 **yuè** 长。 北京 **chūn** 天常常 **guā** 大 **fēng**，**qiū** 天天气最好，不冷、不热，非常 **shū** 服，就是太 **duǎn** 了。

Title and narrative vocabulary

				Simplified	Traditional
chūntiān	chūn 天	*spring*	noun phrase	春天	春天
dī		*low*	adjectival verb	低	低
dōngtiān	duǎn 天	*winter*	noun phrase	冬天	冬天
duǎn		*short*	adjectival verb	短	短
fēng		*wind*	noun	风	風
guā		*blow*	verb	刮	刮
guā fēng		*windy (blow wind)*	verb + object	刮风	刮風
mēn		*humid (in warm weather)*	adjectival verb	闷	悶
qìhòu	气候	*climate*	noun	气候	氣候
qiūtiān	qiū 天	*autumn, fall*	noun phrase	秋天	秋天
xuě		*snow*	noun	雪	雪
yǔ		*rain*	noun	雨	雨
yuè lái yuè	yuè 来 yuè	*more and more*	intensifier phrase	越来越	越來越

Narrative characters

Character	Pinyin	Meaning/function	Radical	Phrases	Traditional character
长	cháng	*long*	长	长短 chángduǎn *length*	長
热	rè	*hot*	灬		熱
夏	xià	*summer**	夂	夏天 xiàtiān *summer*	夏
又	yòu	*both . . . and; again*	又	又 mēn 又热 yòu mēn yòu rè *both humid and hot*	又

The situation: It is several months into the fall semester, and the weather in Beijing is getting colder and colder. Dawei, his classmate Wang Maike, and his roommate Guoqiang are hanging out in the dorm, and Dawei is complaining about the weather.

Part A

大为： 这几天北京真冷。今天 **yīn** 天，最高 **wēndù** 只有零下三、四 **dù**， 我快 **shòu** 不了了。听说明天跟今天一样冷，**érqiě** 会下 **xuě**。

国强： 下 **xuě** 不是很好吗？下 **xuě** 的时候外边特别漂亮。

大为： 下 **xuě** 以后，路上很脏，出去也很不方 **biàn**。

国强： 可是天气 **yùbào** 说后天天气会变好，多 **yún zhuǎn qíng**，**érqiě** 会 **nuǎn** 和一点。

大为： 我还是觉得北京的 **dōng** 天太冷了。我比较喜欢 **qiū** 天，每天都是 **qíng** 天。

Vocabulary Dialogue Part A

				Simplified	Traditional
dù		degree	noun	度	度
duō yún	多 yún	cloudy	adjective phrase	多云	多雲
érqiě		moreover, in addition, also	adverb	而且	而且
fāngbiàn	方 biàn	convenient	adjectival verb	方便	方便
nuǎnhuo	nuǎn 和	warm	adjectival verb	暖和	暖和
qíng		clear	adjectival verb	晴	晴
qíngtiān	qíng 天	clear day	noun phrase	晴天	晴天
shòubùliǎo	shòu 不 了	unable to bear (something)	resultative verb	受不了	受不了
tiānqì yùbào	天气 yùbào	weather forecast	noun phrase	天气预报	天氣預報
wēndù		temperature	noun	温度	溫度
yīn tiān	yīn 天	overcast	noun phrase	阴天	陰天
yùbào		forecast	noun	预报	預報
zhuǎn		turn	verb	转	轉
zhuǎn qíng		turning clear	verb phrase	转晴	轉晴

Dialogue Part A Characters

Character	Pinyin	Meaning/function	Radical	Phrases	Traditional character
比	bǐ	*compare**	比	比较 bǐjiào *relatively*	比
变	biàn	*change*	又		變
较	jiào	*compare**	车	比较 bǐjiào *relatively*	較
亮	liàng	*light, shine*	亠	漂亮 piàoliang *pretty*	亮
零	líng	*zero*	雨	零下 língxià *below zero*	零
漂	piào	*good-looking**	氵	漂亮 piàoliang *pretty*	漂
脏	zāng	*dirty*	月		髒

Part B

国强： 你家 **xiāng** 的天气怎么样？

大为： 我住在南加 **zhōu**，离海边很近。那里的天气，四 **jì** 如 **chūn**，**dōng** 天不 **shī** 冷，夏天不 **mēn** 热。一年四 **jì** 都很 **shū** 服。

国强： 一年四个 **jìjié** 的天气都一样。那就没意思了。北京不一样，一年有四 **jì**， **chūn** 夏 **qiū dōng** 都有。

大为： 我还是觉得我家 **xiāng** 的天气比北京的天气好。夏天 **liáng** 快多了。

国强： 我早就听说加 **zhōu** 的环境好、 **fēngjǐng** 漂亮， **xīwàng** 将来有机会去看看。

大为： 加 **zhōu** 的气候很好。不过这几年 **yǔ** 下得少，夏天太干 **zào**, 常有大火。有人说，这跟全球 **nuǎn** 化有关系。

国强： 我们只有一个地球，这**的** **què** (*díquè*) 是一个 **zhí** 得关心的话题。我的环境管理课也 **tí** 到这方面的问题。

Vocabulary Dialogue Part B

				Simplified	Traditional
bǐ	比	compared with	verb, preposition	比	比
díquè	的 què	really, indeed	adverb	的确	的確
fēngjǐng		scenery	noun	风景	風景
gānzào	干 zào	dry	adj. verb	干燥	乾燥
guānxīn	关心	be concerned about	verb	关心	關心
huàtí	话题	topic	noun	话题	話題
jìjié		season	noun	季节	季節
jiāxiāng	家 xiāng	hometown	noun	家乡	家鄉
Jiāzhōu	加 zhōu	California	proper noun	加州	加州
liángkuai	liáng 快	cool (pleasantly cool)	adjectival verb	凉快	涼快
mēn rè	mēn 热	hot and humid	adjectival phrase	闷热	悶熱
nuǎnhuà	nuǎn 化	warming	verb	暖化	暖化
qiú	球	ball, sphere, world	noun	球	球
quánqiú	全球	global	noun, adjective	全球	全球
quánqiú nuǎnhuà	全球 nuǎn 化	global warming	noun phrase	全球暖化	全球暖化
shī		humid (in cold weather)	adjectival verb	湿	溼
shī lěng	shī 冷	cold and damp	adjectival phrase	湿冷	溼冷
sì jì	四 jì	four seasons	noun phrase	四季	四季

sì jì rú chūn	四 jì 如 chūn	*like spring all year round*	four-character expression	四季如春	四季如春
tídào	tí 到	*mention*	verb	提到	提到
xīwàng		*hope*	verb	希望	希望
zhíde	zhí 得	*worth*	adverb	值得	值得

Dialogue Part B Characters

Character	Pinyin	Meaning/function	Radical	Phrases	Traditional character
管	guǎn	*manage*	竹	管理 guǎnlǐ *management*	管
海	hǎi	*sea, ocean*	氵	海边 hǎibiān *sea shore, sea coast*	海
化	huà	*change, transform*	亻	文化 wénhuà *culture,* **nuǎn** 化 nuǎnhuà *warming*	化
环	huán	*ring-shaped, surround*	王	环境 huánjìng *environment*	環
加	jiā	*Add*	力	加 **zhōu** Jiāzhōu *California,* **cān** 加 cānjiā *participate (in)*	加
境	jìng	*border*	土	环境 huánjìng *environment*	境
将	jiāng	*about to, will*	寸	将来 jiānglái *in the future*	將
理	lǐ	*reason, logic*	王	管理 *management*	理

Part C

Màikè：我同意！说到关心，我一直想问：我的中文老师为什么要管我穿什么衣服呢？昨天老师跟我说我穿得太少了。应该多穿一点。

国强：这几天比较冷。老师一定是 **pà** 你生病，所以让你多穿些衣服。

Màikè：我已经二十多岁了，难道我还不会照 **gù** 自己吗？

国强：**āiyā**, 老师只是关心你。

Màikè：老师关心我的学习，也要关心我穿多少衣服吗？

国强：对，你大概不习惯。这可能是中外文化的不同吧。

Vocabulary Dialogue Part C

				Simplified	Traditional
āiyā		*expression of annoyance or impatience*	*interjection*	哎呀	哎呀
guǎn	管	*manage*	verb	管	管
pà		*fear*	*verb*	怕	怕
shuō dào	说到	*speaking of*	verb	说到	說到
tóngyì	同意	*agree*	verb	同意	同意
zhàogù	照 gù	*take care of*	verb	照顾	照顧

Dialogue Part C Characters

Character	Pinyin	Meaning/ function	Radical	Phrases	Traditional character
病	bìng	*sick*	疒	生病 shēng bìng *become sick*	病

该	gāi	*should, ought to*	讠	应该 yīnggāi *should, ought to*	該
概	gài	*approximate**	木	大概 dàgài *probably*	概
岁	suì	*years of age*	山		歲
应	yìng	*respond**	广	应该 yīnggāi *should, ought to*	應
照	zhào	*illuminate; take a photo*	灬	照片 zhàopiàn *photos*, 照照片 zhào zhàopiàn *take photos*, 照 **gù** zhàogù *take care of*	照

Supplementary Vocabulary

环境保护 (环保)	huánjìng bǎo hù (huánbǎo)	*environmental protection*
回收	huíshōu	*recycle*
污染	wūrǎn	*pollution*
空气污染	kōngqì wūrǎn	*air pollution*
水污染	shuǐ wūrǎn	*water pollution*
垃圾	lājī	*garbage, trash*
废气	fèiqì	*exhaust*
太阳能	tàiyángnéng	*solar energy*
资源	zīyuán	*resources*

Stroke Order Flow Chart

Character   **Total Strokes**

Narrative

Character													Total Strokes
长	丿	二	长	长									4
热	一	十	扌	扚	执	执	执	热	热				10
夏	一	二	厂	百	百	百	百	夏	夏	夏			10
又	丁	又											2

Dialogue A

Character													Total Strokes
比	一	比	比	比									4
变	丶	二	广	亦	亦	亦	变	变					8
较	一	土	车	车	车	车	轩	轩	较	较			10
亮	丶	二	亠	古	声	高	亭	亮					9
零	一	厂	一	雨	雨	雨	雫	零	零	零	零		13
漂	丶	冫	氵	汒	沪	沪	湹	湹	湹	漂	漂	漂	14
脏	丿	刀	月	月	月	胪	胪	胪	脏	脏			10

Dialogue B

Character													Total Strokes
管	丿	𠂆	竹	竹	竻	竻	竻	竻	管	管	管	管	14
海	丶	冫	氵	汒	汇	汇	海	海	海	海			10
化	丿	亻	亻	化									4
环	一	二	王	王	玎	玎	环	环					8
加	丁	力	力	加	加								5
境	一	十	土	圹	圹	圹	垃	培	培	培	墇	境	14
将	丶	冫	斗	丬	州	州	将	将	将				9
理	一	二	王	王	玊	珇	珇	珇	理	理	理		11

Dialogue C

Character													Total Strokes
病	丶	二	广	广	疒	疒	疒	病	病	病			10
该	丶	讠	讠	讠	该	该	该	该					8
概	一	十	扌	木	朾	朾	朾	相	梍	梍	椕	概	13
岁	丨	山	山	少	岁	岁							6
应	丶	二	广	广	应	应	应						7
照	丨	刀	日	日	日	昭	昭	昭	昭	昭	昭	照	13

Use and structure

21.1.   yuè 来 yuè (越来越) + AdjV *more and more AdjV*

To say that something has *more and more* of some quality, say:

> Subject **yuè 来 yuè** adjectival verb.
> 最近几年北京的夏天热得 **yuè 来 yuè** 早，热的时间也 **yuè 来 yuè** 长。
> *In the past few years, Beijing's summer has become hotter and hotter, and the period of time when it is hot has become longer and longer.*

Since **yuè 来 yuè** indicates change, sentences with **yuè 来 yuè** often end in 了 to emphasize the change or new situation.

> 这几年东西 **yuè 来 yuè** 贵了。
> *These past few years things have gotten more and more expensive.*

Yuè 来 yuè is an intensifier, used the same way as 很 *very*, 太 *too*, 真 *really*, etc. It always occurs before an adjectival verb.

> **Practice**   *Workbook: Focus on Structure 21.1, 21.3; Focus on Communication 21.2.*

21.2.   Weather expressions: 下 xuě (下雪) *it is snowing*, 下 yǔ (下雨) *it is raining*, guā fēng (刮风) *it is windy*

In English, weather expressions often begin with the word *it*: *it is snowing, it is raining, it is windy*, etc. In Mandarin, these equivalent expressions occur without a subject. They begin with the verb:

> 下 **xuě** *it is snowing* (literally: *falls snow*)
> 下 **yǔ** *it is raining* (literally: *falls rain*)
> **guā fēng** *it is windy* (literally: *blows wind*)
> 明天会下 **xuě**。
> *It may snow tomorrow.*
> **Chūn** 天常常 **guā fēng**。
> *It is often windy in the spring.*

Do not include a subject in these weather expressions in Mandarin. That is, do not say things like: ⊗他下 **xuě** *"it" is snowing*.

Chinese and English also differ in the way that they express the intensity of rain, snow, or wind. The difference is illustrated in the following chart.

English	Chinese
It was **very** windy yesterday.	昨天 **guā** 大 **fēng** 了。
It will snow **heavily** tomorrow. (Tomorrow there will be a lot of snow.)	明天会下大 **xuě**。
It rained **heavily** this morning. (There was a lot of rain this morning.)	今天早上下大 **yǔ** 了。

In sum, in Chinese, the way to express the severity of the rain, snow, or wind is to put the description right before the word for rain, snow, or wind: 下大 **yǔ**, 下大 **xuě**, **guā** 大 **fēng**.

The direction of the wind also occurs right before the word **fēng** *wind*, for example:

> ***Guā*** 南 **fēng** 。
> *There is a southern wind. (The wind is blowing from the south.)*
> ***Guā*** 西北 **fēng** 。
> *There is a northwest wind. (The wind is from the northwest.)*

> **Practice** ▶ *Workbook: Focus on Structure 21.1, 21.3; Focus on Communication 21.4, 21.5, 21.6, 21.7.*

21.3.   Talking about temperature

Temperature is stated as number + dù (degrees).

To state the temperature for today say:

> 今天的 **wēndù** 是（三十五）**dù**.
> *Today's temperature is (35) degrees.*

To talk about temperature *below zero* say:

> 零下**(四) dù**
> *(4) degrees below zero.*

To ask about temperature say:

> 明天的 **wēndù** 是多少 **dù**?
> *What will the temperature be tomorrow?*

To talk about the highest temperature say:

> 最高 **wēndù**
> *the highest temperature*

To talk about the lowest temperature say:

> 最 **dī wēndù**
> *the lowest temperature*
> 最高 **wēndù** 只有零下三、四 **dù**。
> *The highest temperature will be only 3 or 4 degrees below zero.*

> **Practice** ▶ *Workbook: Focus on Structure 21.1, 21.3; Focus on Communication 21.4, 21.5, 21.6, 21.7.*

21.4.   Verb 不了 (buliǎo) *unable to verb*

不了, pronounced **buliǎo**, is a verb suffix that indicates that the subject is unable to do the action associated with the verb. V 不了 is often called the *potential form* of resultative verbs. In this lesson, we see it as part of the word **shòu** 不了 (shòubuliǎo). **Shòu** means to endure or bear something. **Shòu** 不了 means that you are unable to bear or endure some situation. **Shòu** 不了 can often be translated into English as *can't stand* some situation.

这几天北京真冷，我快 **shòu** 不了了。
These past few days Beijing has been really cold, I almost can't stand it.

The 不了 suffix can be used with any verb to say that the subject cannot do the action of the verb: 去不了 *unable to go*, 买不了 *unable to buy*, etc.

那个地方比较远，如果没有车你去不了。
That place is relatively far (from here). If you don't have a car you can't go.
已经十年了，我还忘不了她。
It's already been 10 years, (and) I still can't forget her.
我的电脑坏了，用不了了。
My computer is broken. I can't use it anymore.
国强的生日我去不了了，我得 **zhǔnbèi** 明天的考试。
I can't go to Guoqiang's birthday. I have to prepare for tomorrow's test.

Remember that 了 is pronounced **liǎo** in this suffix. When you see 不了 together, you should always assume that it is the verb suffix **buliǎo**. We will learn more about the potential form of verbs in later lessons.

Practice ▸ *Workbook: Focus on Structure 21.4, 21.5; Focus on Communication 21.2.*

21.5. Saying that things are alike or are not alike with 一样

All members of a group are alike

To say that all of the members of a group of nouns are alike, say:

NP 一样。
一年四个 **jìjié** 的天气都一样。
The weather in all of the four seasons of the year is the same.

Two noun phrases are alike

To say that two noun phrases (two people, places, things, ideas, situations, etc.) are alike, say the following. Notice that the two noun phrases can be linked with either 跟 or 和:

NP₁ 跟/和 NP₂ 一样。
这件衣服和那件衣服一样。
This article of clothing and that article of clothing are alike.

Two noun phrases are alike in some way

To say that two noun phrases (two people, places, things, ideas, situations, etc.) are alike or the same in some way, that is, that they have the same quality, say the following. Here again, the two noun phrases can be linked with either 跟 or 和:

NP₁ 跟/和 NP₂ 一样 **AdjV**
昨天跟今天一样冷。
Yesterday and today equally cold.

Chūn 天和 **qiū**天一样 **shū**服。
Spring and fall are equally comfortable.
这件衣服和那件衣服一样贵。
This article of clothing is as expensive as that article of clothing.

Two noun phrases are not alike, or are not alike in some way

To say that two noun phrases are not alike, or are not alike in some way, say 不一样 as follows. Notice that the negation is 不 and it always occurs before 一样.

这件衣服和那件衣服不一样。
This article of clothing and that article of clothing are not the same.
这件衣服和那件衣服不一样贵。
This article of clothing and that article of clothing are not equally expensive.

Asking whether two noun phrases are alike

To ask whether two noun phrases are alike, you can use a 吗 question or you can ask 一样不一样?

这件衣服和那件衣服一样吗？
这件衣服和那件衣服一样不一样？
Are these two articles of clothing alike?

Asking whether two noun phrases are alike in some way

To ask whether two noun phrases are alike in some way, use the 吗 form of yes-no questions:

这件衣服和那件衣服一样贵吗？
Is this article of clothing as expensive as that article of clothing?
Chūn 天跟 **qiū** 天一样漂亮吗？
Are spring and fall equally pretty?

> **Practice** ▸ *Workbook: Focus on Structure 21.6, 21.8, 21.9, 21.10; Focus on Communication 21.2, 21.4.*

21.6.   不是 VP 吗？ *Isn't it the case that VP?*

(subject) 不是 VP 吗？   means *isn't it the case that . . . ?* or *isn't it true that . . . ?*

下 **xuě** 不是很好吗？
Isn't snow good? (Literally: *Isn't it the case that snowing is a good thing?*)
美国大学不是都很贵吗？
Isn't it the case that American colleges are all very expensive?

(subject) 不是 VP 吗？   asks the listener to confirm something that the speaker believes to be true. These questions are often rhetorical questions, that is, questions that don't require an answer.

> **Practice** ▸ *Workbook: Focus on Structure 21.10.*

21.7.   变 + AdjV *become AdjV*

变 + AdjV means *become AdjV*. To say that something will become AdjV, say:

> subject 会变 AdjV.
> 天气 **yùbào** 说后天天气会变好。
> *The weather forecast says that the day after tomorrow the weather will become good.*
> 如果你不早一点买，飞机票就会变贵。
> *If you don't buy (them) a little early, airline tickets will become more expensive.*
> 每天都跟同学 **liàn** 习，你的中文就会变好。
> *If you practice with your classmates every day, your Chinese will get better.*
> 早睡早起会让你的 **shēntǐ** 变好。
> *Going to bed early and getting up early will make your body better.*
> (*If you go to sleep early and get up early, your health will improve.*)

To say that something *became AdjV*, say:

> **subject 变 AdjV 了**
> 最近天气变冷了。
> *The weather has recently become cold.*
> 二年 **jí** 的中文课，汉字变多，**yǔ** 法也变难了。
> *In second-year Chinese, there are more characters and the grammar gets harder.*
> 好久不见，你变漂亮了！
> *I haven't seen you in a long time, you've become beautiful!*

In these sentences, 了 emphasizes the change of situation.

> **Practice** ▶ *Workbook: Focus on Structure 21.2; Focus on Communication 21.4.*

21.8.   Comparisons with 比

比 is used to make comparisons. It occurs in the structure NP$_1$ 比 NP$_2$ AdjV and indicates that NP$_1$ has more of the quality of the adjectival verb than NP$_2$.

> **NP₁ 比 NP₂ AdjV**
> 我家 **xiāng** 的天气比北京的天气好。
> *The weather in my hometown is better than the weather in Beijing.*
> **Dōng** 天比 **qiū** 天冷。
> *Winter is colder than fall.*

To say that one noun phrase has *a little more* of some quality than another, say:

> **NP₁ 比 NP₂ AdjV 一点**
> 北京比上海冷一点。
> *Beijing is a little colder than Shanghai.*

When asking yes-no questions that involve 比 comparisons, use the 吗 form:

> 北京比上海冷吗？
> *Is Beijing colder than Shanghai?*

We will learn more about comparisons in later lessons.

Practice ▷ *Workbook: Focus on Structure 21.7, 21.8, 21.9, 21.10; Focus on Communication 21.2, 21.4.*

21.9.   A difference between two noun phrases: NP₁ 跟/和 NP₂ 的不同

To say that something is a difference between two noun phrases, say:

NP₁ 跟/和 **NP₂** 的不同
这是中国文化和美国文化的不同。
This is a difference between Chinese culture and American culture.

The two noun phrases being compared can sometime be expressed with a single phrase:

这可能是**中外**文化的不同吧。
I suspect that this is probably a difference between Chinese culture and other cultures.

Practice ▷ *Workbook: Focus on Structure 21.9.*

21.10.   The suffix 化 *-ize, -ify*

In addition to its occurrence in words like 文化 *culture*, 化 also functions as a suffix for adjectives, adjectival verbs, and nouns.

When it serves as a suffix for adjectives and adjectival verbs, Adj-化 can often be translated as a verb with the English suffix *-ify*:

美 *beautiful*   美化 *beautify*
绿 *green*   绿化 *greenify*
老 *old*   老化 *(to) age, become older*
美化环境会让人觉得很高兴。
Beautifying the environment can make people feel very happy.
绿化 **chéng** 市可以让生活变好。
Greenifying the city can make life better.
如果你不照 **gù** 自己，会老化得特别快。
If you don't take care of yourself, you will age very quickly.

When it serves as a suffix for nouns, 化 can often be translated as either a noun or a verb with the English suffix *-ize*:

美国 *America*   美国化 *Americanize*
中国 *China*   中国化 *Sinicize*
现 **dài**（**xiàndài**）*modern*   现 **dài** 化 *modernize*
zhèng 治 *politics*   **zhèng** 治化 *politicize*
chéng 市 *city*   **chéng** 市化 *urbanize*
不要把每一件事 **qing** 都 **zhèng** 治化。
Don't politicize everything.
Chéng 市化带来了很多环境问题。
Urbanization brings with it a lot of environmental problems.

Practice   *Workbook: Focus on Structure 21.3.*

21.11.   zhí 得 (值得) + V *worth V-ing*

Zhí 得 occurs directly before action verbs. **Zhí** 得 + action verb means *worth V-ing*. Guo-qiang uses it in the conversation in the dialogue about global warming:

这是一个 **zhí** 得关心的话题。
This is a topic worth caring about.
听说那个电 **yǐng zhí** 得看。
I've heard that that movie is worth seeing.

21.12.   的 què (díquè) *indeed, really*

的 **què (díquè)** is an adverb that provides the speaker's perspective on a situation. It indicates that the speaker is emphatic about what he or she states. In Part B of the dialogue, Guoqiang uses it when talking about global warming:

这的 **què (díquè)** 是一个 **zhí** 得关心的话题。
This really is a topic worth caring about.

的 **què (díquè)** emphasizes the speaker's opinion about a statement. It can be omitted from the sentence without changing its basic meaning. That is, if Guoqiang did not want to be so emphatic, he could have said:

这是一个 **zhí** 得关心的话题。
This is a topic worth caring about.

Narrative structure: the opinion paragraph

The narrative in this lesson illustrates the structure of an *opinion paragraph,* a paragraph in which the writer indicates their opinion and provides reasons to support it. As in most paragraphs, the topic is usually stated in the first sentence. It is the main point of the first sentence.

大为虽然在北京已经住了一年多了，可是他还是不习惯北京的天气。
Although Dawei has already lived in Beijing for more than a year, he is still not used to Beijing's weather.

Although this sentence contains information about how long Dawei has lived in Beijing, the main point of the sentence is that Dawei is not used to Beijing weather. If you read through the paragraph, you will find that his actual opinion of the weather is not stated, but it is implied by the words used to describe the weather.

The paragraph is structured around the four seasons, beginning with **dōng** 天. Let's make a list of the seasons and find the main word or phrases that the narrator uses to describe each season:

dōng 天: **xuě** 下得不多, 可是非常冷 (*it doesn't snow much but it is extremely cold*)
夏天: 又 **mēn** 又热， **yǔ** 下得也很少 (*hot and humid, there isn't much rain*)
chūn 天: **guā** 大 **fēng** (*very windy*)
qiū 天: 天气最好。。。 就是太 **duǎn** 了。 (*the weather is the best but it's too short*)

We are now ready to read between the lines: What is Dawei's opinion of the weather in Beijing? How do you know? Based on the evidence that the narrator gives, do you share Dawei's opinion? What could you change in the essay to express a positive opinion about the same weather conditions?

As you work on the reading exercises in the workbook, think about how the paragraphs are structured and about the opinions or values implied by the words that are used to describe things or events.

 Sentence pyramids

Supply the English translation for the last line where indicated.

1 冷 一样冷 跟今天一样冷 明天会跟今天一样冷 听说明天会跟今天一样冷。	*cold* *equally cold* *as cold as today* *tomorrow it will be as cold as today.* _____
2 下 **xuě** 每天都下 **xuě** 这个星期每天都下 **xuě**。	*it snows* *it snows every day* *This week it is snowing every day.*
3 热 又 **mēn** 又热 夏天又 **mēn** 又热。	*hot* *both humid and hot* *It is both humid and hot in the summer.*
4 早 **yuè** 来 **yuè** 早 热得 **yuè** 来 **yuè** 早 夏天热得 **yuè** 来 **yuè** 早 北京的夏天热得 **yuè** 来 **yuè** 早 最近几年北京的夏天热得 **yuè** 来 **yuè** 早。	*early* *earlier and earlier* *it gets hot earlier and earlier* *it gets hot in the summer earlier and earlier* *Beijing summers get hot earlier and earlier* *Recently, Beijing summers have gotten hot earlier and earlier.*
5 **fēng** **guā fēng** **guā** 大 **fēng** 常常 **guā** 大 **fēng** **chūn** 天常常 **guā** 大 **fēng** 北京 **chūn** 天常常 **guā** 大 **fēng** 。	*wind* *windy* *very windy* *it is often very windy* *it is often very windy in the spring* _____

6 **dù** 四 **dù** 零下三、四 **dù** 只有零下三、四 **dù** **wēndù** 只有零下三、四 **dù** 最高 **wēndù** 只有零下三、四 **dù**。	*degree* *4 degrees* *3 or 4 degrees below zero* *it's only 3 or 4 degrees below zero* *the temperature is only 3 or 4 degrees below zero* *The highest temperature is only 3 or 4 degrees below zero.*
7 **shòu** 不了 我快 **shòu** 不了了。	*can't stand it* *I just about can't stand it.*
8. 不是很好吗 下 **xuě** 不是很好吗?	*isn't it good?* *Isn't snow good?*
9 很脏 路上很脏 下 **xuě** 以后，路上很脏。	*very dirty* *the roads are very dirty* *After it snows, the roads are very dirty.*
10 变好 天气会变好 后天的天气会变好 天气 **yùbào** 说后天的天气会变好。	*become good* *the weather will turn good* *the day after tomorrow the weather will turn good* _____
11 **qíng** **zhuǎn qíng** 多 **yún zhuǎn qíng** 天气会变好，多 **yún zhuǎn qíng**。	*clear* *turn clear* *cloudy turning clear* *The weather will improve, cloudy turning clear.*
12 四 **jì** 如 **chūn** 那里的天气，四 **jì** 如 **chūn**。	*like spring all year* *The weather there, it's like spring all year.*
13 一样 天气都一样 一年四个 **jìjié** 的天气都一样。	*the same* *the weather is all the same* *The weather is the same all four seasons of the year.*
14 都有 **chūn** 夏 **qiū dōng** 都有 一年有四 **jì**，**chūn** 夏 **qiū dōng** 都有。	*have them all* *has spring, summer, fall, and winter* _____

15 天气好 北京的天气好 比北京的天气好 我家 **xiāng** 的天气比北京的天气好。	*the weather is good* *Beijing's weather is good* *better than Beijing's weather* *The weather in my hometown is better than Beijing's weather.*
16 关系 有关系 跟全球 **nuǎn** 化有关系 这跟全球 **nuǎn** 化有关系。	*connection* *has a connection* *is related to global warming* _____
17 话题 **zhí** 得关心的话题 一个 **zhí** 得关心的话题 这是一个 **zhí** 得关心的话题。	*discussion topic* *discussion topic worth caring about* *a discussion topic worth caring about* _____
18 穿什么衣服 管我穿什么衣服 为什么要管我穿什么衣服 我的中文老师为什么要管我穿什么衣服呢?	*wear what clothing* *care about what clothing I wear* *why care about what clothing I wear* _____?
19 衣服 穿衣服 多穿些衣服 让你多穿些衣服 老师 **pà** 你生病，所以让你多穿些衣服。	*clothing* *wear clothing* *wear more clothing* *make you put on more clothing* *The teacher is afraid you will become sick so (s/he) makes you put on more clothing.*
20 自己 照 **gù** 自己 不会照 **gù** 自己吗? 难道我还不会照 **gù** 自己吗? 我已经二十多岁了，难道我还不会照 **gù** 自己吗?	*self* *take care of (my) self* *unable to take care of (my) self?* *Do you mean to say I am still unable to take care of myself?* _____
21 学习 学生的学习 老师关心学生的学习。	*study* *students' studies* *Teachers are concerned about students' studies.*

22 不同 中外文化的不同 这可能是中外文化的不同。	*difference; not the same* *a difference between Chinese and foreign cultures* *This is perhaps a difference between Chinese culture and foreign cultures.*

 Language FAQs

Four-character expressions

One important feature of formal written Chinese is the use of four-character expressions. Some four-character expressions capture a meaning or convey an idea. 四 **jì** 如 **chūn** *like spring all year long* (literally: *four seasons as if spring*) is this type of expression.

Some four-character expressions are abbreviations of longer expressions, formed by eliminating a syllable or more from the contributing parts. Here are four-character expressions used in this lesson that are formed in this way:

chūn 夏 **qiū dōng** (from **chūn** 天、夏天、 **qiū** 天、 **dōng** 天) *spring, summer, fall, winter*

全球 **nuǎn** 化 (from 全地球 **nuǎn** 化) *global warming*

和 and 的： One character, two pronunciations

In this lesson, we learn two words with characters that have more than one pronunciation, 和 and 的. We have already learned that when the character 和 is pronounced **hé** when it means *with*. In this lesson, we see that when it occurs as part of the word **nuǎn** 和 *warm* it is pronounced **huo**. We have already learned that 的 is usually pronounced **de**. In the word 的 **què**, however, it is pronounced **dí**. 和 and 的 are two of a small number of characters associated with more than one pronunciation depending upon the word in which it occurs. In Chinese, these characters are called **pò** 音字 (破音字), or *broken sound characters*. We have learned other **pò** 音字 in earlier lessons:

行: pronounced **xíng** in the expression 行不行？ *okay?* and pronounced **háng** in the word **yín** 行 (银行 **yínháng**) *bank*.

觉: pronounced **jué** in the word 觉得, and pronounced **jiào** in the word **shuì** 觉.

得: pronounced **děi** when it occurs as an independent word meaning *must*, and pronounced **de** when it occurs in the word 觉得 and when it introduces adverbial complements as in 说得快.

The four seasons of the year

Notice that when listing the four seasons of the year in Chinese, you begin with spring:

chūn 夏 **qiū dōng** (春夏秋冬) *spring summer fall winter*

The list begins with spring because in the traditional Chinese calendar, the start of the new year is also the first day of spring.

Two meanings of 穿 *put on, wear*

The verb 穿 has two meanings, *put on* and *wear*. How can it have both meanings? Because after you put something on, you are wearing it. Context will make clear whether you should translate 穿 as *put on* or *wear*. Sometimes either translation is possible:

我的中文老师为什么要管我穿什么衣服呢?
Why does my Chinese teacher care what clothes I put on (what clothes I wear)?

Many Mandarin words that refer to a change of situation like 穿 also refer to the resulting state. Here are two more examples: 病 *to get sick, to be sick,* 坐 *to sit down, to be seated.*

 # Notes on Chinese culture

The role of the teacher in Chinese culture

The role of the teacher in Chinese culture was defined over two thousand years ago in the teachings of Confucius, a philosopher and teacher who lived 551–479 BCE. In Chinese culture, the responsibility of the teacher to the student is not limited to the classroom or school context. Instead, the teacher is responsible for the well-being of his or her students in all aspects of their lives. As Màikè discovers, Chinese teachers often feel that it is their responsibility to teach their foreign students to dress and behave appropriately when in China. American students need to show that they are grateful for the concern of their teachers, and they should do their best to follow their advice.

Dressing for cold weather in Chinese culture

In Chinese culture, people dress according to the weather but also according to the seasons as determined in the traditional Chinese lunar (agricultural) calendar. The traditional calendar distinguishes 24 different seasons, each with distinct type of weather conditions and associated expectations about how you should dress.

Expressing temperature in the Fahrenheit and Celsius scales

China, like most countries, expresses temperature using the Celsius scale, in which zero degrees is the temperature at which water freezes, and 100 degrees is the temperature at which water boils. The United States and a small number of other countries use the Fahrenheit scale to express temperature. Zero degrees Celsius is 32 degrees Fahrenheit. Minus 3 or 4 degrees Celsius is about 25 degrees Fahrenheit.

The official heating season in China

In northern China, the government determines the official beginning and end of the heating season. Heat can be turned on in buildings beginning on November 15, and it must be turned off by March 15. Since the weather in many cities in the north may become cold before November 15, people have to be prepared to dress for the weather even when they are indoors. Official government policy decrees that south of the Yangzi River buildings cannot have central heating at all. Tourist hotels are exempt from these policies, however.

Narrative in English

Although Dawei has already lived in Beijing for more than a year, he is still not used to Beijing's weather. In the winter in Beijing there isn't much snow, but it is extremely cold (and) the temperature is very low. The summer is both humid and hot, and it doesn't rain much. In recent years, it has gotten hot in the summer earlier and earlier and the period when it's hot has gotten longer and longer. In the spring in Beijing, it is often very windy. The weather in the fall is the best; it's not cold, it's not hot, it's extremely comfortable, it's just that it's too short.

Dialogue in English

Part A

Dawei: These past few days it's been really cold in Beijing. Today it's cloudy and today's high will only be 3 or 4 degrees below zero. I just about can't stand it. I've heard that tomorrow will be as cold as today and in addition it is going to snow.

Guoqiang: Isn't snow good? When it snows, the outdoors is particularly beautiful.

Dawei: After it snows the streets are dirty, and it is extremely inconvenient to go out.

Guoqiang: But the weather forecast says that the weather will turn nice the day after tomorrow, cloudy turning clear, and it is going to warm up a little.

Dawei: I still think the weather in Beijing is too cold. I prefer fall. It's clear every day.

Part B

Guoqiang: What is the weather like in your hometown?

Dawei: I live in southern California, near the coast. The weather there is like spring all year long. It's not cold and damp in the winter, and it's not hot and muggy in the summer. It's comfortable all year long.

Guoqiang: All of the seasons of the year are the same. That's not interesting. Beijing is not the same. The year has all four seasons: spring, summer, fall, and winter.

Dawei: I still think the weather in my hometown is better than Beijing's weather. It's a lot cooler in the summer.

Guoqiang: I have long since heard it said that California's climate is good and the scenery is pretty. I hope that in the future I have the chance to go and take a look.

Dawei: California's climate is good. However, these past few years there hasn't been much rain, the summers have been dry, and there are often big fires. Some people say this has to do with global warming.

Guoqiang: This really is a topic worth caring about. My environmental management class has also brought up this topic.

Part C

Maike: I agree. Speaking of caring about things, I've long wanted to ask, why does my Chinese teacher care about what clothing I wear? Yesterday the teacher said I wasn't wearing enough clothing and that I should put on some more clothes.

Guoqiang: It's been relatively cold these past few days. The teacher must be afraid that you'll get sick, so s/he wants to make you put on more clothes.

Maike: I'm already more than 20 years old. Do you mean to say I still can't take care of myself?

Guoqiang: Oh for heaven's sake, the teacher is just being concerned about you.

Maike: The teacher is concerned about my studies and also concerned about how much clothing I wear?

Guoqiang: Yes. You are probably not used to it. This is perhaps a difference between Chinese culture and foreign culture.

Lesson **22**

Duànliàn
身体
Working out

Communication goals
By the end of this lesson, you will be able to:

- Talk about different forms of indoor and outdoor sports and exercise.
- Compare two entities in terms of their similarities and differences.
- Decline an invitation by presenting an earlier commitment.

Literacy goals
By the end of this lesson, you will be able to:

- Use Chinese word formation strategies to identify and create new words.
- Write a comparison paragraph indicating the similarities and differences of two entities.

Key structures
- 在 **X** 上 *from the perspective of X, when it comes to X*
- **xiāng** 同 *similarities* and 不同 *differences*
- 为了 *for the purpose of, in order to*
- **gèng** + AdjV *even more AdjV*
- **lìng** 外 *in addition*
- 走进来 *walk in* and other directional expressions

- AdjV 是 AdjV . . . 可是 *it's AdjV all right, but*
- **lián** NP 都/也 VP *can't even VP*
- A 没有 B 那么/这么 AdjV *A is not as AdjV as B*
- **gòu** *enough*
- 来自 NP *come from NP*
- 到 **dǐ** *after all, finally*

Narrative

美国的大学生跟中国的大学生在 duànliàn 身体上有 xiāng 同 的地方，也有不同的地方。**Xiāng** 同的是年 qīng 人都知道 yùndòng 是为了让身体 **gèng jiànkāng**，喜欢 yùndòng 的人每周都要 duànliàn 几次。他们 pǎo bù、打 lán 球、pá山，跳舞，或者到 jiàn 身房去duànliàn 。不同的是中国的学生很多喜欢 tī zú 球、打 pái 球或打 pīngpāng 球，而美国大学生的 yùndòng，除了美 shì zú 球、bàng 球和 huá chuán 以外，还有室 nèi 的重 liàng xùn 练，yújiā 等等。夏天yóu yǒng ，冬天huá雪、huá bīng 。Lìng 外，美国人非常重视体 yù 活 dòng,很多美国的大学生参加校队，差不多每个周末都有比 sài 。

Narrative vocabulary

				Simplified	Traditional
bàngqiú	bàng 球	*baseball*	noun phrase	棒球	棒球
bǐsài	比 sài	*competition*	noun	比赛	比赛
dǎ bàngqiú	打 bàng 球	*play baseball*	verb + object	打棒球	打棒球
dǎ páiqiú	打 pái 球	*play volleyball*	verb + object	打排球	打排球
dǎ pīngpāng qiú	打 pīngpāng 球	*play ping-pong*	verb + object	打乒乓球	打乒乓球
děngděng	等等	*etcetera*	sentence final phrase	等等	等等
duànliàn		*exercise*	verb	锻炼	鍛煉
ér	而	*and, but, or*	conjunction	而	而

gèng		*even more*	intensifier	更	更
huá		*row*	verb	划	划
huá bīng		*ice skating*	verb + object	滑冰	滑冰
huá chuán		*row boats, crew*	verb + object	划船	划船
huá xuě	huá 雪	*skiing*	verb + object	滑雪	滑雪
huódòng	活 dòng	*activity, movement*	noun; verb	活动	活動
jiànkāng		*healthy*	adjectival verb	健康	健康
jiànshēn fáng	jiàn 身房	*gym*	noun phrase	健身房	健身房
lìngwài	lìng 外	*in addition, besides*	adverb	另外	另外
Měishì	美 shì	*American-style*	noun phrase	美式	美式
Měishì zúqiú	美 shì zú 球	*American-style football*	noun phrase	美式足球	美式足球
niánqīng	年 qīng	*young*	noun	年轻	年輕
niánqīng rén	年 qīng 人	*young people*	noun phrase	年轻人	年輕人
pá		*climb*	verb	爬	爬
pá shān	pá 山	*climb a mountain*	verb + object	爬山	爬山
páiqiú	pái 球	*volleyball*	noun phrase	排球	排球
pǎo bù		*run, jog*	verb + object	跑步	跑步
pīngpāng qiú	pīngpāng 球	*ping-pong*	noun phrase	乒乓球	乒乓球
shìnèi huódòng	室 nèi 活 dòng	*indoor activities*	noun phrase	室内活动	室內活動
tī		*kick*	verb	踢	踢

tī zúqiú	tī zú 球	*play soccer, football*	verb + object	踢足球	踢足球
tǐyù	体 yù	*sports, physical training*	noun	体育	體育
tǐyù huódòng	体 yù 活 dòng	*sports activities, exercise*	noun phrase	体育活动	體育活動
wèile	为了	*for the sake of, for the purpose of*	preposition	为了	為了
xiāngtóng	xiāng 同	*similar*	noun	相同	相同
xiàoduì	校队	*school team*	noun phrase	校队	校隊
yóu yǒng		*swimming*	verb + object	游泳	游泳
yújiā		*yoga*	noun	瑜伽	瑜伽
yùndòng		*movement, sports*	noun	运动	運動
zhòngliàng xùnliàn	重 liàng xùn 练	*weight training*	noun phrase	重量训练	重量訓練
zhòngshì	重视	*take seriously, consider important*	verb	重视	重視
zúqiú	zú 球	*soccer, football*	noun phrase	足球	足球

Narrative characters

Character	Pinyin	Meaning/ function	Radical	Phrases	Traditional character
参	cān	*participate**	厶	参加 cānjiā *participate*	參
除	chú	*except, besides; remove*	阝	除了 chúle *except, besides*	除

冬	dōng	*winter*	夂	冬天 dōngtiān *winter*	冬
队	duì	*team*	阝	校队 xiàoduì *school team*	隊
而	ér	*and, but, or*	而	而且	而
或	huò	*or, perhaps*	戈	或者 huòzhě *perhaps*	或
练	liàn	*practice*	纟	练习 liànxí *practice,* 训练 xùnliàn *to train*	練
身	shēn	*body**	身	身体 shēntǐ *body*	身
视	shì	*vision**	礻	电视 diànshì *television,* 重视 zhòngshì *value*	視
体	tǐ	*body**	亻	身体 shēntǐ *body*	體
跳	tiào	*jump*	足	跳舞 tiàowǔ *dance*	跳
舞	wǔ	*dance*	舛	跳舞 tiàowǔ *dance*	舞
雪	xuě	*snow*	雨	下雪 xià xuě *to snow,* huá 雪 huáxuě *skiing*	雪
者	zhě	*or**	少	或者 huòzhě *perhaps*	者

Dialogue

Part A

国强： 我走进来的时候，看见 **Màikè** 了。他要去打 **lán** 球， **yuē** 我们跟他一起去。

大为： 这么冷的天， **lián** 手都 **shēn** 不出来，还能打球吗？

国强： 今天冷是冷，可是没有前两天那么冷。 你太怕 冷了。把书收起来，跟我们一起去吧!

大为： 你去吧。我今天没空出去玩。小文明天有化学课的考试，问我能不能陪她准备考试。

Dialogue Part A Vocabulary

				Simplified	Traditional
huàxué	化学	*chemistry*	noun	化学	化學
lián		*even*	adverb	连	連
shēn		*extend*	verb	伸	伸
yuē		*make an appointment, arrange to meet*	verb	约	約

Dialogue Part A Characters

Character	*Pinyin*	*Meaning/ function*	*Radical*	*Phrases*	*Traditional character*
备	bèi	*prepare**	夂	准备 zhǔnbèi *prepare*	備
复	fù	*resume, renew**	夂	复习 fùxí *review*	復
空	kòng	*free time*	穴	有空 yǒu kòng *have free time,* 没空 méi kòng *do not have time*	空
怕	pà	*fear*	忄		怕
收	shōu	*collect, gather up*	攵	收 **shi** shōushi *straighten up, clean up*	收
准	zhǔn	*accurate*	冫	准备 zhǔnbèi *prepare*	準

Part B

国强： 那好吧。不过我告诉你，生 mìng 在 yú yùndòng. 一 yùndòng 就不冷了。

大为： 生 mìng 在 yú yùndòng 是什么意思？

国强： 这 jù话的意思就是 yùndòng 对你的 jiànkāng 很重要。你就是 duànliàn 得不 gòu 。

大为： 我想我 duànliàn 得比你多得多。不下雨的时候我每天都 qí 自行车去上课。这是 duànliàn 吧。Lìng 外，在教室 lóu 、宿舍 lóu ，和图书馆，我都走 lóutī. 我的宿舍在五 lóu, 我每天都走上去，再走下来，不坐电 tī 。这也是 duànliàn 吧。

国强： 这是 duànliàn 也是 jiéyuē 能 yuán 。

大为： Jiéyuē 能 yuán 是什么意思？

国强： 能 yuán 就是"energy." 有一些能 yuán 来自大自然里的东西，比方说水、 shíyóu 等等。Jiéyuē 就是少用，少用大自然的东西就是 bǎohù 地球，也就是环 bǎo 。好了，说了半天你到 dǐ 去不去打球？

大为： 不去。一会儿帮小文复习 wán，她要跟美丽去上 yújiā 课。我就跟她们去 jiàn 身房。Jiàn 身房比外边暖和多了。

Dialogue Part B Vocabulary

				Simplified	Traditional
bǎohù		*protect*	verb	保护	保護
bǐfāng shuō	比方说	*for example*	phrase	比方说	比方說
dà zìrán	大自然	*nature*	noun	大自然	大自然
dàodǐ	到 dǐ	*after all*	adverb	到底	到底
dìqiú	地球	*earth*	noun	地球	地球
diàntī	电 tī	*elevator*	noun	电梯	電梯
gòu		*enough*	verb	够	夠
huánbǎo	环 bǎo	*environmental protection*	noun phrase (abbreviation of 环 jìng bǎohù)	环保	環保
huánjìng bǎohù	环 jìng bǎohù	*environmental protection*	noun phrase	环境保护	環境保護

jiàoshì lóu	教室 lóu	classroom building	noun phrase	教室楼	教室樓
jiéyuē		conserve	verb	节约	節約
jiéyuē néngyuán	jiéyuē 能源	conserve energy	verb + object	节约能源	節約能源
jù		classifier for *speech utterances*	classifier	句	句
lái zì	来自	come from	verb + preposition	来自	來自
lóutī		staircase, stairs	noun	楼梯	樓梯
néngyuán	能 yuán	energy	noun	能源	能源
qí		ride astraddle	verb	骑	騎
qí zìxíngchē	qí 自行车	ride a bicycle	verb + object	骑自行车	騎自行車
shēngmìng	生 mìng	life	noun	生命	生命
shēngmìng zàiyú yùndòng	生 mìng 在 yú yùndòng	movement is the essence of life	conversational expression	生命在于运动	生命在於運動
shíyóu		oil, petroleum	noun	石油	石油
zhòngyào	重要	important	adjectival verb	重要	重要
zìxíngchē	自行车	bicycle	noun	自行车	自行車

Dialogue Part B Characters

Character	Pinyin	Meaning/ function	Radical	Phrases	Traditional character
教	jiāo, jiào	teach	攵	教室 jiàoshì classroom, 家教 jiājiào tutor	教

| 暖 | nuǎn | *warm** | 日 | 暖和 nuǎnhuo *warm* 暖化 nuǎnhuà *warming* | 暖 |
| 雨 | yǔ | *rain* | 雨 | 下雨 xià yǔ *(it's) raining* | 雨 |

体 yù 活 dòng
Sports and physical fitness activities

dǎ bàngqiú	打 bàng 球	*play baseball*
dǎ lánqiú	打 lán 球	*play basketball*
dǎ páiqiú	打 pái 球	*play volleyball*
dǎ pīngpāng qiú	打 pīngpāng 球	*play ping-pong*
huá bīng	huá bīng	*ice skating*
huá chuán	huá chuán	*rowing, crew*
huá xuě	huá 雪	*skiing*
pá shān	pá 山	*mountain climbing*
pǎo bù	pǎo bù	*jogging*
tī zúqiú	tī zú 球	*play football*
yóu yǒng	yóu yǒng	*swim*
yújiā	yújiā	*yoga*
wán Měishì zúqiú	玩美 shì zú 球	*play American football*
zhòngliàng xùnliàn	重 liàng xùn 练	*weight training*

Stroke Order Flow Chart

Character **Total Strokes**

Narrative

参	ㄥ	ㄙ	厶	尹	矢	矣	参	参						**8**
除	㇏	阝	阝	队	阶	陉	除	除						**9**
冬	ノ	ク	夂	夂	冬									**5**
队	㇏	阝	阴	队										**4**
而	一	丆	兀	丙	而	而								**6**
或	一	厂	戸	口	亘	或	或	或						**8**
练	㇑	㇗	纟	纟	纬	纺	练							**8**
身	ノ	亻	勹	自	自	身	身							**7**
视	丶	㇇	礻	礻	礻	礼	视	视						**8**
体	ノ	亻	仁	什	付	休	体							**7**
跳	丶	口	口	甲	足	足	足	趴	跙	跳	跳	跳		**13**
舞	ノ	一	二	仁	仨	無	無	無	舞	舞	舞	舞	舞	**14**
雪	一	冖	二	雨	雨	雪	雪	雪	雪	雪	雪			**11**
者	一	十	土	耂	者	者	者	者						**8**

Dialogue A

备	ノ	ク	夂	冬	各	各	备	备						**8**
复	ノ	一	仁	仁	自	百	复	复	复					**9**
空	丶	丷	宀	宀	穴	空	空	空						**8**
怕	㇑	㇚	忄	忄	忄	怕	怕	怕						**8**
收	㇄	㇐	収	收	収	收								**6**
准	丶	㇀	冫	亻	亣	冹	冹	准	准	准				**10**

Dialogue B

教	一	十	土	耂	耂	孝	孝	孝	敎	教				**11**
暖	㇑	冂	日	日	旷	旷	旷	�	暖	晚	暖	暖		**13**
雨	一	冂	冂	雨	雨	雨	雨							**8**

Use and structure

22.1.   Subject 在 X 上 *as for X, when it comes to X*

In Lesson 18, we learned the structure 在 **NP** 方面 when expressing the meaning *when it comes to NP* or *as for NP* (*Use and Structure* 18.9).

他在 **yǔ** 法那方面，有的时候会有问题。
Sometimes he has problems when it comes to grammar.

In this lesson, we learn a similar structure that you can use when presenting a subject from a particular perspective, say:

Subject 在 NP (or VP) 上
美国的大学生跟中国的大学生在 <u>**duànliàn** 身体上</u>有 **xiāng** 同的地方，也有不同的地方。
When it comes to exercising, American students and Chinese students have similarities and differences.

在学习上，他比你用功得多。
When it comes to studying, he is much more hard working (he works harder) than you.

中文和英文在 **yǔ** 法上有很大的不同。
In terms of grammar, Chinese and English have a lot of big differences.

这几年中国在经济上有很大的进 **bù**。
These past few years, China's economy has made a lot of progress.

在教 **hái** 子上，中国人和美国人很不一样。
When it comes to educating children, Chinese people and Americans are very different.

The structures 在 **NP** 方面 and 在 **NP** (or **VP**) 上 are very similar in function. The main difference between them is that 在 **NP** 方面 is more formal. Both are good structures to use when beginning a comparison of two or more people, places, or things.

> **Practice**   *Workbook: Focus on Structure 22.1.*

22.2.   **xiāng** 同的地方 *similarities*, 不同的地方 *differences*

To say that things have similarities, say:

(NP) 有 **xiāng** 同的地方
(the noun phrases) have similarities

To say that things have differences, say:

(NP) 有不同的地方
(the noun phrases) have differences

美国的大学生跟中国的大学生在 **duànliàn** 身体上有 **xiāng** 同的地方，也有不同的地方。
When it comes to exercising, American students and Chinese students have similarities and differences.

To state what the similarities or differences are, say:

Xiāng 同的(地方)是 . . .
The similarities are . . .

不同的(地方)是 . . .
The differences are . . .

Xiāng 同的是年 **qīng** 人都知道 **yùndòng** 是为了让身体 **gèng jiànkāng** 。
The similarities are that young people all know that exercise makes your body (you) healthier.

This structure is relatively formal and is most commonly used in writing and in formal speech. It introduces the fact that there are similarities or differences between things and can be followed by specific examples.

 Practice   *Workbook: Focus on Structure 22.1, 22.2, 22.3.*

22.3.   为了 *for the purpose of, in order to*

为了 focuses on the purpose of some action. It precedes either an NP or a VP and may be translated as *for the purpose of, in order to,* or *because of.* In this lesson, 为了 occurs before a VP.

年 **qīng** 人都知道 **yùndòng** 是为了让身体 **gèng jiànkāng** 。
Young people all know that exercise is for the purpose of making the body even more healthy.

我每天走路去上学，不坐校车，是为了 **duànliàn** 身体。
The reason I walk to school and don't take a school bus is in order to exercise.

他不让你去是为了 **bǎohù** 你。
The reason he doesn't let you go is (in order) to protect you.

为了陪你去看电 **yǐng**，我只好明天再准备考试了。
In order to accompany you (to go with you) to see a movie, I'll just have to prepare for the test again tomorrow.

为了 **bǎohù** 地球，我们都应该 **jiéyuē** 能 **yuán** 。
In order to protect the earth, we all have to conserve energy.

 Practice   *Workbook: Focus on Structure 22.15; Focus on Communication 22.2.*

22.4.   gèng AdjV *even more AdjV* and 还 AdjV *even more AdjV*

Gèng is an intensifier and always precedes an adjectival verb. It adds a comparative meaning of *even more* to the adjectival verb and often occurs in comparison structures.

红色的比 **lán** 色的 **gèng** 好看。
The red one is even better looking than the blue one.

Sentences with **gèng** often follow comparisons with 比.

Lán 色的比 **huáng** 色的好。红色的 **gèng** 好。
The blue one is better than the yellow one. The red one is even better.

The intensifier 还 may also occur in comparisons with 比 to indicate *even more adjectival verb*.

他觉得收 **shi** 房间比 **pá** 山，打球还累。
He thinks that cleaning his room is even more tiring than mountain climbing or playing ball.

> **Practice**   Workbook: Focus on Structure 22.4.

22.5.   Abbreviating conjunctions: 或者 and 或

Two-syllable conjunctions like 或者 *or* can be abbreviated as single-syllable words when the abbreviation does not result in ambiguity. That is the situation in the following line from the narrative:

中国的学生很多喜欢 **tī zú** 球、打 **pái** 球或打 **pīngpāng** 球.
Chinese students like to play soccer, volleyball, or ping-pong.

22.6.   Lìng 外 *in addition*

Lìng 外 (另外) *in addition* introduces additional information on the topic being discussed.

Lìng 外，很多美国的大学生参加校队，差不多每个周末都有比 **sài** 。
In addition, lots of American college students participate in school teams and have competitions almost every weekend.

我不喜欢北京的冬天。每天都很冷，**lìng** 外，下雪的时候走路很不方 **biàn** 。
I do not like Beijing's winters. It's very cold every day, and in addition, when it snows walking is not convenient.

> **Practice**   Workbook: Focus on Structure 22.5; Focus on Communication 22.3.

22.7.   等等 *etcetera*

Ending a list with 等等, or with one single 等, adds the meaning conveyed by the word *etcetera* (*etc.*) in English. That is, it indicates that the list does not include every item that could be included, but that the items on the list are typical of the kinds of items that could also be included.

> 美国学生喜欢玩美 **shì zú** 球、打 **bàng** 球， **tī zú** 球等等。
> *American students like to play American football, baseball, soccer, etc.*

> 她做了很多菜，有饺子、 **chǎo** 白菜、 **jī tāng** 等等。
> *She made a lot of dishes. There's dumplings, stir-fried cabbage, chicken soup, etc.*

> **Practice** ▶   *Workbook: Focus on Structure 22.13.*

22.8.   Verbs used in playing ball and in other sports: 打 *lánqiú play basketball*, tī *zúqiú play soccer (football)*, 玩 *zúqiú play soccer (football)*

In English we say that you play a sport or a game, that is, you *play* football, basketball, soccer, volleyball, baseball, ping-pong, etc. In Chinese, the verb that is used with a ball sport depends upon the body part that is involved in hitting the ball. If it is the hand that is used in hitting the ball, the verb that is used is 打 *hit*: 打 **lán** 球 *play basketball*, 打 **pái** 球 *play volleyball*, 打 **pīngpāng** 球 *play ping-pong*, 打 **bàng** 球 *play baseball*, etc. If it is the foot that is used in hitting the ball, the verb that is used is **tī** *kick*: **tī zú**球 *play soccer*. If you want to say that you are playing a game for fun and not for competition, the verb you can use is 玩 *play*: 玩 **lán** 球 *play basketball*, 玩美 **shì zú**球 *play American football*.

> **Practice** ▶   *Workbook: Focus on Structure 22.3, 22.4, 22.5, 22.9, 22.10, 22.11; Focus on Communication 22.4, 22.8.*

22.9.   而 *and, while, but*

而 is a conjunction that is used in written and formal spoken texts. It can be used to link verb phrases or entire sentences. When it is used, it indicates that the phrases or sentences that it joins are balanced opposites of each other. Depending upon the context, it may be translated as *and*, *but*, or *while*.

When 而 is used, the phrases or clauses that it joins are typically balanced, not just in meaning (as direct opposites of each other), but also in structure. Notice that in the following sentences, the "conjuncts" of 而 have very similar structures.

> 不同的是中国的学生很多喜欢 **tī zú** 球、打 **pái** 球或打 **pīngpāng** 球，而美国大学生喜欢玩美 **shì zú** 球、打 **bàng** 球和 **huá chuán** 。
> *The difference is that Chinese students like to play soccer, volleyball, or ping-pong, while American students like to play American-style football and baseball and row crew.*

中文课已经开始十分钟了。 学生都来了，而老师还没到。
Chinese class already started 10 minutes ago. The students have all arrived but the teacher has not yet arrived.

今天的考试，我的同学都考得很好，而我因为忘了很多字，考得不太好。
As for today's test, my classmates all did well, while I forgot a lot of characters and did poorly.

这儿的冬天很长而夏天特别 **duǎn** 。
The winter here is very long and the summer is especially short.

When 而 links verb phrases, the phrases are often identical except that one is affirmative and the other is negated.

他跟现在的年 **qīng** 人不同，不喜欢上网，而喜欢看书 。
He is different from today's young people. He doesn't like to use the internet but likes to read books.

你为什么喜欢看美国电 **yǐng** 而不喜欢看中国电 **yǐng** ？
Why do you like to watch American movies and not Chinese movies?

Here are additional examples in which 而 links verb phrases. Notice that the verb phrases express opposites in each sentence.

美国人喜欢的是 **bàng** 球而不是 **zú** 球。
What Americans like is baseball and not soccer.

他有兴趣的课是中国经济而不是中国文化。
The class that he is interested in is economics and not Chinese culture.

教得好的是王老师而不是李老师，你别选李老师的课吧。
The one who teaches well is Professor Wang, not Professor Li. Don't take Professor Li's class.

Practice   *Workbook: Focus on Structure 22.3; Focus on Communication 22.2, 22.3.*

22.10.   More directional verbs: 进来 *come in*, 出来 *come out*, 下来 *come down*, 上去 *go up*

In Lesson 17, we learned the directional verbs 回来 *come back* and 回去 *go back* (*Use and Structure* 17.3). In this lesson, we practice forming additional directional verbs.

Directional verbs are always formed by a verb of motion followed by 来 *come* or 去 *go*. The verb of motion indicates the way that the subject is moving, and 来 *come* or 去 *go* indicates the direction of the motion either *towards* (来 *come*) or *away from* (去 *go*) the speaker or narrator. The following are commonly used directional verbs. Notice how the 来 *come* or 去 *go* ending changes the meaning of the expression.

	Directional	*Verbs*
Verb of motion	Verb of motion + 来 *come*	Verb of motion + 去 *go*
进 *enter*	进来 *come in*	进去 *go in*
出 *exit*	出来 *come out*	出去 *go out*
上 *ascend*	上来 *come up*	上去 *go up*
下 *descend*	下来 *come down*	下去 *go down*
过 *pass, go across*	过来 *cross some space moving towards the speaker*	过去 *cross some space moving away from the speaker*

> **Practice** ▶ *Workbook: Focus on Structure 22.6, 22.7, 22.8; Focus on Communication 22.5.*

22.11. Directional complements: Resultative verbs with directional endings 走进来 *walk in*, shēn 出来 *extend out*

We have learned how to form and use resultative verbs in Lessons 19 and 20 (*Use and Structure* 19.2 and 20.6). In this lesson, we see that directional verbs can function as resultative verb endings. When directional verbs are used as resultative verb endings, they are often called *directional complements*. Here are some examples.

Action verb +	Directional verb =	Resultative verb
走 *walk*	进来 *come in*	走进来 *walk in*
shēn *extend*	出来 *come out*	shēn 出来 *extend out*
pǎo *run*	上去 *go up*	pǎo 上去 *run up*
开 *drive*	下去 *go down*	开下去 *drive down*

我走进来的时候，看见 **Màikè** 了。
When I walked in, I saw Maike.

Resultative verbs with directional endings can occur in the potential form (*Use and Structure* 20.6). To create the potential form of these verbs, include 得 or 不 between the action verb and the directional expression:

Resultative verb	*V 得 ending* able to achieve the result	*V 不 ending* unable to achieve the result
走进来 *walk in*	走得进来 *able to walk in*	走不进来 *unable to walk in*
shēn 出来 *extend out*	shēn 得出来 *able to extend out*	shēn 不出来 *unable to extend out*
pǎo 上去 *run up*	pǎo 得上去 *able to run up*	pǎo 不上去 *unable to run up*
开下去 *drive down*	开得下去 *able to drive down*	开不下去 *unable to drive down*

这么冷的天，**lián** 手都 **shēn** 不出来。
On a day as cold as today, you can't even extend out your hand.

When a verb with a directional ending takes an object, the object may occur right before 来 or 去.

他 **shēn** 出手来了。
He extended out his hand (towards the speaker).

她走进教室来了。
She walked into the classroom (where the speaker is located).

他 **pǎo** 出宿舍去了。
He ran out of the dorm (and away from the direction of the speaker).

When the object is the thing that moves in the action, it can also be expressed with a structure that states the object before the verb such as **lián** (see note 22.11) or 把 (*Use and Structure* 19.8):

这么冷的天，**lián** 手都 **shēn** 不出来。
On a day as cold as today, you can't even extend out your hand.

他把手 **shēn** 出来了。
He held out his hand.

When talking about exiting from a location (for example, *walk out of the dorm*), you can also say:

从 location **Verb** 出来   or   从 location **Verb** 出去
come out from a location   or   *go out from a location*

他从宿舍走出来了。
He walked out from the dorm.

他从公园 **pǎo** 出去了。
He ran out from the park.

> **Practice** ▸ *Workbook: Focus on Structure 22.6, 22.7, 22.8; Focus on Communication 22.5.*

22.12.   lián (连) NP *even NP*, lián (连) NP 都/也 V *even NP (is, has, does) V*

Lián (连) NP means *even NP*. The phrase **lián NP** occurs before 都 or 也 + **V(P)** in the following structures:

Lián NP 都/也 VP *even the subject (is, has, does) VP*

我家 每一个人都是老师。<u>我妹妹是老师</u>。 →
In my family, everyone is a teacher. My younger sister is a teacher.

Lián <u>我妹妹</u>也是老师。
Even my younger sister is a teacher.

我认识的人都有男朋友了。<u>我妹妹有男朋友</u>。 →
Everyone that I know has a boyfriend. My younger sister has a boyfriend.

Lián 我妹妹也有男朋友。
Even my younger sister has a boyfriend.

最近大家都开始学中文。我妹妹学中文。→
Recently, everyone has begun studying Chinese. My younger sister studies Chinese.

Lián 我妹妹也学中文。
Even my younger sister studies Chinese.

NP **lián** *time when* 都/也 VP *something happens even at this time*:

他们每天都上课。 他们星期天上课。→
They go to class every day. They go to class on Sunday.

他们 **lián**星期天都上课。
They even go to class on Sunday.

Subject **lián** object NP 都/也 V *subject even "verbs" the object*:

他家每个房间都有书 **jià**。 他的 **cè**所有书 **jià**。→
There is a bookcase in every room of his house. There is a bookcase in the bathroom.

他家每个房间都有书 **jià**, **lián cè**所也有。
There is a bookcase in every room of his house. There is even one in the bathroom.

她会说英文、法文、 **Dé**文、和日文。→
She can speak English, French, German, and Japanese.

她会说英文、法文，和**Dé**文、 **lián**日文都会说。
She can speak English, French, and German. She can even speak Japanese.

The **lián** structure has two functions.

1   It emphasizes the NP that follows **lián**, indicating that something is *even true for that NP*.
2   If the NP that is emphasized is the object of the verb, it *topicalizes* that NP, placing it in a position at the beginning of the sentence, before the verb.

Certain structures in Mandarin, including resultative verbs with directional endings (e.g., 走进来 *walk in*, **shēn** 出来 *extend out*) cannot be followed by an object. When **lián** occurs with resultative verbs with directional endings, it makes it possible to include the object of the resultative verb in the sentence. The two structures are used together in this sentence from the dialogue:

这么冷的天， **lián** 手都 **shēn** 不出来。
On a day as cold as today, you can't even extend out your hand.

Practice ▷ *Workbook: Focus on Structure 22.9; Focus on Communication 22.2.*

22.13.   NP AdjV 是 AdjV (可是...) *NP has the quality of AdjV all right, but...*

When some topic has been mentioned in a conversation and you want to say that it has a particular quality, but that it is less than some expectation or standard, say:

NP AdjV 是 AdjV, (可是...)
NP has the quality AdjV all right, but...

今天冷是冷，可是没有昨天那么冷。
It is cold today, but it is not as cold as yesterday.

Statements made with **AdjV 是 AdjV** are typically followed by a clause that begins with a contrast conjunction, for example, 可是 *but,* 但是 *but,* 不过 *but, however,* etc.

今天冷是冷，可是没有前两天那么冷。
It's cold today all right, but it's not as cold as the previous two days.

他的宿舍大是大，可是 **guì** 子不 **gòu**。
His dorm is big all right, but there aren't enough dressers.

Practice   ➤   *Workbook: Focus on Structure 22.10; Focus on Communication 22.2, 22.3.*

22.14.   NP₁ 没有 NP₂ (那么/这么) AdjV *NP1 is not as AdjV as NP2*

In Lesson 21, we learned to use the 比 comparison structure to say that something has *more of* some quality than something else (*Use and Structure* 21.7). To say that something has *less of* some quality than something else, say:

NP₁ 没有 NP₂ (那么/这么) AdjV
NP1 is not as AdjV as NP2

今天没有昨天那么冷。
Today is not as cold as yesterday.

那么 and 这么 are not required in this structure, though one or the other usually occurs. 那么 is the more commonly used word. 这么 is used when NP₂ is something close to you and you want to emphasize its proximity:

NP₁ 没有 NP₂ 这么 AdjV
NP1 is not as AdjV as NP2

For example, if you were eating dumplings and wanted to say that some other dumplings are not as good as the ones you are eating right now, you could say:

饭馆的饺子没有您的饺子这么好吃。
Restaurant dumplings are not as delicious as your dumplings.

Notice that 那么 and 这么 do not get translated into English.

Practice   ➤   *Workbook: Focus on Structure 22.10, 22.11; Focus on Communication 22.2.*

22.15.   gòu (够) *enough*

Gòu *enough* is an adjectival verb. It often occurs as a resultative verb ending, as in Part B of the dialogue.

你 **duànliàn** 得不**gòu** 。
You don't exercise enough.

你吃得不够。
You didn't eat enough.

我刚学开车，练习得不**gòu** ，还不能自己开车去学校。
I just learned how to drive (and) I haven't practiced enough. I still can't drive myself to school.

Bōshìdùn 的冬天很冷，你准备的衣服不**gòu** 。
Boston's winters are very cold; you have not prepared enough clothing.

When **gòu** occurs as a resultative verb ending, it is often the focus of questions.

外边很冷，他穿得 **gòu** 不 **gòu** ？
It's cold outside. Are you wearing enough (clothing)?

The negative answer is:

（我可能穿得）不**gòu** 。
(It may be that I am wearing) not enough.

The affirmative answer is:

Gòu 了。
Enough.

Màikè: 一张电 **yǐng** 票十五块，你带的钱 **gòu** 不 **gòu** ？
Mike: One movie ticket is $15. Did you bring enough money?

大为：我有三十块，**gòu** 了。
Dawei: I have $30, (it's) enough.

Notice that the English word *enough* occurs in a very different structure from the word **gòu**. In English, you say you *have enough* of some noun. In Mandarin, you say that some noun is *enough*.

<table>
<tr><td><u>Say this:</u></td><td><u>Do not say this:</u></td></tr>
<tr><td>我们的时间 **gòu** ，可以先去吃饭再去看电 **yǐng**。
We have enough time. We can first go eat and then go see a movie.</td><td>⊗我们有 **gòu** 的时间。</td></tr>
</table>

Practice ▶ *Workbook: Focus on Structure 22.15.*

22.16.   NP₁ 比 NP₂ Adj 得多 *NP1 has a lot more of some quality than NP2*

In Lesson 21, we learned how to make simple comparisons with 比 and to say that one NP has a little more of some quality than another (*Use and Structure* 21.7). To say that NP₁ has *a lot more* of some quality than NP₂, say:

NP₁ 比 NP₂ AdjV 得多
北京比上海冷得多。
Beijing is a lot colder than Shanghai.

这件衣服比那件衣服贵得多。
This item of clothing is a lot more expensive than that item of clothing.

Do not include an intensifier before the AdjV in 比 sentences.

<u>**Say this:**</u>

北京比上海冷得多。
Beijing is a lot colder than Shanghai.

<u>**Do not say this:**</u>

⊗ 北京比上海很冷。

> **Practice**   *Workbook: Focus on Structure 22.12.*

22.17.   qí 车 *ride a bike*, 坐车 *ride in a car*, 开车 *drive a car*, huá chuan *row a boat*

We have already learned that Mandarin uses different verbs to indicate driving a vehicle (开车) and being a passenger in a vehicle (坐车). In this lesson, we see that the verb **qí** is used for riding on something that you sit on astraddle. That is, you **qí** a bicycle (**qí** 自行车), and you also **qí** a horse (**qí** 马). The verb for row is **huá** and to row a boat you **huá chuán**.

22.18.   来自 NP *come from NP*

来自 NP means *come from NP*. It is usually used when introducing oneself:

我来自美国。
I come from the United States.

In the dialogue, 国强 uses this structure when explaining the source of some types of energy:

有一些能 **yuán** 来自大自然里的东西...
Some energy comes from things that occur in nature...

你每天用的东西，很多都来自中国。
The things you use every day, a lot of them come from China.

我给你们 **jièshào** 一下，这位是来自加州的李先生。
Let me introduce you. This is Mr. Li who comes from California.

这个球队来自美国，参加过很多比 **sài**，打得特别好。
This team comes from the United States, (they have) participated in a lot of competitions and play particularly well.

Practice ▶ *Workbook: Focus on Structure 22.13.*

22.19.   到 **dǐ** *finally, after all, in the end*

到 **dǐ** *finally, after all* is an adverb that is only used in questions. It occurs after the subject and right before the verb phrase.

说了半天你到 **dǐ** 去不去打球？
We've talked for a long time, are you going to go play ball or not?

我说了半天你到 **dǐ** 想不想跟我们去 **huá** 雪？
I've talked a long time, do you want to go skiing with us or not?

我们认识了这么久，我也没去过她家。所以她家到 **dǐ** 在哪儿我也不知道。
We've known each other for so long, (but) I've never been to her house. So where her house is I actually don't know.

已经一个月了，大考的**chéngjì**到 **dǐ** 什么时候会出来？
It's already been a month, when are the grades for the exam finally going to come out?

门外有 **xié**，门里边也有 **xié**，床下还有两 **shuāng xié** . . . 你到 **dǐ** 有几 **shuāng xié**?
There are shoes outside the door, shoes inside the door, and there are also shoes under the bed . . . how many pairs of shoes do you have in all?

Practice ▶ *Workbook: Focus on Communication 22.2.*

Narrative structure: a comparison paragraph

The narrative in this lesson illustrates the structure of a *comparison paragraph*, a paragraph in which the writer compares two or more things in terms of their similarities and differences. A comparison paragraph generally begins by including the people or things that will be compared, stating that they have similarities and differences.

美国的大学生跟中国的大学生在 **duànliàn** 身体上有 **xiāng** 同的地方，也有不同的地方。
When it comes to exercise, American college students and Chinese college students have similarities and differences.

It then lists the similarities: **Xiāng** 同的是 . . .

Then it lists the differences: 不同的是...

In Mandarin, the similarities and differences that parallel each other are generally listed first. In the narrative in this lesson, the parallel differences are the specific activities: *soccer* vs. *American football*, *volleyball* vs. *baseball*, *ping-pong* vs. *crew*. Additional differences, those that don't have a correspondence in the other comparison group, are listed afterwards. Notice that the expression **lìng** 外 introduces these remaining details as additional differences that don't fit with the parallel differences listed first.

Lìng 外，很多美国的大学生参加学校的校队，差不多每个周末都有比 **sài**。
In addition, a lot of American college students join school teams and participate in competitions just about every week.

 Sentence pyramids

Supply the English translation for the last line where indicated.

I	
不同的地方 也有不同的地方 有 **xiāng** 同的地方，也有不同的地方 在 **duànliàn** 身体上有 **xiāng** 同的地方，也有不同的地方 美国人和中国人在 **duànliàn** 身体上有 **xiāng** 同的地方，也有不同的地方。	*differences* *also has differences* *has similarities and also has differences* *when it comes to exercise, there are similarities and also differences* *When it comes to exercise, Americans and Chinese have similarities and differences.*
2	
yùndòng 喜欢 **yùndòng** 年 **qīng** 人都喜欢 **yùndòng** **Xiāng** 同的是年 **qīng** 人都喜欢 **yùndòng** 。	*physical exercise* *like physical exercise* *young people all like exercise* *The similarity is that young people all like exercise.*
3	
美 **shì zú** 球 玩美 **shì zú** 球 喜欢玩美 **shì zú** 球 而美国大学生喜欢玩美 **shì zú** 球 中国的学生喜欢 **tī zú** 球，而美国大学生喜欢玩美 **shì zú** 球 不同的是中国的学生喜欢 **tī zú** 球，而美国大学生喜欢玩美 **shì zú** 球。	*American football* *play American football* *like to play American football* *and American students like to play American football* *Chinese student like to play soccer, and American students like to play American football* *The difference is that Chinese students like to play soccer, and American students like to play American football.*

4	
校队	*school team*
参加校队	*participate in school teams*
美国的大学生参加校队	*American college students participate in school teams*
很多美国的大学生参加校队	*a lot of American students participate in school teams*
Lìng 外，很多美国的大学生参加校队。	

5	
jiànkāng	*healthy*
gèng jiànkāng	*healthier*
身体 **gèng jiànkāng**	*the body is healthier*
让身体 **gèng jiànkāng**	*makes the body healthier*
Yùndòng 是为了让身体 **gèng jiànkāng**。	*The purpose of exercise is to make the body healthier.*

6	
几次	*several times*
duànliàn 几次	*exercise several times*
都要 **duànliàn** 几次	*all want to exercise several times*
每周都要 **duànliàn** 几次	*every week want to exercise several times*
喜欢 **yùndòng** 的人每周都要 **duànliàn** 几次。	*People who like to exercise all want to work out several times a week.*

7	
看见 **Màikè** 了	*saw Mike*
我走进来的时候，看见 **Màikè** 了。	*When I walked in, I saw Mike.*

8	
出来	*exit*
shēn 出来	*extend out*
shēn 不出来	*unable to extend out*
lián 手都 **shēn** 不出来	*can't even extend my hand out*
这么冷的天，**lián** 手都 **shēn** 不出来。	*It's such a cold day that I can't even extend my hand out.*

9	
冷	*cold*
那么冷	*so cold*
没有前两天那么冷	*not as cold as the previous two days*
可是没有前两天那么冷	*but it isn't as cold as the previous two days*
今天冷是冷，可是没有前两天那么冷。	*It's cold today all right, but it isn't as cold as the previous two days.*

10	
怕冷	*afraid of the cold*
你太怕冷了。	

11 **yùndòng** 生 mìng 在 yú yùndòng 。	*movement/exercise* *Movement/exercise is the essence of life.*
12 重要 对你的 jiànkāng 很重要 **Yùndòng** 对你的 jiànkāng 很重要。	*important* *important for your health*
13 **gòu** **duànliàn** 得不**gòu** 你 **duànliàn** 得不**gòu** 。	*enough* *don't exercise enough*
14 电 **tī** 坐电 **tī** 不坐电 **tī** 我都走上去，走下来，不坐电 **tī** 我在宿舍 **lóu** 都走上去，走下来，不坐电 **tī**。	*elevator* *take the elevator* *not take the elevator* *I walk up and walk down and don't take the elevator*
15 意思 什么意思 **Jiéyuē** 能 yuán 是什么意思?	*meaning* *what does it mean* *What does "Jiéyuē能 yuán" mean?*
16 等等 水、 **shíyóu** 等等 比方说水、 **shíyóu** 等等 能 yuán 来自大自然里的东西，比方说水、 **shíyóu** 等等。	*etcetera* *water, petroleum, etcetera* *for example, water petroleum, etc.* *Energy comes from things that exist in nature, for example, water, petroleum, etc.*
17 少用 **Jiéyuē** 就是少用。	*use less* *To conserve is to use less.*
18 环 **bǎo** 就是环 **bǎo** 少用能 yuán 就是环 **bǎo** 。	*environmental protection* *is environmental protection* *Using less energy is environmental protection.*
19 去不去打球? 你到 **dǐ** 去不去打球?	*going to play ball or not?* *Are you going to play ball after all or not?*
20 **nuǎn** 和多了 比外边 **nuǎn** 和多了 **Jiàn** 身房比外边 **nuǎn** 和多了。	*much warmer* *much warmer than outside* *The gym is much warmer than outside.*

Notes on Chinese culture

生 mìng 在 yú yùndòng

生 mìng 在 yú yùndòng is an expression used in mainland China that refers to the importance of exercise in one's life. In Taiwan, there is a different expression that conveys the same sentiment: 活 **dòng** (*activity, exercise*)：活着就是要 **dòng** *movement is essential to life.*

Turning down an invitation

In Chinese culture, you typically do not turn down an invitation to do something with someone by saying that you are not interested in participating. That kind of direct refusal is considered rude. Instead, it is much more socially acceptable to say that you have something to do during the scheduled time of the event and that you are therefore unable to participate. In the dialogue, it is clear that Dawei does not want to play basketball with Guoqiang and Maike because he doesn't want to be outside in the cold. But he turns down the invitation by noting that he has a prior engagement: he has promised to help Xiaowen to study for a test.

Sports and education

In the United States and Britain, sports are considered a part of a well-rounded education, and even the most academically strong students are encouraged to participate in a sport. In fact, in the United States, very strong athletic performance may improve your chances of being admitted to the college of your choice. In contrast, in China, academics and competitive athletics do not go hand in hand, and Chinese students on an academic path do not spend their time participating in competitive sports. This is another instance of 中外文化的不同!

Narrative in English

When it comes to exercise, American college students and Chinese college students have similarities and differences. The similarities are that young people all know that physical exercise makes you (the body) healthier. People who like to exercise work out several times a week. They jog, play basketball, do mountain climbing, dance, or go to a gym to work out. The differences are that lots of Chinese students like to play soccer, volleyball, or ping-pong, while American students, aside from American football and baseball and rowing, also have indoor weight training, yoga, etc. They swim in the summer and ski and skate in the winter. In addition, Americans highly value physical activity. Lots of American college students participate in school teams and have competitions almost every weekend.

Dialogue in English

Part A

Guoqiang: When I walked in I saw Mike. He wants to go play basketball and invited us to go with him.

Dawei: On a day as cold as today, you can't even extend your hand out, and you're still able to play ball?

Guoqiang: It's cold today all right, but it's not as cold as the previous two days. Put your books away and come with me! You are too afraid of the cold.

Dawei: You go. I don't have time to play today. Xiaowen has a test in culture class tomorrow and asked me to study for the test with her (accompany her in preparing for the test).

Part B

Guoqiang: Okay. But I'm telling you, 生 mìng 在 yú yùndòng (exercise is the essence of life). As soon as you begin to exercise you won't be cold.

Dawei: What does "生 mìng 在 yú yùndòng" mean?

Guoqiang: The meaning of this expression is "movement is important for your health." You don't exercise enough.

Dawei: I think I exercise a lot more than you do. When it isn't raining, I ride my bike to class every day. This is exercise. Also, in classroom buildings, the dorm, and the library, I always walk up and walk down and don't take the elevator. This is exercise.

Guoqiang: This is exercise, and it is also "jiéyuē néngyuán."

Dawei: What do you mean by "jiéyuē néngyuán"?

Guoqiang: "néngyuán" is energy. "jiéyuē" means to use less of something. Using less energy is (a form of) environmental protection. Okay, we've talked for a long time, are you in fact going to play basketball or not?

Dawei: I'm not going. In a while, after I help Xiaowen to review, she's going with Meili to a yoga class. I will go to the gym with them. The gym is a lot warmer than the outdoors.

Lesson 23

Guàng jiē
Going shopping

Communication goals

By the end of this lesson, you will be able to:

- Shop for clothing.
- Compare objects in terms of price, size, color, and appearance and indicate your preferences.
- Compare shopping in a store with shopping online.

Literacy goals

By the end of this lesson, you will be able to:

- Use Chinese word formation strategies to identify and create new words.

Key structures

- 大大小小 *big and small*
- 一 **zhǒng** (一种) NP *a type of NP*
- 不得不**VP** *nothing one can do but VP*
- 只要 *as long as*
- 穿不下 *unable to put (something) on* and **V** 不下 *unable to get something down*

- 越 **V** 越 **AdjV** *the more V the more AdjV*
- 一点都不 AdjV *not even a little AdjV, not AdjV at all*
- 大小 *and other abstract nouns formed from opposites*
- zhèng (正) AdjV *precisely AdjV*
- 看起來 VP *appears to be VP*

Narrative

新年快到了。大大小小的 **shāng** 店都 **tiē** 出了打 **zhé jiǎn jià** 的 **guǎng** 告，让 **gù** 客来花钱买东西。吃 **wán** 早饭，大为、小文和美丽就坐地铁进城去买东西了。小文和美丽特别喜欢 **guàng jiē**。她们说 **guàng jiē** 也是一 **zhǒng** 运动。大为最不喜欢 **guàng shāng** 店。他觉得 **guàng jiē** 比爬山、打球还累，而且花很多时间，**guàng** 半天也不一定找得到想要的衣服。可是女朋友让他去，他不得不去。

Narrative vocabulary

				Simplified	Traditional
bùdébù	不得不	*must*	modal verb	不得不	不得不
dǎ zhé	打 zhé	*sell at a discount*	verb + object	打折	打折
guàng		*visit, stroll through*	verb	逛	逛
guàng jiē		*window shop, stroll along the shopping streets*	verb + object	逛街	逛街
guǎnggào	guǎng 告	*advertisement*	noun	广告	廣告
gùkè	gù 客	*customer*	noun	顾客	顧客
jiǎn jià		*reduce the price*	verb + object	减价	減價
jiē		*street* (cf. 路)	noun	街	街
shāngdiàn	shāng 店	*store*	noun	商店	商店
tiē		*post, hang up*	verb	贴	貼
xīn nián	新年	*New Year*	noun phrase	新年	新年
zhǒng		*type of*	classifier	种	種

Narrative characters

Character	Pinyin	Meaning/function	Radical	Phrases	Traditional character
城	chéng	*city**	土	城市 chéngshì *city*	城
动	dòng	*move*	力	运动 yùndòng *movement, exercise*	動
爬	pá	*climb*	爪	爬山 pá shān *climb a mountain*	爬
且	qiě	*also**	一	而且 érqiě *moreover*	且
铁	tiě	*iron*	钅	地铁 dìtiě *subway*	鐵
务	wù	*business**	力	服务员 fúwùyuán *clerk, waiter* (mainland China usage)	務
新	xīn	*new*	斤	新年 xīnnián *New Year*	新
员	yuán	*person who performs a job**	口	服务员 fúwùyuán *clerk, waiter* (mainland China usage)	員
运	yùn	*move, transport*	辶	运动 yùndòng *movement, exercise*	運

Dialogue

Part A

小文:	大为，你看这条 **qún** 子怎么样？颜色也好，式样也简单，就是贵了点儿。
大为:	你去试一试。贵一点没关系，只要你喜欢就好。
小文 (对美丽):	太小了，我穿不下。(*picks up another one.*) 这件也太小了。现在的衣服怎么越做越小？难道他们觉得大家都很 **shòu** 吗？
美丽:	别这么说，我觉得你一点儿都不 **pàng**! 问问服务员吧。一定有大一号的。

小文 **(对服务员)**：　　服务员，这条 **qún** 子有大一号的吗？我要 **lán** 色的。
服务员：　　　　　　我看看。这条是小号的。这是中号的。这条大小怎么样？
小文：　　　　　　　**Zhèng** 合适 。

Vocabulary Dialogue Part A

				Simplified	Traditional
hào	号	*size*	classifier	号	號
pàng		*fat*	adjectival verb	胖	胖
qúnzi	**qún** 子	*skirt*	noun	裙子	裙子
shì	试	*try, test (something) out*	verb	试	試
shìyàng	式样	*style*	noun	式样	式樣
shòu		*thin*	adjectival verb	瘦	瘦
zhèng		*precisely, exactly*	intensifier	正	正
zhǐyào	只要	*as long as*	sentence adverb	只要	只要

Dialogue Part A Characters

Character	Pinyin	Meaning/ function	Radical	Phrases	Traditional character
单	dān	*alone*, odd-numbered**	十	简单 jiǎndān *simple*	單
简	jiǎn	*simple**	竹	简单 jiǎndān *simple*	簡
式	shì	*style*	弋	式样 shìyàng *style,* 美式 **zú** 球 Měishì zúqiú *American football*	式

条	tiáo	classifier for long, thin objects	木	一条 **kù** 子 yī tiáo kùzi a "pair" of slacks	條
颜	yán	color*	页	颜色 yánsè color	顏
越	yuè	the more*	走	越来越 yuèláiyuè more and more	越

Part B

小文 (对美丽)：你看怎么样？

美丽：不 **cuò**，长短也可以，不过，你要不要试一下别的颜色的？我觉得你 **lán** 色的衣服太多了。

服务员：这条 **qún** 子还有红的、**huáng** 的、**hēi** 的、咖啡色的、和**zǐ**色的。你想试哪个颜色的？

小文：红的吧，春节快到了，买一条红 **qún** 子 **zhèng** 好。上面穿一 **jiàn jīn** 色的毛衣一定很好看。

(小文在试穿红色的 **qún** 子)

服务员：这 **zhǒng** 式样的 **qún** 子今年 **zhèng** 流行，卖得很好。穿在你身上真漂亮。买一条吧。

美丽：红色的比 **lán** 色的更好看。而且，看起来特别 **shòu**。连我都想买一条了。

小文：真的吗？好看是好看，可是，真的不便宜。（对大为:）大为，你看起来很 **wúliáo**，你要不要去看看 **chènshān** 和 **kù** 子？

大为：不必。我都上网买衣服。只要知道大小，连 **xié** 子都可以在网上买，又快又方便。坐在家里动动手，今天买，明天就到。还不必开车出去，**jiǎn** 少空气 **wūrǎn**。

美丽：可是这样不能试穿，也不知道好看不好看。另外，每次上网买东西，送来的时候都有很多纸 **xiāng**，还是不环保吧。

Dialogue Part B Vocabulary

				Simplified	Traditional
bù cuò	不 **cuò**	not bad	neg + verb	不错	不錯
chángduǎn	长短	length	noun	长短	長短
chūnjié	春节	Spring Festival	noun phrase	春节	春節

dàxiǎo	大小	*size* (abstract)	noun	大小	大小
kāfēisè	咖啡色	*brown, coffee colored*	noun	咖啡色	咖啡色
jiǎnshǎo	**jiǎn** 少	*reduce*	verb	减少	減少
jīn		*gold*	adjective	金	金
kōngqì	空气	*air*	noun	空气	空氣
shìchuān	试穿	*try on*	verb	试穿	試穿
wúliáo		*bored*	adjectival verb	无聊	無聊
wūrǎn		*pollution*		污染	污染
xiāngzi	**xiāng** 子	*box*	noun	箱子	箱子
zhǐ xiāng	纸 **xiāng**	*cardboard box/paper box*	noun phrase	纸箱	紙箱
zǐ		*purple*	adjective	紫	紫
zǐ sè	**zǐ** 色	*purple colored*	noun	紫色	紫色

Dialogue Part B Characters

Character	Pinyin	Meaning/ function	Radical	Phrases	Traditional character
保	bǎo	*protect**	亻	保 hù bǎohù *protect,* 环保 huánbǎo *environmental protection*	保
必	bì	*must*	心	不必 bù bì *no need to*	必

便	biàn	convenient*	亻	方便 fāngbiàn convenient	便
春	chūn	spring	日	春天 chūntiān spring, 春节 Chūnjié Spring Festival (Chinese New Year)	春
短	duǎn	short	矢	长短 chángduǎn length	短
更	gèng	even more	日		更
节	jié	festival*, classifier for classes	艹	春节 Chūnjié Spring Festival (Chinese New Year), 一节课 yī jié kè one class, 节约 jiéyuē conserve	節
连	lián	even	辶		連
另	lìng	in addition*	口	另外 lìngwài in addition	另
便	pián	inexpensive*	亻	便宜 piányi cheap, inexpensive	便
送	sòng	send, deliver, give as a present	辶		送
宜	yí	suitable*	宀	便宜 piányi inexpensive, cheap	宜

Stroke Order Flow Chart

Character   **Total Strokes**

Narrative

															Total
城	一	十	圠	圹	圻	城	城	城							9
动	一	二	云	云	动	动									6
爬	一	厂	厂	爪	爪	爪	爬								8
且	丨	冂	月	月	且										5
铁	丿	仁	仨	钅	钅	针	针	铁	铁						10
务	丿	夕	夂	务	务										5
新	丶	亠	宁	立	立	辛	辛	亲	亲	新	新	新			13
员	丨	冂	口	尸	吊	员	员								7
运	一	二	云	云	运	运	运								7

Dialogue A

															Total
单	丶	丷	丷	兴	兴	畄	旦	单							8
简	丿	仁	仁	竻	竻	竻	竹	竹	简	简	简	简	简		13
式	一	二	干	王	式	式									6
条	丿	夕	夂	冬	条	条	条								7
颜	丶	亠	宁	立	产	产	彦	彦	彦	彦	彦	颜	颜	颜	15
越	一	十	土	丰	丰	走	走	赵	越	越	越				12

Dialogue B

															Total
保	丿	亻	仁	伊	伊	伊	保	保							9
必	丶	心	心	心	必										5
便	丿	亻	亻	仁	佰	佰	便	便							9
春	一	二	三	声	夫	未	春	春	春						9
短	丿	丿	上	乡	矢	矢	知	知	知	短	短				12
更	一	一	一	亩	百	更	更								7
节	一	十	艹	节	节										5
连	一	七	车	车	车	连	连								7
另	丶	冂	口	号	另										5
送	丶	丷	丷	兰	关	关	关	诶	送						9
宜	丶	宀	宀	宀	官	官	官	宜							8

Use and structure

23.1.   大大小小 *big and small*

One-syllable adjectival verbs like 大 *big* and 小 *small*, when used to describe a noun, can sometimes be repeated to indicate *all of the noun*.

大大小小的 **shāng** 店都 **tiē** 出了打 **zhé jiǎn jià** 的 **guǎng** 告，让 **gù** 客来花钱买东西。
All of the big and small stores put up advertisements for discounts to get the customers to spend money and buy things.

23.2.   一 zhǒng (一种) NP *a type of NP*

Zhǒng (种) *type of, kind of* is a classifier. Like all classifiers, it must follow a number, or the question word 几, or the words 这 *this*, 那 *that*, or 哪 *which?* The phrase with **zhǒng** precedes and describes a noun:

一 **zhǒng** 生活
a type of life
一种能 **yuán**
a type of energy
这 **zhǒng** 式样的 **qún** 子今年 **zhèng** 流行，卖得很好。
This style of skirt is right in fashion this year, (it's) selling well.
你想买哪 **zhǒng chènshān** ？
What kind of shirt do you want to buy?

> **Practice** ▶   *Workbook: Focus on Structure 23.2; Focus on Communication 23.5.*

23.3.   不得不 VP *nothing one can do but VP, no alternative but to VP*

To say that you have no alternative but to do something that you don't necessarily want to do, say 不得不 VP:

女朋友让他去，他不得不去。
His girlfriend asked him to go (shopping) and there was nothing he could do but go.

不得不 VP is often used in the first person, when describing one's own situation.

这件衣服是我的男朋友送给我的。我不得不穿。
This clothing was given to me by my boyfriend. I have to wear it.

> **Practice** ▶   *Workbook: Focus on Structure 23.2; Focus on Communication 23.2, 23.3.*

23.4.   只要 S/VP₁ 就 VP₂ *as long as S/VP₁, then VP₂*

只要 is a connecting phrase that indicates that something will happen provided that some condition is met. It is equivalent to the English expressions *as long as* or *provided that.* 只要 may occur at the beginning of a sentence or right after the subject. The adverb 就 typically occurs in the second clause, right before the verb phrase.

> 只要 S 就 VP
> 贵不贵没关系，只要你喜欢就好。
> *It doesn't matter whether it is expensive. As long as you like it, it is okay.*
> Subject 只要 **VP₁** 就 VP₂
> 你只要会说一点中文，在中国 **lǚyóu** 就没问题。

As long as you can speak a little Chinese, traveling in China is not a problem.

> **Practice**   *Workbook: Focus on Structure 23.3; Focus on Communication 23.2, 23.3, 23.5.*

23.5.   穿不下 *unable to put (something) on* and V 不下 *unable to get something down*

(V)不下 is a resultative ending. Like all resultative endings, it serves as a suffix to an action verb. 不下 always occurs in the potential form, typically in the negative form. **Verb** 不下 means *unable to do the action of the verb to make the object go down*. In the dialogue, 小文 uses it to describe the fact that she can't put on the skirt because it is too small:

> 太小了，我穿不下。
> *It's too small. I can't put it on.*

Here are examples with other verbs that occur with the ending 不下:

> 我今天早上吃太多了，现在吃不下。
> *I ate a lot today. I can't eat anything at all now.*
> 我的宿舍太小，放不下这么多东西。
> *My dorm (room) is too small, (it) can't fit this many things.*
> 你别再买书了，你看，书 **jià** 已经放不下了。
> *Don't buy any more books, you see, the bookcase already can't fit any more.*
> 我的车可能坐不下那么多人，如果你们也要去，就自己开车吧。
> *My car can probably not fit that many people. If you also want to go, drive yourselves.*
> 今天的饺子我很喜欢，吃了很多，真的吃不下了。
> *I really liked today's dumplings. I ate a lot, and I really can't eat any more.*

> **Practice**   *Workbook: Focus on Structure 23.4.*

23.6.   越 VP₁ 越 VP₂ *the more VP₁, the more VP₂*

This structure, like the phrase 越来越 (*Use and Structure* 21.1), indicates change over time. In note 21.1 we learned that 越来越 is an intensifier. It occurs before an adjectival verb to say that something has more and more of the quality of the adjectival verb.

> 这几天的天气越来越热。
> *It is getting hotter and hotter these days.*
> 那个老师的考试越来越难。
> *That teacher's tests are getting harder and harder.*

The structure 越 VP₁ 越 VP₂ is used to say that the more there is of VP₁, the more there is of VP₂.

In this structure, VP₁ can be an action verb, a stative verb, or an adjectival verb. VP₂ is usually an AdjV, but it may be a phrase involving an action verb or stative verb.

In the sentence from Dialogue A that includes this structure, VP₁ is an action verb and VP₂ is an AdjV:

现在的衣服怎么越做越小。
How is it that clothing these days get smaller and smaller? (the more they are made, the smaller they get)

Here are additional examples.

他越吃越 pàng 。
The more he eats, the fatter he gets.
刚开始学汉字我觉得很难，可是越学越容易。
When I first started to study Chinese characters, I thought it was difficult, but the more you study them the easier it gets.

In this sentence, VP₁ is a stative verb phrase, and VP₂ is also a stative verb phrase:

我越喜欢他, 他越不喜欢我。
The more I like him, the more he doesn't like me.

In this sentence, VP₁ consists of an AdjV, and VP₂ also consists of an adjectival verb:

这 zhǒng qún 子，越长越流行。
This kind of skirt, the longer it is the more stylish it is.

| **Practice** | *Workbook: Focus on Structure 23.5.* |

23.7.   一点儿都 NEG V *not even a little V, not V at all*

一点都 **NEG** V expresses the meaning *not even a little V* or *not V at all*. It can be used with adjectival verbs, modal verbs, stative verbs, or action verbs.

一点都 **NEG V with adjectival verbs, modal verbs, and stative verbs**

When used with adjectival verbs, modal verbs, or stative verbs, negation is always 不.

我觉得你一点儿都不 **pàng** 。
I think you are not even a little fat.
我一点都不喜欢。
I don't like it at all.
他一点都不会。
He can't do it at all.
她一点都不**pà**。
She's not afraid at all.

When used with modal verbs, or stative verbs, if the verb phrase includes an object, the object is generally stated at the beginning of the sentence.

我不想看那个电 yǐng。	→	那个电 yǐng, 我一点都不想看。
I don't want to watch that movie.	→	*I have no interest at all in watching that movie.*
我不能吃鱼。	→	我一点鱼都不能吃。
I can't eat fish.	→	*I can't eat fish at all.*

一点都 NEG V with action verbs

When used with action verbs, if the verb takes an object, the object is stated before the verb phrase, usually right after 一点.

If the sentence refers to an action in present, future, or general time, negation is 不.

她不喝酒.   →   她一点酒都不喝。
She doesn't drink alcohol. She doesn't drink alcohol at all.

我不看电视。 →   我一点电视都不看。
I don't watch television. I don't watch television at all.

When talking about an action that did not occur or was not completed in the past, negation is 没.

我没吃东西。   →   我一点东西都没吃。
I didn't eat anything. I didn't eat anything at all.
我没做功课。   →   我一点功课都没做。
I didn't do homework. → *I didn't do any homework at all.*

Practice ▶ *Workbook: Focus on Structure 23.6; Focus on Communication 23.2, 23.3, 23.5.*

23.8. Talking about sizes

Chinese sizes are indicated with the classifier 号:

小号 *small,* 中号 *medium,* 大号 *large,* 特大号 *extra large*

To ask for *one size larger,* say 有大一号的吗?

Practice ▶ *Workbook: Focus on Communication 23.5.*

23.9. 大小 *size* and other abstract nouns composed from opposites

大小 *size* is a noun composed of two one-syllable adjectival verbs that indicate the two opposite ends of the scale in terms of size:

大   ←→   小
big   *small*

Combining opposites is a common way to form abstract nouns in Mandarin. The following are additional examples of Mandarin abstract nouns formed from opposite adjectival verbs:

长短 *length:*
长   ←→   短
long   *short*

pàngshòu *relative weight:*
pàng ←→   shòu
fat   *thin*

难易 *degree of difficulty*

难   ←→   容易
difficult   *easy*

大小 and these other nouns formed from opposites are *abstract*. That means that they can be used to talk about the abstract notion of *size, weight, difficulty,* etc., but they are not used when talking about what size you wear, how much you weigh, or how difficult or easy some particular task is. The following sentences illustrate this point with the word 大小.

If you want to say:	*Say this:*	*Do not say this:*
I wear size medium.	我穿中号的衣服。 or 我穿中号(的)。	⊗ 我的大小是中号。
What size do you wear?	你穿几号的衣服?	⊗ 你的大小是几号?
I don't know my size.	我不知道我穿几号的衣服。	⊗ 我不知道我的大小。

Here are additional sentences that illustrate the acceptable use of 大小.

这条 **qún** 子的大小怎么样?
How is the size of this skirt?
这几个字的大小 **zhèng** 合适，不大, 也不小。
The size of these characters is just right, not (too) big and not (too) small.
这条 **qún** 子，大小合适，可是颜色不好。
As for this skirt, the size is right but the color isn't good.

23.10.   zhèng (正) AdjV

Zhèng (正) is an intensifier and always occurs before an adjectival verb. It indicates that the subject has *precisely* the qualities of the adjectival verb.

这 **zhǒng** 式样的 **qún** 子今年 **zhèng** 流行，卖得很好。
This style of skirt is right in fashion this year, (it's) selling well.

> *Practice* ▸ *Workbook: Focus on Communication 23.5.*

23.11.   穿在你的身上 Verb + PP

Like the verb 放 *put, place* discussed in *Use and Structure 19.11*, the prepositional phrase 在 **NP** follows the verb 穿 *put on, wear*.

穿在你身上真漂亮。
Wearing (it) on your body is really pretty.

Generally speaking, when the prepositional phrase 在 **NP** indicates where an action occurs, it precedes the verb:

他们在市中心 **guàng jiē**。
They shop downtown.

When the prepositional phrase 在 **NP** indicates where something winds up as a result of an action, it follows the verb:

他把书放在 **zhuō** 子上。
He put the book on the table.

Practice ▸ *Workbook: Focus on Communication 23.3, 23.5.*

23.12. 看起来 VP *appears to be VP*

看起来 indicates that a situation *appears to be* a certain way. As these two sentences from the dialogue illustrate, 看起来 expresses the speaker's opinion about a situation.

红色的比 **lán** 色的更好看。 而且，看起来特别 **shòu** 。
The red one is better looking than the blue one. Also, it makes you look especially thin.
你看起来很 **wúliáo** 。
You appear bored.

Here are additional sentences with 看起来。

他今天看起来不太高兴。
He doesn't appear to be very happy today.
你的房间看起来比我的大。
Your room looks bigger than mine.
你看起来很高兴，今天考得很好，是不是？
You look happy. You did well on the test, right?

Practice ▸ *Workbook: Focus on Structure 23.7; Focus on Communication 23.2, 23.5.*

 # Sentence pyramids

Supply the English translation for the last line where indicated.

I

guǎng 告	*advertisement*
jiǎn jià 的 **guǎng** 告	*advertisements about reducing prices*
打 **zhé jiǎn jià** 的 **guǎng** 告	*advertisements about discounts and reducing prices.*
tiē 出了打 **zhé jiǎn jià** 的 **guǎng** 告	*posted advertisements about discounts and reducing prices*
shāng 店都 **tiē** 出了打 **zhé jiǎn jià** 的 **guǎng** 告	*stores all posted advertisements about discounts and reducing prices*
大大小小的 **shāng** 店都 **tiē** 出了打 **zhé jiǎn jià** 的 **guǎng** 告。	*Large and small stores all posted advertisements about discounts and reducing prices.*

2
累
比爬山、打球还累
guàng jiē 比爬山、打球还累
大为觉得 **guàng jiē** 比爬山、打球还累。

tired
more tiring than mountain climbing and playing ball
Shopping is more tiring than mountain climbing and playing ball.

3
不得不去
他不得不去
女朋友让他去，他不得不去。

can't not go (must go)
he must go
(If) his girlfriend makes him go, he must go.

4
简单
式样也简单
颜色也好，式样也简单
这条**qún**子，颜色也好，式样也简单。

simple
(the) style is simple
the color is good and the style is simple

5
穿不下
我穿不下
这条 **qún** 子太小了，我穿不下。

can't put it on (it won't fit)
I can't put it on
This skirt is too small, I can't put it on.

6
越做越小
怎么越做越小？
现在的衣服怎么越做越小？

made smaller and smaller
why made smaller and smaller?
Clothing nowadays, why are they made smaller and smaller?

7
大家都很 **shòu**
他们觉得大家都很 **shòu**
难道他们觉得大家都很 **shòu** 吗？

everyone is very thin
they think that everyone is very thin
Do they think that everyone is very thin?

8
不 **pàng**
一点儿都不 **pàng**
你一点儿都不 **pàng**
我觉得你一点儿都不 **pàng**！

not fat
not at all fat
you are not at all fat

9
大一号
有大一号的
这条 **qún** 子有大一号的吗？

one size bigger
have (clothing that is) one size bigger

10
试一下别的颜色的
你要不要试一下别的颜色的？

try a different color (of something)
Do you want to try a different color (of something)?

11

zǐ 色的
咖啡色的、和 zǐ 色的
huáng 的、hēi 的、咖啡色的、和 zǐ 色的
这条 qún 子还有红的、huáng 的、
hēi 的、咖啡色的、和 zǐ 色的。

purple
coffee colored (brown), and purple
yellow, black, brown, and purple
This skirt exists in red, yellow, black, brown,
and purple.

12

流行
今年 zhèng 流行
这 zhǒng qún 子今年 zhèng 流行
这 zhǒng 式样的 qún 子今年 zhèng 流行。

popular, trendy
(it's) very popular this year
This kind of skirt is very popular this year
This kind of style of skirt is very popular (very
trendy) this year.

13

特别 shòu
看起来特别 shòu
而且，看起来特别 shòu。
红色的比 lán 色的更好看。 而且，
看起来特别 shòu。

particularly thin
appear particularly thin
in addition, appear particularly thin
The red one is prettier than the blue one. In
addition, (you) appear particularly thin.

14

真的不便宜
好看是好看，可是 真的不便宜。

really not cheap
It's pretty all right, but it's really not cheap.

15

wúliáo
很 wúliáo
你看起来很 wúliáo。

bored
very bored
_____

16

买衣服
我都上网买衣服。

buy clothing
I always go online to buy clothing.

17

方便
又快又方便
在网上买，又快又方便。

convenient
both fast and convenient
Buying online is both fast and convenient.

18

在网上买
连 xié 子都可以在网上买
只要知道大小，连 xié 子都可以在
网上买。

buy online
even shoes you can buy online
As long as you know (the) size, you can even
buy shoes online.

19

wūrǎn
空气 wūrǎn
jiǎn 少空气 wūrǎn
不必开车出去，jiǎn 少空气 wūrǎn。
网上买东西，不必开车出去，jiǎn
少空气 wūrǎn。

pollution
air pollution
reduce air pollution
no need to drive a car to go, reduce air pollution
(When you) buy things online, you don't need to
drive a car to go, (and you) reduce air pollution.

20	
试穿	*try it on*
不能试穿	*you can't try it on*
网上买东西，不能试穿。	*(When you) buy things online, you can't try it on.*

21	
环保	*environmentally friendly*
不环保	*not environmentally friendly*
还是不环保	*it's not environmentally friendly*
都有很多纸 **xiāng**，还是不环保	*there are always a lot of paper boxes, it's not environmentally friendly*
送来的时候都有很多纸 **xiāng**，还是不环保	*When they ship them there are always a lot of paper boxes, it's not environmentally friendly.*
每次上网买东西，送来的时候都有很多纸 **xiāng**，还是不环保吧。	

 Language FAQs

New Year and Spring Festival

There are a number of different expressions that refer to the Chinese New Year. This lesson introduces two: 新年 *New Year* and 春 **jié** *Spring Festival*. 春 **jié** *Spring Festival* refers to the entire two weeks of the Chinese New Year holiday season, which begins on the first day of the new year and continues through the Lantern Festival.

Going shopping

The expressions 买东西, **guàng shāng** 店 and **guàng jiē** all refer to going shopping. Shopping is a recreational activity in China, much as it is in the West, and the expressions **guàng shāng** 店 and **guàng jiē** focus on shopping as recreation, involving visits to many stores over a period of time but not necessarily a final purchase. In recent years, online shopping in China has become very popular, and brick-and-mortar stores are no longer the preferred shopping destination for many shoppers.

 Notes on Chinese culture

Shopping for the New Year

The period before the Chinese New Year is an important shopping season in China. Most stores offer sales and many people buy new clothing. Red is the color associated with happiness in Chinese culture, and many people wear something red during the New Year season. In Lesson 25, we will learn more about the traditions associated with the Chinese New Year.

Narrative in English

New Year is almost here. Big and small stores are all posting advertisements about discounts and reduced prices, making the customers come and spend money buying things. After eating breakfast, Dawei, Xiaowen, and Meili rode the subway to the city to buy things. Xiaowen and Meili really like to go shopping. They say that shopping is a type of exercise. Dawei dislikes shopping more than anything. He thinks that shopping is more tiring than mountain climbing and playing ball. Moreover, it takes a lot of time. You shop for half a day (a long time) and don't necessarily find the clothing you want to buy. But his girlfriend made him go and he has to go (can't not go).

Dialogue in English

Part A

Xiaowen:	Dawei, what do you think about this skirt? The color is good, the style is simple, it's just that it's a little expensive.
Dawei:	Go try it on. It's not important if it is a little expensive. As long as you like it, it is okay.
Xiaowen (to Meili):	It's too small, I can't put it on. (*picks up another one*) This one is also too small. Clothing nowadays, why is it that the more they make the smaller they get? (They are made smaller and smaller.) Do they think that everyone is very thin?
Meili:	Don't talk this way. I think you are not at all fat! Let's ask the clerk. They certainly have larger sizes.
Xiaowen (to the clerk):	Clerk, this skirt, do you have one size larger? I want a blue one.
Clerk:	Look. This one is a small. This one is a medium. What do you think of this size?
Xiaowen:	Just right.

Part B

Xiaowen (to Meili):	What do you think?
Meili:	Not bad, and not too short. However, do you want to try a different color? I think you have too many blue clothes.
Clerk:	This skirt comes in red, yellow, black, brown, and purple. What color do you want to try?
Xiaowen:	The red one, Spring Festival will be here soon. Buying a red skirt is just right. (If I) wear a gold sweater on top it will certainly look very good. (*Xiaowen tries on the red skirt*)
Clerk:	This (type of) style of skirt is very popular this year, it is selling very well. It is very attractive on you. Buy one!

Meili: The red one is even prettier than the blue one. In addition, you look very thin. Even I want to buy one.

Xiaowen: Really? It's nice looking all right, but it's really not cheap. (*to Dawei:*) Dawei, you look bored. Do you want to go look at shirts and slacks?

Dawei: There is no need to do it. I buy all of my clothes online. As long as you know the size, you can even buy shoes online, it is quick and convenient. Sitting at home and moving my fingers, you buy it today and it arrives tomorrow. And you don't have to drive a car to go, it reduces air pollution.

Meili: But in this way you can't try (things) on, and you don't know if they look good or not. In addition, every time you go online to buy things, (when they) send it there are a lot of paper boxes, it's also not environmentally friendly.

Lesson 24

Jiǎn 价, 打折
Discounts and bargains

Communication goals

By the end of this lesson, you will be able to:

■ Discuss the price, size, and appearance of clothing.
■ Compute discounts and bargain with shopkeepers to reduce prices.
■ Persuade others to do something.

Literacy goals

By the end of this lesson, you will be able to:

■ Use the clothing radical to identify characters that refer to clothing.

Key structures

■ Question words as indefinite expressions: 什么都 VP *(verb) everything* and 什么都 NEG VP *not (verb) anything*
■ 再 **ActV**, 又 **ActV** 了 *do an action again*
■ 你这儿 *People as locations*
■ AdjV 得 VP/S *so AdjV that VP/S*
■ 不但 VP₁/S 而且 VP₂/S *not only . . . but also . . .*
■ The verb **ná** *take* and the preposition 把
■ 不是 NP₁ 就是 NP₂ *if it isn't NP₁ it is NP₂*
■ 连一 classifier (NP) 都/也 NEG V *not even V one (NP)*

Narrative

大为、小文和美丽去市中心 **guàng** 街。小文和美丽跟服务员 **tǎo** 价还价，用三百块买了两条式样相同，颜色不同的裙子。另外，小文买了两件衬衫和一条裤子。美丽买了一双黑 **pí** 鞋、一条 **wéijīn**，一 **fù ěrzhào**，和一 **fù** 手 **tào**。只有大为什么都没买。因为他们买了很多东西，坐地铁不方便，所以他们是坐出 **zū** 汽车回学校的。

Narrative vocabulary

				Simplified	Traditional
chūzū qìchē (chūzūchē)	出 zū 汽车 (出 zū 车)	taxi	noun phrase	出租汽车 (出租车)	出租汽車 (出租車)
ěrzhào		earmuffs	noun	耳罩	耳罩
fù		pair of, a set of	classifier	副	副
pí xié	pí 鞋	leather shoes	noun phrase	皮鞋	皮鞋
shǒutào	手 tào	glove	noun	手套	手套
tǎo jià-huán jià	tǎo 价还价	bargain back and forth	verb phrase	讨价还价	討價還價
wéijīn		scarf	noun	围巾	圍巾

Narrative characters

Character	Pinyin	Meaning/ function	Radical	Phrases	Traditional character
百	bǎi	hundred	白	一百块 yī bǎi kuài one hundred dollars	百

衬	chèn	*shirt**	衤	衬衫 chènshān *shirt*	襯
黑	hēi	*black*	黑	黑色 hēisè *black colored*	黑
价	jià	*price*	亻	**tǎo** 价还 价 tǎo jià-huán jià *bargain back and forth*, 价钱 jiàqian *price*, jiǎn 价 jiǎn jià *reduce the price*	價
街	jiē	*street*	行	**guàng** 街 guàng jiē *go window shopping, stroll along the streets*	街
裤	kù	*slacks**	衤	裤子 kùzi *slacks*	褲
汽	qì	*steam, gas*	氵	汽车 qìchē *car*, 出 **zū**(汽)车 chūzū (qì)chē *taxi*	汽
裙	qún	*skirt**	衤	裙子 qúnzi *skirt*	裙
衫	shān	*shirt**	衤	衬衫 chènshān *shirt*	衫
鞋	xié	*shoe*	革	鞋子 xiézi *shoe*, 运动鞋 yùndòngxié *athletic shoes, sneakers, gym shoes*, **pí** 鞋 píxié *leather shoe*	鞋

Dialogue

Part A

美丽：	我也想买这条裙子，可是价钱真的太贵了。买两条便宜一点吧。
服务员：	这样，买两条就打八折。本来一条一百九十块，现在一条一百五十二。
小文：	那两条还要三百 **líng** 四块。三百怎么样？下次我们再来你这儿买。
服务员：	这位小姐真会 **tǎo** 价还价。好吧，算你们三百。不过，别告诉别人。
美丽：	好极了！

Dialogue Part A Vocabulary

				Simplified	Traditional
běnlái	本来	*originally*	adverb	本来	本來
jiàqian	价钱	*price*	noun	价钱	價錢
suàn	算	*calculate, count*	verb	算	算
xiǎojie	小姐	*young lady, miss*	noun	小姐	小姐

Dialogue Part A Characters

Character	Pinyin	Meaning/function	Radical	Phrases	Traditional character
极	jí	*extremely**	木	好极了 hǎojíle *terrific, great*	極
位	wèi	polite classifier for *people*	亻	您是哪位? nín shì nǎwèi? *Who are you?*	位
折	zhé	*bend, twist, fold (clothes)*	扌	打折 dǎ zhé *give a discount*	折

Part B

美丽 (对小文):	小文你看，好可爱的 **ěrzhào** 。我早就想买 **ěrzhào** 了。最近这么冷， 冷得我 **ěrduo** 都没有感觉了。
小文:	北京的冬天这么冷，非得戴 **ěrzhào** 不可。这 **fù** 好，不但暖和，而且颜色也合适，跟你那件咖啡色的大衣很 **pèi** 。
服务员:	我们有跟这 **fù ěrzhào** 一样颜色的手 **tào** 和 **wéijīn** 。要不要试试?
美丽:	好，麻烦你给我 **ná** 过来，好不好?
小文:	你们这儿怎么 **fù** 钱?
服务员:	现金、现金 **kǎ** 、信用 **kǎ** 、二 **wéi** 码扫码都可以。您方便就好。
小文:	可以用 **Wēi** 信 **Zhīfù** 吧?
服务员:	当然可以。在这儿扫一下码就行了。您要发票吗?
小文:	不用了。
服务员:	谢谢!

Dialogue Part B Vocabulary

				Simplified	*Traditional*
bùdàn	不但	*not only*	conjunction	不但	不但
èrwéi mǎ	二 **wéi** 码	*QR code*	noun phrase	二维码	二維碼
fāpiào	发票	*receipt*	noun	发票	發票
fù		*pay*	verb	付	付
kǎ		*card*	noun	卡	卡
kě'ài	可爱	*cute*	adjectival verb	可爱	可愛
gǎnjué	感觉	*feeling*	noun	感觉	感覺
ná		*bring, take*	verb	拿	拿
pèi		*match*	verb, adjectival verb	配	配
sǎo mǎ	扫码	*scan a code* (cf. sǎo 扫 *sweep, scan*)	verb + object	扫码	掃碼

Wēixìn	Wēi 信	*WeChat*	proper noun	微信	微信
Wēixìn Zhīfù	Wēi 信 Zhīfù	*WeChat Pay*	proper noun	微信支付	微信支付
xiànjīn	现金	*cash*	noun	现金	现金
xiànjīn kǎ	现金 kǎ	*debit card*	noun phrase	现金卡	现金卡
xìnyòng kǎ	信用 kǎ	*credit card*	noun phrase	信用卡	信用卡

Dialogue Part B Characters

Character	Pinyin	Meaning/ function	Radical	Phrases	Traditional character
戴	dài	*wear on the head, neck, and upper extremities*	戈	戴耳罩 dài ěrzhào *wear earmuffs*	戴
感	gǎn	*feel**	心	感冒 gǎnmào *a cold*, 感觉 gǎnjué *feeling*	感
金	jīn	*gold, metal*	金	金色 jīnsè *gold colored*, 现金 xiànjīn *cash*, 现金 **kǎ** xiànjīnkǎ *debit card*	金
码	mǎ	*number, symbol, code**	石	号码 hàomǎ *number (telephone number)*, 扫码 sǎo mǎ *scan a code*	码
扫	sǎo	*sweep, scan*	扌	扫地 sǎo dì *sweep the floor*, 扫码 sǎo mǎ *scan a code*	扫
信	xìn	*trust*	亻	短信 duǎnxìn *text message*, 信用 **kǎ** xìnyòng kǎ *credit card*, **Wēi** 信 Wēixìn *WeChat*	信

Part C

小文： 大为，你在做什么？是不是又在玩手机，**làng** 费时间？ 你要不要买几条裤子或看看大衣？你的裤子太旧了。

大为： 我的裤子看起来旧，但不是旧的。这种样子的裤子今年 **zhèng** 流行。

小文： 运动鞋和袜子，今天都打六折。价钱便宜多了， 你不想看看吗？

大为： 我什么都不要买。 我今天就陪你们来买东西。

美丽： 那我们就走吧，今天买太多东西了，坐出 **zū** 车回去吧 （大为把手机 **ná** 出来叫车。）

大为： 好，五分钟以后到，我们出去等吧。

Dialogue Part C Vocabulary

				Simplified	Traditional
dàyī	大衣	*coat, overcoat*	noun	大衣	大衣
làngfèi	**làng** 费	*waste*	verb	浪费	浪費
yùndòng xié	运动鞋	*sneakers*	noun	运动鞋	運動鞋

Dialogue Part C Characters

Character	Pinyin	Meaning/ function	Radical	Phrases	Traditional character
费	fèi	*expense, spend, waste*	贝	**làng** 费 làngfèi *waste,* 学费 xuéfèi *tuition*	費
双	shuāng	*pair*	又	一双鞋 yī shuāng xié *a pair of shoes*	雙
袜	wà	*socks**	衤	袜子 wàzi *socks*	襪
种	zhǒng	*kind of*	禾	这种衣服 zhè zhǒng yīfu *this kind of clothing*	種

Part D

(那天晚上，在宿舍楼前边)
大为：   国强，快过来帮忙。我 **ná** 不了这么多东西。
国强：   买了这么多东西，不是大 **jiǎn** 价，就是不要钱。
大为：   怎么会不要钱？ 这些都是小文的。他们两个一共花了一 **qiān** 多
          块。 我什么都没买。
国强：   你连一双袜子都没买吗?
大为：   没有。小文和美丽 **guàng** 了三家商店，我一直帮她们 **ná** 东西，
          累死了。她们去喝咖啡，让我把东西先 **ná** 回来。
国强：   不买东西你还去了一天。真是 **yuàn** 者上 **gōu** 。
大为：   我快饿死了，用手机叫外卖吧。你想吃什么?

Dialogue Part D Vocabulary

				Simplified	Traditional
bāng máng	帮忙	help out, lend a hand	verb + object	帮忙	幫忙
yuàn zhě shàng gōu	**yuàn** 者上 **gōu**	willingly swallowed the bait, willingly got caught	proverb	愿者上钩	願者上鉤

Dialogue Part D Characters

Character	Pinyin	Meaning/ function	Radical	Phrases	Traditional character
饿	è	hungry	饣	饿死了 èsǐle *starving to death*	餓
楼	lóu	building; floor of a building	木	楼 **tī** lóutī *staircase*	樓
商	shāng	commerce*	口	商店 shāngdiàn *(a) shop*	商
死	sǐ	dead	歹	累死了 lèisǐle *dead tired*, 饿死了 èsǐle *starving to death*	死

Clothing terms and associated classifiers
Clothing vocabulary introduced through Lesson 24

clothing item	characters	Pinyin	classifier	traditional characters
shirt	衬衫	chènshān	件 (jiàn)	襯衫
coat, overcoat	大衣	dàyī	件 (jiàn)	大衣
gloves	手 **tào** (手套)	shǒutào	副 (fù)	手套
earmuffs	耳罩	ěrzhào	副 (fù)	耳罩
socks	袜子	wàzi	双 (shuāng)	襪子
shoes	鞋子	xié(zi)	双 (shuāng)	鞋子
leather shoes	**pí** 鞋 (皮鞋)	pí xié	双 (shuāng)	皮鞋
sneakers	球鞋 运动鞋	qiúxié yùndòng xié	双 (shuāng)	球鞋 運動鞋
slacks	裤子	kùzi	条 (tiáo)	褲子
skirt	裙子	qúnzi	条 (tiáo)	裙子
scarf	围巾	wéijīn	条 (tiáo)	圍巾

Supplementary clothing vocabulary

clothing item	characters	pinyin	classifier	traditional characters
dress	连衣裙	**liányī qún**	件 (jiàn)	連衣裙
jacket	夹克	**jiá kè**	件 (jiàn)	夾克
overcoat	外套	**wàitào**	件 (jiàn)	外套
pajamas	睡衣	**shuì yī**	套 (tào)	睡衣
sweater	毛衣	**máoyī**	件 (jiàn)	毛衣
sweatshirt	运动衫	**yùndòng shān**	件 (jiàn)	運動衫
swimsuit	泳衣	**yǒng yī**	件 (jiàn)	泳衣

T-shirt	T 恤	**T xù**	件 **(jiàn)**	T 恤
vest	背心	**bèixīn**	件 **(jiàn)**	背心
sandals	凉鞋	**liáng xié**	双 **(shuāng)**	凉鞋
slippers	拖鞋	**tuō xié**	双 **(shuāng)**	拖鞋
jeans	牛仔裤	**niúzǎi kù**	条 **(tiáo)**	牛仔裤
necktie	领带	**lǐng dài**	条 **(tiáo)**	领带
shorts	短裤	**duǎn kù**	条 **(tiáo)**	短裤
suit	西装	**xī zhuāng**	套 **(tào)**	西装
hat	帽子	**mào zi**	顶 **(dǐng)**	帽子

The clothing radical 衤 yī

Some radicals provide consistent clues about the meaning of the characters in which they occur. The radical 衤 **yī** is one of them. Characters with the radical 衤 **yī** almost always refer to an item of clothing. Here are characters presented in this lesson with the radical 衤 **yī**. When you see an unfamiliar character with this radical, your first guess should be that it refers to an article of clothing. 衤 **yī** is an alternative form of the character 衣 **yī** in the word 衣服 *clothing*.

衬	衬衫 **chèn**(shān)	*shirt*
衫	衬衫 (chèn)**shān**	*shirt*
裤	裤子 **kù(zi)**	*slacks*
裙	裙子 **qún(zi)**	*skirt*
袜	袜子 **wà(zi)**	*socks*

Stroke Order Flow Chart

Character   **Total Strokes**

Narrative

Char															Total
百	一	丆	丆	百	百	百									6
衬	丶	ラ	衤	衤	衤	补	衬	衬							8
黑	丶	冂	冂	皿	回	甲	里	里	里	黑	黑	黑			12
价	丿	亻	亻	价	价	价									6
街	丿	彳	彳	彳	往	往	往	往	往	往	街	街			12
裤	丶	ラ	衤	衤	衤	衤	衤	衤	裤	裤	裤	裤			12
汽	丶	氵	氵	氵	汽	汽	汽								7
裙	丶	ラ	衤	衤	衤	衤	衤	裙	裙	裙	裙	裙			12
衫	丶	ラ	衤	衤	衤	衤	衫	衫							8
鞋	一	十	艹	艹	艹	芑	苦	苩	革	革	革	鞋	鞋	鞋	15

Dialogue A

Char								Total
极	一	十	才	木	杁	极	极	7
位	丿	亻	亻	仁	仵	位	位	7
折	一	扌	扌	扩	扩	折	折	7

Dialogue B

Char																		Total
戴	一	十	土	士	吉	吉	查	壴	壴	壴	壴	壴	壴	真	戴	戴	戴	17
感	一	厂	厂	厂	咸	咸	咸	咸	咸	咸	感	感	感					13
金	丿	人	仝	今	全	全	金	金										8
码	一	丆	石	石	石	矿	码	码										8
扫	一	十	扌	扫	扫	扫												6
信	丿	亻	亻	信	信	信	信	信	信									9

Dialogue C

Char										Total
费	一	一	弓	弗	弗	弗	弗	费	费	9
双	又	又	双	双						4
袜	丶	ラ	衤	衤	衤	衤	衤	袜	袜	10
种	丿	二	千	禾	禾	禾	和	和	种	9

Dialogue D

Char													Total
饿	丿	𠂉	饣	饣	饣	饣	饣	饿	饿	饿			10
楼	一	十	才	木	木	杙	杼	栏	株	楼	楼	楼	13
商	丶	亠	亠	产	产	商	商	商	商	商	商		11
死	一	丆	歹	歹	死	死							6

Use and structure

24.1. Using question words as indefinite expressions: 什么都/也 VP *everything, anything* and 什么都/也 NEG VP *nothing, not anything*

Question word phrase + 都 + verb (affirmative sentences)

Mandarin content question words include 什么 *what,* 谁 *who,* 哪 *which,* 哪儿 *where,* 什么时候 *when,* 几 *how many,* etc. In affirmative sentences, content question words take on the "indefinite" meaning *every* or *any* when they are followed by 都 and the verb phrase.

Note the following:

■ The question word may occur by itself or it may be part of a noun phrase (for example 什么地方). When it occurs as part of a noun phrase, we refer to the phrase as a question word phrase.

■ To have indefinite meaning, the question word or the question word phrase must occur before the verb.

The following sentences illustrate the use of question words as indefinite expressions for the various question words.

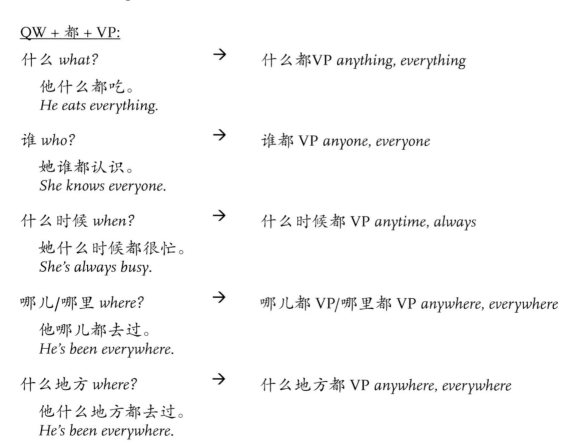

QW + 都 + VP:

什么 *what?* → 什么都VP *anything, everything*

他什么都吃。
He eats everything.

谁 *who?* → 谁都 VP *anyone, everyone*

她谁都认识。
She knows everyone.

什么时候 *when?* → 什么时候都 VP *anytime, always*

她什么时候都很忙。
She's always busy.

哪儿/哪里 *where?* → 哪儿都 VP/哪里都 VP *anywhere, everywhere*

他哪儿都去过。
He's been everywhere.

什么地方 *where?* → 什么地方都 VP *anywhere, everywhere*

他什么地方都去过。
He's been everywhere.

Question word phrase + 也 or 都 + NEG + VP

When noun phrases with content question words are followed by 也 or 都 + negation (不 or 没) + VP, they convey the meaning *none* or *not any*. The following sentences illustrate this for the various question words.

QW + 也 or 都 + NEG + VP:

什么 *what?* → 什么也/都 NEG VP *nothing*

我什么都没买。
I didn't buy anything.

只有大为什么都没买。
Only Dawei didn't buy anything.

谁 *who?* → 谁也/都 NEG VP *no one*

他谁都不喜欢。
He doesn't like anyone.

什么时候 *when?* → 什么时候也/都 NEG VP *never*

他什么时候都不忙。
He's never busy.

哪儿/哪里 *where?* → 哪儿也/都VP/哪里也/都 NEG VP *nowhere*

她哪儿也没去过。
She hasn't been anywhere.

什么地方 *where?* → 什么地方也/都 NEG VP *nowhere*

她什么地方也没去过。
She hasn't been anywhere.

> **Practice**   *Workbook: Focus on Structure 24.1, 24.2; Focus on Communication 24.1, 24.2, 24.3.*

24.2.   打折 *give a discount*, 打八折 *20% off*

The expression 打折 means *give a discount*.

春节快到了，商店都在打折。
The Spring Festival is almost here, and stores are giving discounts.

To indicate the percentage of the discount, add a number before 折:

打八折 *20% off*
打六折 *40% off*
打五折 *50% off*

To indicate a discount that is a two-place fraction, for example, 15% off, say:

打八五折 *15% off*

Notice that English and Chinese indicate discounts in opposite ways. In English, the percentage of a discount means the percentage of the original price that the item is reduced to; the higher the percentage, the greater the discount. In Chinese, 折 indicates the percentage of the original price that you pay; the lower the 折 the greater the discount. 10% off is not a great sale, but 打一折 is a terrific sale: 90% off the original price!

To ask whether a discount is offered, say:

打折吗？ **or** 打不打折？
Do you give a discount?

To ask how big the discount is, say:

打几折？
How much is the discount?

Study the following table to see how to express an equivalent discount in English and Chinese for an item whose original price is ¥100.

10% off	打九折	¥90
20% off	打八折	¥80
30% off	打七折	¥70
40% off	打六折	¥60
50% off	打五折	¥50
60% off	打四折	¥40
70% off	打三折	¥30
80% off	打二折	¥20
90% off	打一折	¥10

Practice ▸ *Workbook: Focus on Structure 24.3; Focus on Communication 24.5, 24.6.*

24.3. 再 VP and 又 VP 了 saying that a situation occurs again

The adverbs 再 and 又 are used when saying that a situation occurs again. 再 is used when saying that a situation will occur again *in the future*.

下次我们再来你这儿买。
Next time we'll come to your place again to shop.
我不知道你这么喜欢吃我做的饺子，这样，明天再做一些。
I didn't know you liked to eat my dumplings this much. How about this, I'll make a few again tomorrow.
这一次大家都考得不好，老师说下个星期再考一次。
This time everyone did poorly on the test. Teacher said that we will have a test again next week.

又 is used when saying a situation has occurred again in the past, or that it started in the past and is continuing into the present time. When 又 is used with an action verb, the verb or verb phrase is typically followed by 了.

今天又下雨了。
It rained again today. (It is raining again today.)
我又忘了他的名字了。
I forgot his name again.
你怎么又来晚了？
Why did you arrive late again?

再 and 又 are adverbs (like 都, 也, 还, 只, 就, etc.), and they occur at the beginning of the verb phrase, before any prepositional phrases:

他又给他的女朋友打电话了。
He phoned his girlfriend again.
我想再到中国去 **lǚyóu** 。
I'd like to go to China to travel again.

We have already learned how to use 再 and 又 in other structures. In Lesson 13 of this course, we learned that 再 can be used when indicating sequence (*Use and Structure* 13.10):

你得先过马路，再往北走。
First you have to cross the street, then you go north.

In Lesson 19 (*Use and Structure* 19.7), we learned to use 又 before each of a pair of adjectival verbs to express the meaning of *both AV₁ and AV₂*:

我们的宿舍又脏又 **luàn**.
Our dorm room is both dirty and messy.

> **Practice** ▶ *Workbook: Focus on Structure 24.4; Focus on Communication 24.1.*

24.4.   People as locations 你这儿

In Chinese, words referring to people (pronouns, names) cannot be destinations. That is, you cannot say "来我" to mean *come to me*. To use a pronoun or a noun referring to a person as a location, you must add 这儿/这里 *here* or 那儿/那里 *there* after the pronoun or noun.

下次我们再来<u>你这儿</u>买。
Next time we will come again to shop at your place.
我明天去<u>我 **āyí** 那儿</u>吃晚饭。
Tomorrow I'm going to my aunt's place to eat dinner.

24.5.   AdjV 得 VP/S *so AdjV that VP/S*

Adjectival verbs indicate qualities: *difficult, pretty, cold*, etc. We have seen that intensifiers such as 很 *very*, 非常 *extremely*, 有一点 *a little*, etc. modify those qualities, so you can say that something is 有一点难 *a little difficult*, or 非常漂亮 *extremely pretty*, or

很冷 *very cold*, etc. Sometimes you want to say that something is *so (difficult, pretty, cold, etc.) that something happens*. In Mandarin, you express this meaning with the structure:

AdjV 得 **VP/S** *so AdjV that VP/S*
我冷得 **ěrduo** 都没有感觉了。
I'm so cold that my ears are numb.

As the structure rule indicates, 得 can be followed by either a VP or an entire sentence. Here are examples of each.

AdjV 得 **VP**

忙得没有时间吃饭。
I am so busy that I don't have time to eat.
他累得走不了路了。
He was so tired that he couldn't walk.
我冷得只想 **dāi** 在家里睡觉。
I am so cold that I just want to stay home and sleep.
我忙得忘了给女朋友打电话。
I was so busy that I forgot to phone my girlfriend.

AdjV 得 **S**

忙得我没有时间吃饭。
I am so busy that I don't have time to eat.
天气冷得我不想出去。
It's so cold that I don't want to go out.

This structure can also be used with 连. See note 24.11.

> **Practice**   *Workbook: Focus on Structure 24.5, 24.6; Focus on Communication 24.1, 24.2, 24.3.*

24.6.   不但 VP$_1$ /S 而且 VP$_2$/S *not only . . . but also . . .*

In Lesson 21, we learned the word 而且 *moreover, furthermore, in addition*. 而且 often occurs paired with 不但 *not only* in the expression 不但 VP$_1$/S 而且VP$_2$/S *not only . . . but also . . .*:

那件衬衫不但便宜而且好看。
That shirt is not only cheap but it's also pretty.
我的同屋不但很 **cōng** 明而且很用功。
My roommate is not only smart, he's also hard working.

Notice that 不但 and 而且 may be followed by a VP or by a sentence.

这 **fù ěrzhào** 不但暖和而且颜色也合适。
These earmuffs are not only warm, they are also the right color.
这 **fù ěrzhào** 不但价钱很便宜，而且颜色也合适。
(As for) these earmuffs, they are not only inexpensive, but they are also the right color.

> **Practice**   *Workbook: Focus on Structure 24.6; Focus on Communication 24.2, 24.3.*

24.7.   戴 vs. 穿 *wear*

As noted in *Use and Structure* 20.12, 戴 and 穿 both mean *wear* but they are specialized for different parts of the body.

戴 is used when talking about wearing items on the head, neck, or arms:

> 戴 **ěrzhào** *wear earmuffs*   戴手 **tào** *wear gloves*   戴口 **zhào** *wear a face mask*

戴 is also the verb to use when saying that you wear *scarves, hats, earrings, necklaces, neckties,* or *rings.*
穿 is used when talking about wearing items on the torso or legs:

> 穿鞋 *wear shoes*   穿裤子 *wear slacks*
> 穿裙子 *wear a skirt*   穿衬衫 *wear a shirt*

> **Practice** ▶ *Workbook: Focus on Structure 24.8; Focus on Communication 24.7.*

24.8.   ná (拿) *bring, take* and the preposition 把

Ná (拿) is an action verb that means to transport an object by hand from one place to another.

Ná is translated into English as *bring* when it is followed by a directional expression ending with 来 *come.*

> 麻烦你给我 **ná** 过来，好不好？
> *May I trouble you to bring it over for me?*

Ná is translated into English as *take* when followed by a directional expression ending with 去 *go* or 走 *go,* or 回 *return,* or when the context otherwise makes it clear that movement is away from the speaker or point of reference.

> 我得把这些书都 **ná** 回图书馆去。
> *I have to take these books back to the library.*

Ná often occurs as the main verb with the preposition 把 (*Use and Structure* 19.8). Sentences with 把 and **ná** can usually be paraphrased as:

> 把 (*take/get a hold of*) something and **ná** (*bring/take it*) somewhere
> 他把东西 **ná** 进来了。
> *He took (*把*) the things and brought (***ná***) them in.* = *He brought in the things.*
> 我们把书 **ná** 回家吧。
> *Let's take (*把*) the books and bring (***ná***) them home.* = *Let's bring home the books.*
> 谁把我的钱 **ná** 走了？
> *Who took (*把*) my money and took (***ná***) it away?* = *Who took my money (away)?*

> **Practice** ▶ *Workbook: Focus on Structure 24.9; Focus on Communication 24.1.*

24.9.   帮 *help* and 帮（别人的）忙 *help (others)*

帮 *help* is a verb that can be followed by an object (the person you are helping) and an action.

请帮我把东西 **ná** 进来。
Please help me bring the things in.
我得帮我的同屋收 shi 屋子。
I have to help my roommate clean up the room.
对不起我不能去，我得帮我妈妈买东西 。
Sorry, I can't go. I have to help my mom shop.
你能不能帮我看一下这几个字写得对不对。
Can you help me by taking a look to see if these characters are written correctly?

帮忙 is a verb + object phrase. Although it is translated into English as *help*, it literally means *help with busy-ness*. When you use the phrase 帮忙 to say that you are *helping someone,* you say:

帮（**person** 的）忙
他常帮朋友的忙。
He often helps his friends.
你应该帮别人的忙。
You should help other people.
谢谢你，你帮了我一个大忙。
Thank you. You helped me a lot.

When you use the phrase 帮忙, you cannot not include the action that you are helping someone to do. If you want to include the action, use the verb 帮:

她常帮她的男朋友买衣服。
She often helps her boyfriend shop for clothing.

24.10.   不是 NP₁，就是 NP₂ *if it isn't NP₁, it is NP₂*

不是 **NP₁**，就是 **NP₂** indicates that two noun phrases are alternatives, and that either one or the other is always true.

There are several variations in the way that the structure is used.

It can be used to present two different explanations, when the speaker is sure that one or the other is correct. This is how Guoqiang uses it in the dialogue.

买了这么多东西，看起来不是大 **jiǎn** 价，就是不要钱。
(They've) bought so many things, it looks like if it wasn't a big sale, it's that they were giving things away for free.

It can be used to indicate that some action always involves one of two NPs.

美丽每天都穿红色的衣服，不是红色的衬衫，就是红色的裙子。
Meili wears red clothing every day. If it isn't a red shirt, it's a red skirt.

每天的生活都一样。不是上课就是做功课。
Every day is the same. If I'm not going to class I'm doing homework.

Practice ▶   *Workbook: Focus on Structure 24.10, 24.11; Focus on Communication 24.2.*

24.11. 连 NP 都/也 NEG V *not even NP*, and 连一 classifier (NP) 都/也 NEG V *not even one NP*

In Lesson 22, we learned to use 连 + NP to talk about *even NP*.

我家每个人都学中文，连我妹妹都学中文。
Everyone in my family studies Chinese. Even my little sister studies Chinese.

We have seen that 连 always occurs before a noun phrase, and that 连 + NP must occur before the verb phrase of the sentence (*Use and Structure* 22.11).

In this lesson, we learn to use 连 when the VP includes negation.

连NP 都/也 NEG V(P) *even NP does not V(P)*

连 **NP** occurs before 都 /也 **NEG V(P)** in the following structures:

连 **Subject NP** 都/也 **NEG VP** *even the subject (is not, has not, does not) VP*

这个问题太难，连最 **cōng** 明的学生都不会写。
This question is too difficult. Even the smartest student couldn't do it.
这件事她没告诉别人，连她最好的朋友都不知道。
She hasn't told anyone about this matter. Even her best friend doesn't know.

Subject 连 **time when** 都/也 **NEG VP** *something does not happen even at this time:*

他每天都不吃早饭，连星期天都不吃。
He doesn't eat breakfast. He doesn't even eat it on Sunday.

Subject 连 **object NP** 都/也 **NEG V** *subject doesn't even "verb" the object:*

他什么运动都不喜欢，连 **pīngpāng** 球都不打。
He doesn't like any sports. He doesn't even play ping-pong.
她这几天忙 zhe 准备考试，连男朋友的电话都不接。
These past few days she has been busy preparing for exams; she hasn't even answered her boyfriend's phone calls.
我昨天太累了，连晚饭都没吃就去睡觉了。
I was too tired yesterday; I didn't even eat dinner and went right to bed.

连一classifier (NP) 都/也 NEG V *not (be, have do) even one NP*

When the NP takes the form 一 classifier (NP) and the verb phrase is negated, the meaning of the sentence is *not even one (NP)*.

我 **guàng** 了一天的商店，连一双袜子都没买。
I shopped the whole day and didn't even buy a pair of socks.
他刚到这个新学校，连一个朋友都没有。
He has just arrived at this new school and doesn't even have one friend.

我的钱都花 **wán** 了，现在连一毛钱都没有。
I've spent all of my money and don't even have a dime.
我今天忙死了，到现在连一**bēi** 水也没喝。
I've been busy to death today, up until now I haven't even drunk one cup of water.

Practice ▶   *Workbook: Focus on Structure 24.5.*

 # Sentence pyramids

Supply the English translation for the last line where indicated.

I **tǎo** 价还价 跟服务员 **tǎo** 价还价 小文和美丽跟服务员 **tǎo** 价还价了。	*bargain back and forth* *bargain back and forth with the clerk* *Xiaowen and Meili bargained back and forth with the clerk.*
2 裙子 颜色不同的裙子 式样相同，颜色不同的裙子 她买了两条式样相同，颜色不同的裙子。	*skirt* *different colored skirt* *skirts of identical styles and different colors* *She bought two skirts of identical styles and different colors.*
3 手 **tào** 一 **fù** 手 **tào** 一 **fù** **ěrzhào**，和一 **fù** 手 **tào** 一条 **wéijīn**，一 **fù** **ěrzhào**，和一 **fù** 手 **tào** 一双黑 **pí** 鞋、一条 **wéijīn**，一 **fù** **ěrzhào**，和一 **fù** 手 **tào** 美丽买了一双黑 **pí** 鞋、一条 **wéijīn**，一 **fù** **ěrzhào**，和一 **fù** 手 **tào**。	*gloves* *a pair (set) of gloves* *a set of earmuffs and a pair of gloves* *a scarf, a set of earmuffs, and a pair of gloves* *a pair of black leather shoes, a scarf, a set of earmuffs, and a pair of gloves* _____
4 没买 什么都没买 大为什么都没买。	*didn't buy* *didn't buy anything* _____
5 回学校 坐出 **zū** 汽车回学校 他们是坐出 **zū** 汽车回学校的。	*return to school* *take a taxi back to school* *They took a taxi back to school.* (provided as a detail of a completed event)

6 打折 打八折 买两条就打八折。	*give a discount* *20% off*
7 一百五十二 一条一百五十二 现在一条一百五十二 本来一条一百九十块，现在一条 一百五十二。	*one hundred fifty-two dollars* *one is one hundred fifty-two dollars* *right now one is one hundred fifty-two dollars* *Originally one cost one hundred ninety dollars, right now one is one hundred fifty-two dollars.*
8 打折 打几折？	*give a discount* *How much is the discount?*
9 打折 打六折 都打六折 今天都打六折了 袜子，今天都打六折了 运动鞋和袜子，今天都打六折了。	*give a discount* *40% off* *all 40% off* *today all are 40% off* *socks today are all 40% off*
10 买 来你这儿买 再来你这儿买 下次我们再来你这儿买。	*shop, buy* *come to your place to shop* *come to your store again to shop*
11 太贵了 真的太贵了 价钱真的太贵了。	*too expensive* *really too expensive* *The price is really too expensive.*
12 便宜 便宜一点 算便宜一点 算便宜一点吧 买两条算便宜一点吧。	*cheap* *a little cheaper* *calculate it a little cheaper* *why don't you calculate it a little cheaper* *If we buy two, why don't you sell it a little cheaper?*
13 **tǎo** 价还价 会 **tǎo** 价还价 真会 **tǎo** 价还价 这位小姐真会 **tǎo** 价还价。	*bargain over the price* *can bargain over the price* *really knows how to bargain over the price*

14	
别人	*other people*
告诉别人	*tell other people*
别告诉别人。	

15	
买 ěrzhào	*buy earmuffs*
想买 ěrzhào	*want to buy earmuffs*
我早就想买 ěrzhào 了。	*I have long wanted to buy earmuffs.*

16	
感觉	*feeling*
有感觉	*have feeling*
没有感觉了	*not have feeling, be numb*
ěrduo 都没有感觉了	*ears don't have any feeling*
我冷得 ěrduo 都没有感觉了。	*I am so cold that my ears have no feeling (are numb).*

17	
戴 ěrzhào	*wear earmuffs*
得戴 ěrzhào	*must wear earmuffs*
非得戴 ěrzhào 不可	*must wear earmuffs*
冬天这么冷，非得戴 ěrzhào 不可	*the winter is so cold you must wear earmuffs*
北京的冬天这么冷，非得戴 ěrzhào 不可。	

18	
合适	*suitable*
颜色也合适	*the color is also right*
不但暖和，而且颜色也合适	*not only warm, but also the color is also right*
这 fù ěrzhào ，不但暖和，而且颜色也合适 。	*This set of earmuffs, not only are they warm but the color is also right.*

19	
很 pèi	*match*
跟你的大衣很 pèi	*matches your overcoat*
跟你那件咖啡色的大衣很 pèi	*matches that brown overcoat of yours*
这 fù ěrzhào 跟你那件咖啡色的大衣很 pèi 。	*These earmuffs match that brown overcoat of yours.*

20	
手 tào 和 wéijīn	*gloves and scarf*
一样颜色的手 tào 和 wéijīn	*the same color gloves and scarf*
跟这 fù ěrzhào 一样颜色的手 tào 和 wéijīn	*the same color gloves and scarf as this pair of earmuffs*
我们有跟这 fù ěrzhào 一样颜色的手 tào 和 wéijīn 。	

21	
好不好？	*okay?*
给我 **ná** 过来，好不好？	*give (it) to me, okay?*
麻烦你给我 **ná** 过来，好不好？	*Let me trouble you to give (it) to me, okay?*

22	
可以	*okay*
二 **wéi** 码扫码都可以	*scanning the QR code is okay*
信用 **kǎ**、二 **wéi** 码扫码都可以	*credit card, scanning the QR code are both okay*
现金 **kǎ**、信用 **kǎ**、二 **wéi** 码扫码都可以	*debit card, credit card, scanning the QR code are all okay*
现金、现金 **kǎ**、信用 **kǎ**、二 **wéi** 码扫码都可以。	*Cash, debit card, credit card, and scanning the QR code are all okay.*

23	
Wēi 信 **Zhīfù**	*WeChat Pay*
可以用 **Wēi** 信 **Zhīfù** 吧？	*Can I use WeChat Pay?*

24	
扫码	*scan the code*
在这儿扫码。	_____

25	
发票	*receipt*
您要发票吗？	*Do you need a receipt?*

26	
玩手机	*play with (your) cell phone*
在玩手机	*playing with (your) cell phone*
又在玩手机	*playing with (your) phone again*
你是不是又在玩手机？	*Are you on your cell phone again?*

27	
làng 费时间	*waste time*
不要 **làng** 费时间。	_____

28	
不是旧的	*not old*
但不是旧的	*but (they) are not old*
看起来旧，但不是旧的	*(they) look old but (they) are not old*
我的裤子看起来旧，但不是旧的。	_____

29	
不是大 **jiǎn** 价，就是不要钱	*if it wasn't a big sale, then it's that they didn't want money (it was free)*
买了这么多东西，不是大 **jiǎn** 价，就是不要钱。	*(They) bought so many things, either it was a big sale or it was free.*

30 一 **qiān**块 一 **qiān** 多块 花了一 **qiān** 多块 一共花了一 **qiān** 多块 他们两个一共花了一**qiān** 多块。	*one thousand dollars* *more than one thousand dollars* *spent more than one thousand dollars* *altogether spent more than one thousand dollars* *The two of them together spent more than one thousand dollars.*
31 没买 一双袜子都没买 连一双袜子都没买 大为连一双袜子都没买。	*didn't buy* *didn't buy one pair of socks* *didn't even buy one pair of socks*
32 **ná**回来 先 **ná** 回来 把东西先 **ná** 回来 她们让我把东西先 **ná** 回来。	*bring back* *first bring back* *take the things back first* *They made me bring the things back first.*
33 **yuàn** 者上 **gōu** 真是 **yuàn** 者上 **gōu** 还 **péi** 女朋友 **guàng** 了一天商店，真是 **yuàn** 者上 **gōu** 你不想，去还 **péi** 女朋友 **guàng** 了一天商店，真是 **yuàn** 者上 **gōu** 。	*you knew what you were getting into* *really is a case of knowing what you were getting into* *still accompanied your girlfriend shopping for a whole day. You knew what you were getting into.* *You didn't want to go and still accompanied your girlfriend shopping for a whole day. You knew what you were getting into.*
34 外卖 手机 **ná** 出来叫外卖吧！	*food delivery* *Take out your phone and order some food for delivery!*

 Language FAQs

一 **fù** 手 **tào** or 一双手 **tào** *a pair of gloves*

The classifier 双 is used when referring to things that come in pairs, for example 一双鞋 *a pair of shoes*. The classifier **fù** also refers to things that come in pairs, but it has a more specialized meaning as well. It refers to things that come in sets that are not generally separated such as eyeglasses. Earmuffs are connected to each other, so they can be counted with the classifier **fù**: 一 **fù ěrzhào** *a set of earmuffs*. Gloves come in matched pairs, but they are not connected and can be counted with the classifier 双 or **fù**: 一双手 **tào**, 一 **fù**手 **tào** *a pair of gloves*.

Notes on Chinese culture

Bargaining

In China, in privately owned stores (but not in chain stores), it is common to **tǎo 价还价** or haggle over the price. Shopkeepers generally expect their customers to ask for the price of goods to be lowered, and a good shopper always gives it a try. In this dialogue, Xiao Wen and Meili are in a good position to bargain, since it is right before the Chinese New Year when most shops have sales, and because they are buying many items in the same store. If you become a regular customer in a store, you are more likely to be offered a better price or a better deal than customers without this 关系 *connection* with the store owner or clerk. Therefore, one goal of a good shopper is to get a good price, but the other is to establish a connection with the store in order to get better deals in the future.

Mobile pay in China

In China, the most common way to pay for purchases is with a mobile app. You pay by scanning a QR code for the item. The payment is then deducted from a linked Chinese bank account. Even the smallest purchases such as dumplings from a street vendor can often be purchased by scanning a QR code. Currently, WeChat Pay and Alipay are the most widely used mobile pay systems. As of this writing, foreigners can also use these systems by linking a credit card and creating a declining balance account.

Ride hailing

China has its own ride-hailing company, 滴滴出行 Dī Dī Chūxíng, that operates similarly to ride-hailing services elsewhere. You use an app to call a car, and you pay with your mobile pay app.

外卖 Ordering meals and snacks online

Food delivery from restaurants has made its way into Chinese culture. To place an order you need to download a food delivery app and you need to have a mobile pay account. Check with your Chinese friends to learn their favorite food delivery apps, place your order, and watch the path of the food from the restaurant to you.

小姐 *Miss, young lady*

The word 小姐 is used in Taiwan in more or less the same way as the word *Miss* is used in English, to address a young woman who is a clerk or waitress, or as the title of an unmarried woman (for example, 高小姐 *Miss Gao*). But in mainland China, the term is much more limited in use, and it often has negative connotations. 小姐 were daughters in wealthy, land-owning families in pre-revolutionary times. Like the terms 先生 *Mr.* and 太太 *Mrs.*, 小姐 *Miss* was banned as a term of address in mainland Chinese speech because of its capitalist connotations. 先生 *Mr.*, 太太 *Mrs.*, and 小姐 *Miss* are slowly begin-ning to return to use in mainland China, but they are still not neutral terms of address. When the clerk says 这位小姐真会 **tǎo** 价-**huán** 价 *this young lady certainly knows how to bargain*, she is jokingly evoking the 小姐 in pre-revolutionary wealthy households, who would have been good with money and would have known fine products. (See also Lesson 15.)

How do you address the clerk?

In mainland China, the neutral word for addressing or referring to the sales person in a store or a server in a restaurant is 服务员, literally, *service person*. In Taiwan and other parts of the Chinese-speaking world, the expression 服务员 is not used, and the expressions 小姐 *Miss* (for female servers) or 先生 *Mr.* (for male servers) are commonly used.

How do you politely ask for service?

In English, we often ask for things politely by forming our request as a ques-tion. For example, in a restaurant, if you want a cup of coffee, you may say, "Can I have a cup of coffee?" In fact, if you want to order a cup of coffee, all you really have to do is say "Give me a cup of coffee." The "Can I have . . ." question form is just a way that we make requests polite in English. In Chi-nese culture, you do *not* begin requests with "我可以不可以 . . ." or any expression that asks if you *can* have something. Instead, to make a request polite, you can preface it with an expression that acknowledges that your request causes someone to do extra work. In this lesson, we see Meili begin her request with the expression 麻烦你, literally, *I am bothering you*:

麻烦你给我 **ná** 过来，好不好？
Can I trouble you to bring them over here for me?

She could also have used the polite expression 请 and said:

请你给我 **ná** 过来，好不好？
Please bring them over here for me.

The most neutral way for her to make the request would be to say:

给我 **ná** 过来。
Bring it over here for me.

Since the sales person is there to serve her, there is no need for her to be overly polite, and some Chinese people say that the use of 麻烦你 or 请 makes the request too polite.

The story behind yuàn 者上 gōu

Chinese proverbs often have their origin in a classical Chinese story. Here is the story behind **yuán** 者上 **gōu** *You did this of your own free will*. During the

Shang dynasty (16th- to 11th-century BCE), there was an honest official named Jiang Shang who left the services of the corrupt Shang king to live in seclusion and wait for a time when he might be called upon to serve a righteous ruler. He passed his days fishing, but he did so in an unusual way. His line did not have a fishhook, for he believed that when the fish were ready, they would come to him of their own free will. One day, while he was fishing, he was approached by King Wen, a benevolent ruler from the state of Zhou, who asked him to serve as his advisor. Jiang Shang joined King Wen's court and he proved to be a wise advisor who contributed to the strength of the state of Zhou.

Narrative in English

Dawei, Xiaowen, and Meili went downtown for some shopping. Xiaowen and Meili bargained with the clerk, and for ¥300 they bought two skirts identical in style and different in color. In addition, Xiaowen bought two shirts and a pair of slacks. Meili bought a pair of black leather shoes, a scarf, a pair of earmuffs, and a pair of gloves. Only Dawei didn't buy anything at all. Because they bought a lot of things, it wasn't convenient to take the subway, so they took a taxi back to school.

Dialogue in English

Part A

Meili:	I want to buy this red skirt, but the price is really too high. If we buy two, how about making it a little cheaper?
Clerk:	How about this, if you buy two I'll give you 20% off. Originally one skirt cost ¥190, now one will cost ¥152.
Xiaowen:	For those two (skirts) you still want ¥304. How about ¥300? Next time we'll come back to your place to shop.
Clerk:	This young lady certainly knows how to bargain. Okay, I'll charge you ¥300. But don't tell anyone.
Meili:	Great!

Part B

Meili (to Xiaowen):	Xiaowen, look, such cute earmuffs! I've wanted to buy earmuffs for a long time. Recently it has been so cold, so cold that my ears are numb.
Xiaowen:	Beijing's winter is so cold, you have to wear earmuffs. This pair is good. It's not only warm, the color is right. It matches your brown coat.
Clerk:	We have gloves and scarves that are the same color as these earmuffs. Would you like to try them on?
Meili:	Okay. Can I trouble you to bring them over here for me?

Xiaowen:	How do you pay here?
Clerk:	Cash, debit card, credit card, and scanning a QR code are all okay. Whatever is convenient for you is good.
Xiaowen:	Can we use WeChat Pay?
Clerk:	Of course you can. You just scan the code here. Do you need a receipt?
Xiaowen:	No.
Clerk:	Thank you!

Part C

Xiaowen:	Dawei, what are you doing? Are you on your cell phone again wasting time? Do you want to buy a few pairs of slacks or look at a coat? Your slacks are too old.
Dawei:	My slacks (may) look old but they are not old. This kind of slacks is right in style this year.
Xiaowen:	Athletic shoes and socks are all 40% off today. The price is so much cheaper, don't you want to look?
Dawei:	I'm not buying anything. Today I'm just accompanying you shopping.
Meili:	Well, let's go. We bought too much today. Let's take a taxi back. (*Dawei takes out his cell phone and calls a car.*)
Dawei:	Okay, it'll arrive in 5 minutes. Let's go outside and wait.

Part D

(*That evening, in front of the dorm*)

Dawei:	Guoqiang, hurry over and help. I can't hold so many things.
Guoqiang:	You've bought so many things. Either they were having a big sale, or they were giving things away for free.
Dawei:	How could they be free? These things are all Xiaowen's. Those two together spent over ￥1000. I didn't buy anything.
Guoqiang:	You didn't even buy a pair of socks?
Dawei:	No. Xiaowen and Meili shopped in three stores, and I helped them carry their things. I'm dead tired. They've gone to drink coffee and they've had me bring the things back.
Guoqiang:	You didn't buy anything and you were still gone for a whole day? You knew what you were getting into. (*Boy were you a sucker!*)
Dawei:	I am starving to death. Use your phone to order some delivery. What do you feel like eating?

Lesson **25**

过春节
Celebrating the New Year festival

Communication goals

By the end of this lesson, you will be able to:

- Explain the basic traditions of the Chinese New Year holiday.
- Explain the symbolic significance of items associated with the Chinese New Year.

Literacy goals

By the end of this lesson, you will

- Be familiar with the use of homophonous characters to convey or imply double meanings.

Key structures

- **AdjV** 不得了 *extremely AdjV*
- **VP** 的 NPs with the main noun omitted
- **V** 着 indicating an ongoing or background event
- **V duration** 的 **object**, another way to express duration
- 一边 VP₁ 一边 VP₂ two actions at the same time
- 从来 **NEG VP** *don't ever VP, have never done VP*
- The adverbs 刚刚 *just completed an action,* 刚才 *just a moment ago,* 等到 *when an action is completed*

Narrative

春节正是学校放 **hán** 假的时候。今年 **hán** 假高美丽没有回家，因为马小文请高美丽跟她一起回家过春节。美丽很高兴能到中国人的家跟中国人一起过春节。小文的家在西 **'ān**，离北京比较远。他们是坐火车回去的。因为全中国有很多的人都要在这个时候回家去看家人，所以坐火车的人非常多。车上 **jǐ** 得不得了。有坐着的，有站着的。有站着睡觉的，还有 **tǎng** 在火车 **zuò** 位 **dǐ** 下睡觉的。他们坐了九个多钟头的火车才到家。

到家的时候，虽然都已经累极了，可是一看到小文的家人，她们就一点也不觉得累了。因为是除**xī**夜，小文的家有很多人。除了她的父母以外，还有小文的 **yéye**，奶奶，和叔叔一家，和一些 **qīnqi**。小文把美丽介绍给家人。然后他们就跟全家一起准备年夜饭。大家一边做饭，一边 **liáo** 天。他们说到已经过去的一年，也 **tán** 到每个人在新的一年里的计划。

Narrative vocabulary

				Simplified	Traditional
bùdéliǎo	不得了	*amazing, awful; extremely, unbearably*	adj VP	不得了	不得了
chúxī	除 **xī**	*Chinese (lunar) New Year's Eve*	noun	除夕	除夕
chúxīyè	除 **xī** 夜	*Chinese (lunar) New Year's Eve*	noun	除夕夜	除夕夜
dǐxià	**dǐ** 下	*below*	noun	底下	底下
hánjià	**hán** 假	*winter vacation*	noun phrase	寒假	寒假
jǐ		*crowd, squeeze*	verb	挤	擠
liáo tiān	**liáo** 天	*chat*	verb + object	聊天	聊天
nǎinai	奶奶	*grandmother (father's mother)*	kinship term	奶奶	奶奶
niányè fàn	年夜饭	*New Year's Eve family dinner*	noun phrase	年夜饭	年夜飯
qīnqi		*relatives*	noun	亲戚	親戚

tán		*talk, converse*	verb	谈	談
tǎng		*lie down*	verb	躺	躺
Xī'ān	西 ān	*Xi'an (city in central northwest China, capital of Shaanxi Province)*	proper name	西安	西安
yéye		*grandfather (father's father)*	kinship term	爷爷	爺爺
yībiān	一边	*on one side, at the same time*	noun, adverb	一边	一邊
zhàn	站	*stand (cf. station, Lesson 11)*	verb	站	站
zuòwèi	**zuò** 位	*seat*	noun	座位	座位

Narrative characters

Character	Pinyin	Meaning/ function	Radical	Phrases	Traditional character
划	huà	*plan, mark*	刂	计划 jìhuà *plan*	劃
计	jì	*calculate*	讠	计划 jìhuà *plan*	計
假	jià	*holiday, vacation**	亻	放假 fàng jià *begin vacation*, **shǔ** 假 shǔ jià *summer vacation*, **hán** 假 hán jià *winter vacation*	假
介	jiè	*introduce**	人	介绍 jièshào *introduce*	介

绍	shào	introduce*	纟	介绍 jièshào *introduce*	紹
叔	shū	uncle*	又	叔叔 shūshu *uncle*	叔
夜	yè	evening, night	夕	夜里 yèlǐ *in the middle of the night,* 年夜饭 niányè fàn *New Year's Eve family dinner*	夜
着	zhe zháo	(verb suffix)*	目	忙着 mángzhe *being busy,* 坐着 zuòzhe *sitting;* 睡不着 shuìbuzháo *unable to fall asleep*	著
正	zhèng	precisely	止		正

Dialogue

Part A

美丽:	叔叔、**Āyí**，您家的年夜饭真 **fēngfù**，太好吃了。我吃得太饱，什么都吃不下了。
马妈妈:	吃 **wán** 饭，我们先吃点水果、喝点茶，然后一起来包饺子。
美丽:	为什么刚刚吃 **wán** 饭，就要包饺子呢?
马妈妈:	中国人过年很多人都吃饺子。在年三十，也就是除 **xī**夜，十二点以前包好，等到半夜的时候吃。
小文:	半夜一到就是新的一年了。父母会给孩子红包，我们也都大了一岁了。美丽，你知道你是 **shǔ** 什么的吗?
美丽:	我知道。我是 **shǔ** 龙的。我想我是一个黄头发蓝眼睛的"龙的 **chuán** 人"吧。
小文:	你听，外边放 **biānpào** 的 **shēng** 音越来越大了。真热 **nao**。
马爸爸 (对小文):	带美丽出去看看吧。

Dialogue Part A Vocabulary

				Simplified	Traditional
bāo	包	*wrap*; classifier for *bags* (see also 红 *bāo*)	verb; classifier	包	包
biānpào		*fireworks*	noun	鞭炮	鞭炮
chuánrén	**chuán** 人	*descendant*	noun	传人	傳人
fàng	放	*set off (firecrackers)* (cf. *put*, Lesson 19)	verb	放	放
fēngfù		*abundant*	adjectival verb	丰富	豐富
guò nián	过年	*celebrate the Chinese New Year*	verb phrase	过年	過年
hóngbāo	红包	*red envelope with money inside given as a gift*	noun phrase	红包	紅包
lóng de chuánrén	龙的 **chuán** 人	*descendant of the dragon*	noun phrase	龙的传人	龍的傳人
nián sānshí	年三十	*the last day of the year*	noun phrase	年三十	年三十
rènao	热 **nao**	*lively*	adjectival phrase	热闹	熱鬧
shēngyīn	**shēng** 音	*sound*	noun	声音	聲音
shǔ		*belong to*	verb	属	屬
tóufa	头发	*hair*	noun	头发	頭髮

Dialogue Part A Characters

Character	Pinyin	Meaning/ function	Radical	Phrases	Traditional character
包	bāo	*wrap; classifier for packages*	勹	包饺子 *bāo jiǎozi wrap dumplings*, 红包 *hóngbāo red gift envelope*	包
饱	bǎo	*full (of food)*	饣	吃饱了 *chībǎo le ate until full*	飽
孩	hái	*child**	子	孩子 *háizi child*	孩
黄	huáng	*yellow*	黄	黄色 *huángsè yellow colored*	黄
睛	jīng	*eyeball**	目	眼睛 *yǎnjing eye*	睛
蓝	lán	*blue*	艹	蓝色 *lánsè blue colored*	藍
龙	lóng	*dragon*	龙		龍
眼	yǎn	*eye**	目	眼睛 *yǎnjing eye*	眼

Part B

美丽：小文，你家门上的"春"字贴 **dào**(倒) 了。

小文：不是"春"字贴 **dào** 了，是"春"到了。"春" ... 到了。

美丽：我明白了。"**Dào**"跟"到"同音。把"春"字贴 **dào** 了意思是说春天到了，春天来了，对不对？

小文：没错。对了，刚才我们吃的鱼好吃吗？

美丽：好吃极了。我从来没吃过这么好吃的鱼。

小文：你知道吗，年夜饭一定会有鱼。吃的"鱼"跟"年年有 **yú**"的"**yú**"同音。"**yú**"就是有多的，没用 **wán** 的。还有，年夜饭里的鱼不要吃 **wán**， **biǎoshì** 有多的， **shèng** 下的，意思是让你在新的一年里生活得更好，有用不 **wán** 的东西。

美丽：没想到同音字跟中国文化有这么大的关系。

小文：十二点到了。新的一年到了。

美丽：新年快乐。

小文：**Gōng** 喜发 **cái**，红包拿来！

Dialogue Part B Vocabulary

				Simplified	Traditional
biǎoshì		*express, indicate, show*	verb	表示	表示
cónglái (+ neg)	从来 **(+ neg）**	*never before*	adverb + neg	从来	從來
dào		*upside down*	verb	倒	倒
gāngcái	刚才	*just before now*	adverb	刚才	剛才
gōngxǐ fācái	**gōng** 喜 发 **cái**	*congratulations and be prosperous*	New Year's greeting expression	恭喜发财	恭喜發財
méi xiǎngdào	没想到	*didn't expect that*	neg + verb	没想到	沒想到
míngbai	明白	*understand*	verb	明白	明白
niánnián yǒu yú	年年有 **yú**	*have more than you need every year*	proverb	年年有余	年年有餘
shèngxia	**shèng** 下	*leftover (be leftover), remain*	verb	剩下	剩下
tóngyīn	同音	*same sound, homophonous*	adjectival phrase	同音	同音
tóngyīn zì	同音字	*characters with identical pronunciations*	noun phrase	同音字	同音字
xīn nián kuàilè	新年快乐	*Happy New Year*	New Year greeting	新年快乐	新年快樂
yú		*surplus*	noun	余	餘

Dialogue Part B Characters

Character	Pinyin	Meaning/ function	Radical	Phrases	Traditional character
乐	lè	*happy**	丿	快乐 kuàilè *happy,* 可乐 kělè *cola,* 可口可乐 Kěkǒukělè *Coca Cola*	樂
拿	ná	*take*	手		拿
贴	tiē	*paste*	贝		貼
鱼	yú	*fish*	鱼		魚

Stroke Order Flow Chart

Character   **Total Strokes**

Narrative

Character	Stroke Order										Total Strokes
划	一	七	戈	戈	戈	划					6
计	丶	讠	讠	计							4
假	丿	亻	亻	亻	伊	伊	伊	伊	伊	假	11
介	丿	人	个	介							4
绍	乚	纟	纟	纫	纫	织	绍	绍			8
叔	丨	卜	上	才	未	未	叔	叔			8
夜	丶	一	广	广	疒	夜	夜	夜			8
着	丶	丷	丷	丷	兰	羊	羊	养	养	着	11
正	一	丁	下	正	正						5

Dialogue A

Character	Stroke Order												Total Strokes
饱	丿	饣	饣	饣	竹	饲	饲	饱					8
孩	乛	了	孑	孑	孒	孩	孩	孩	孩				9
黄	一	十	艹	世	共	昔	昔	苗	黄	黄	黄		11
睛	丨	冂	月	月	目	目	目	日丰	睛	睛	睛	睛	13
蓝	一	十	艹	艹	艿	苂	茷	萃	萃	萃	蓝	蓝	13
龙	一	九	九	龙	龙								5
眼	丨	冂	月	月	目	目	目	目	眼	眼	眼		11

Dialogue B

Character	Stroke Order									Total Strokes
乐	一	匚	乐	乐	乐						5
拿	丿	人	个	今	合	合	合	盒	盒	拿	10
贴	丨	冂	贝	贝	则	贴	贴	贴	贴		9
鱼	丿	夕	夕	危	危	角	鱼	鱼			8

Use and structure

25.1.   AdjV 得不得了 *extremely AdjV, unbearably AdjV*

不得了 means *terrible, awful, unbearable, amazing.* It can occur as the main verb of the sentence, and when it does, it can have either negative or positive connotations, though it is often used sarcastically.

那个人真不得了。
That person is really amazing.

不得了 also occurs in the structure **AdjV** 得不得了. When used in this way, it is an intensifier suffix for adjectival verbs, similar to the intensifier suffix 极了 *extremely.*

车上 **jǐ** 得不得了。
On the train it was extremely (unbearably) crowded.
昨天的考试难得不得了。
Yesterday's test was awfully difficult.

> **Practice**   *Workbook: Focus on Structure 25.1, 25.8; Focus on Communication 25.2.*

25.2.   NP with the main noun omitted

We have learned that descriptions of a noun always occur before the noun, typically followed by 的, and that when the main noun is understood from context, it may be omitted. You always know where the main noun would go if it were present: it would directly follow 的. In the following sentences from the dialogue, the main noun is omitted four times. The implied "missing" noun is 人 *people.*

有坐着的(人)，有站着的(人)。
There were (people) sitting (sitters), there were (people) standing (standers).
有站着睡觉的(人)，还有 **tǎng** 在火车 **zuò** 位 **dǐ** 下睡觉的(人)。
There were (people) sleeping while standing, and there were (people) lying under the seats sleeping.

> **Practice**   *Workbook: Focus on Communication 25.6.*

25.3.   Talking about duration and background events: V 着 and V₁ 着 (object) VP₂

In Lesson 17 (*Use and Structure* 17.2), we learned to use 忙着 + VP to indicate that someone is *busy doing the action of the verb.* 着 is an aspectual suffix that focuses on duration. In this lesson, we learn to use 着 to indicate that the subject is in the middle of some situation, or that a situation has some duration.

V着

The suffix 着 often follows verbs like 坐 *sit*, 站 *stand*, and **tǎng** *lie* that refer to situations with duration, that is, situations that can be maintained for an indefinite period of time. When 着 follows these verbs, it emphasizes the duration of the situation.

有坐着的(人)，有站着的(人)。
There were (people) sitting (sitters), there were (people) standing (standers).

V₁着 (object) VP₂

V 着 is also often used when talking about two situations that occur at the same time. The structure that is used to express this is:

V₁着 (object) VP₂
他站着睡觉。
He slept standing.

The structure V₁着 (object) VP₂ is used when VP₂ is the main action and V₁ is a background situation, something that is taking place when the main action occurs. V₁, the verb that is suffixed with 着 can be any kind of verb. The verb in VP₂ must be an action verb.

别穿着睡衣去买东西。
Don't go shopping in your pajamas.
他拿着一瓶水走进来。
Holding a bottle of water, he walked in. (He walked in holding a bottle of water.)
别 **tǎng** 着看电视。
Don't watch television lying down. (Don't lying down watch television.)

> **Practice** ▶ Workbook: *Focus on Structure 25.2, 25.3, 25.7; Focus on Communication 25.4.*

25.4. NP 的 dǐ 下 *below NP, under NP*

Dǐ 下 *below NP, under NP* is a directional expression like 里边 *inside*, 外边 *outside*, etc. To say *under some noun phrase*, say **NP 的 dǐ下**. As this sentence from the narrative illustrates, 的 may be omitted.

有站着的，有坐着的，还有 **tǎng** 在火车 zuò 位 (的) dǐ下睡觉的。
There were (people) sleeping while standing, and there were (people) lying under the seats sleeping.

To review the use of directional expressions and the stating of location with respect to a reference point in Mandarin, see *Use and Structure 13.7*.

> **Practice** ▶ Workbook: *Focus on Structure 25.8.*

25.5. Another way to express duration: V duration 的 object

In Lesson 12, we learned to indicate the duration of a situation by stating the duration directly after the verb (*Use and Structure 12.11*).

他们坐火车坐了九个多小时才到家。
They rode the train for nine hours and only then arrived home.

In this lesson, we learn a variation of this structure:

> V duration 的 object
> 他们坐了九个多钟头的火车才到家。
> *They rode the train for nine hours and only then arrived home.*
> 我听了半个钟头的音乐。
> *I listened to music for half an hour.*

To use this structure to ask how long someone has done an action, state the question phrase where the duration phrase occurs, for example:

> **(subject) V 多长时间的 object**
> **(subject) V 多久的 object**
> 从西ān 到北京要坐多久的火车?
> *How many hours do you have to ride a train from Xi'an to Beijing? (How long is train ride from Xi'an to Beijing?)*
> 你每天看几个钟头的电视?
> *How many hours of television do you watch every day?*

> **Practice** ▷ *Workbook: Focus on Structure 25.4, 25.7; Focus on Communication 25.2.*

25.6.   一边VP₁, 一边VP₂ *do VP₁ and VP₂ at the same time*

To say that two actions with duration happen at the same time, and that neither action is subordinate to the other, say:

> 一边VP₁, 一边VP₂
> 大家一边做饭, 一边 **liáo** 天。
> *Everyone is cooking and talking.*

The structure 一边VP₁, 一边VP₂ can only be used when VP₁ and VP₂ both indicate actions. Compare this with the structure V₁着 (object) VP₂ introduced in *Use and Structure* 25.3.

> 我喜欢一边吃饭, 一边上网。
> *I like to eat and use the internet at the same time.*
> 你不应该一边开车一边打电话。
> *You shouldn't drive a car and talk on the phone at the same time.*

> **Practice** ▷ *Workbook: Focus on Structure 25.5; Focus on Communication 25.2, 25.4, 25.5.*

25.7.   刚刚 + VP *just did an action*

刚刚 has the same use and structure as the adverb 刚 introduced in Lesson 10 (*Use and Structure* 10.17). It is used to say that you have *just* done an action or that an action *has just happened.* 刚刚 emphasizes that the action was just completed a very, very short time ago.

> 为什么刚刚吃 **wán** 饭, 就开始包饺子呢?
> *Why is it that we've just finished eating and we begin making dumplings? (Why are we starting to make dumplings right after finishing dinner?)*

Even though 刚 and 刚刚 refer to actions that have just been completed, the sentences in which they occur typically do not include 了.

Practice ▶ *Workbook: Focus on Communication 25.2.*

25.8. 等到 *when*

等到 *when* is an adverb that indicates a sequence of two actions. It is used in the following way:

等到 Action$_1$, Action$_2$

等到 emphasizes the fact that the first action has to be complete as a precondition for the second action to occur. You can think about 等到 as meaning "*wait until* the first action happens and then the second action will happen."

As we see in the dialogue, 等到 may occur with the structure 的时候 *when* introduced in Lesson 16 (*Use and Structure* 16.3).

等到半夜的时候吃(饺子)。
When it is midnight (we) eat dumplings.
等到爸爸回家，我们就吃饭。
When dad comes home we will eat.
这条裙子太短了。等到夏天再穿吧。
This skirt is too short. Wait until summer to wear it.
我这个星期特别忙。等到我忙 **wán** 了就帮你，好吗？
I'm really busy this week. Wait until I am finished with everything and I will help you, okay?

Practice ▶ *Workbook: Focus on Communication 25.1, 25.2, 25.5.*

25.9. 刚才 + S/VP *just before*

刚才 can occur before a sentence or a verb phrase, and it refers to actions that just happened a short time ago. It is often possible to translate it in English with the word *just* or *just a little while ago.*

刚才我们吃的鱼好吃吗？
Was the fish that we just ate good?
刚才国强来找你，我告诉他你不在。
When Guoqiang came looking for you a moment ago, I told him you weren't here.
刚才你试穿的裙子比现在这条好看。你还是回去买那条吧。
The skirt you tried on just before is nicer looking that this one. You should go back and buy that one.

Practice ▶ *Workbook: Focus on Structure 25.7; Focus on Communication 25.1.*

25.10.   从来 NEG (VP) *never do (VP), never have done (VP) before*

从来 is an adverb that is always followed by negation, either 不 or 没.

从来不 **VP** is used when saying that someone *never does some action*:

> 他从来不喝酒。
> *He doesn't drink alcoholic beverages.*
> 我从来不上网买东西。
> *I don't ever go shopping on the internet.*

从来没 **VP** is used when saying that someone *never did some action in the past.* Notice that when saying that someone has never done some action in the past, the verb is often followed by the verb suffix 过.

> 我从来没吃过这么好吃的鱼。
> *I have never eaten such a delicious fish before.*
> 我从来没看过这么漂亮的地方。
> *I have never seen such a beautiful place before.*
> 我一直很想去中国，可是从来没去过。
> *I've always wanted to go to China but I have never gone.*

> **Practice**   *Workbook: Focus on Structure 25.6, 25.7, 25.8; Focus on Communication 25.1, 25.2.*

25.11.   没想到 + S *I never thought that . . .*

When you want to say that you never thought that something would be the case, you can begin your sentence with the expression 没想到:

> 没想到同音字跟中国文化有这么大的关系。
> *I never thought that homophonous characters would have such a big connection with Chinese culture. (I never thought that Chinese characters would play such a large role in Chinese culture.)*
> 没想到你第一次包饺子就包得这么好。
> *I never expected that the first time you made dumplings you would wrap them so well.*
> 没想到火车这么 **jǐ**，连一个 **zuò** 位也没有。
> *I never expected that the train would be so crowded. There isn't even one (empty) seat.*

> **Practice**   *Workbook: Focus on Structure 25.7, 25.8; Focus on Communication 25.1.*

Sentence pyramids

Supply the English translation for the last line where indicated.

1 不得了 **jǐ** 得不得了 车上 **jǐ** 得不得了。	*amazing, extremely* *extremely crowded* *The train was extremely crowded.*
2 **dǐ** 下 **zuò** 位 **dǐ** 下 **tǎng** 在 **zuò** 位 **dǐ** 下 有的人 **tǎng** 在 **zuò** 位 **dǐ** 下。	*underneath* *underneath the seat* *lie underneath the seat* _____
3 睡觉 站着睡觉 他们站着睡觉。	*sleep* *sleep standing up* _____
4 有站着的 有坐着的，有站着的。 车上 **jǐ** 得不得了。有坐着的，有站着的。	*there were (people) standing* *there were (people) sitting, there were (people) standing* *The train was extremely crowded. There were (people) sitting, there were (people) standing.*
5 远 比较远 离这儿比较远 她家离这儿比较远。	*far* *relatively far* *relatively far from here* _____
6 火车 九个钟头的火车 他们坐了九个钟头的火车。	*train* *nine hours' worth of train* *They rode the train for nine hours.*
7 **liáo** 天 一边 **liáo** 天 一边包饺子一边 **liáo** 天 大家一边包饺子一边 **liáo** 天。	*chat* *on the one hand chat* *wrap dumplings and chat at the same time* *Everyone was making dumplings and chatting at the same time.*

8 热 **nao** 真热 **nao** 。 **shēng** 音越来越大了。真热 **nao** 。 放 **biānpào** 的 **shēng** 音越来越大了。 真热 **nao** 。 外边放 **biānpào** 的 **shēng** 音越来越大了。真热 **nao** 。	*lively* *really lively* *the sound is louder and louder. Really lively.* *The sound of setting off fireworks is louder and louder. It is really lively.* ————————————————
9 饱 太饱了 吃得太饱了 我吃得太饱了。	*full* *too full* *eat until I was too full* ————————————————
10 饱 吃饱了 你吃饱了吗?	*full* *ate until full* *Are you full?*
11 **fēngfù** 真 **fēngfù** 年夜饭真 **fēngfù** 您家的年夜饭真 **fēngfù** 。	*abundant* *really abundant* *New Year's Eve meal is really abundant* *The New Year's Eve meal at your house is really abundant.*
12 时候 **hán** 假的时候 学校放 **hán** 假的时候 正是学校放 **hán** 假的时候 春节正是学校放 **hán** 假的时候。	*time* *the time of winter vacation* *when schools begin winter vacation* *is exactly when schools begin winter vacation* ————————————————
13 包饺子 然后包饺子 喝点茶，然后包饺子 吃点水果、喝点茶，然后包饺子 我们先吃点水果、喝点茶，然后包饺子。	*wrap dumplings* *afterwards wrap dumplings* *drink a little tea, afterwards wrap dumplings* *eat a little fruit, drink a little tea, afterwards wrap dumplings* ————————————————
14 包饺子 开始包饺子 就开始包饺子 吃 **wán** 饭，就开始包饺子 刚刚吃 **wán** 饭，就开始包饺子 为什么刚刚吃 **wán** 饭，就开始包饺子呢?	*wrap dumplings* *begin to wrap dumplings* *begin to wrap dumplings* *after eating, begin wrapping dumplings* *as soon as (we) finish eating, (we) begin to wrap dumplings* ————————————————

15	
年夜饭	*New Year's Eve dinner*
准备年夜饭	*prepare New Year's Eve dinner*
全家一起准备年夜饭。	*The entire family together prepares the New Year's Eve dinner.*

16	
好吃	*delicious*
非常好吃	*extremely delicious*
鱼非常好吃	*the fish is extremely delicious*
我们吃的鱼非常好吃	*the fish that we ate was extremely delicious*
刚才我们吃的鱼非常好吃。	*The fish that we just ate was extremely delicious.*

17	
鱼	*fish*
好吃的鱼	*delicious fish*
这么好吃的鱼	*this delicious a fish (such a delicious fish)*
没吃过这么好吃的鱼	*have never eaten such a delicious fish*
我从来没吃过这么好吃的鱼。	*I have never eaten such a delicious fish before.*

18	
过年	*New Year holiday*
跟中国人过过年	*spend the New Year holiday with Chinese people*
没跟中国人过过年。	*have not spent the New Year holiday with Chinese people*
我从来没跟中国人过过年。	

19	
春天到了	*spring has arrived*
意思是说春天到了	*the meaning is spring has arrived*
把"春"字贴 **dào** 了意思是说春天到了。	*(When) you paste the character 春 upside down the meaning is spring has arrived.*

20	
同音	*same sound*
吃的"鱼"跟"年年有 **yú**"的"**yú**"同音。	*The word for the fish that you eat and the word "**yú**" in the phrase "年年有 **yú**" have the same sound (same pronunciation).*

21	
同音字	*homophonous characters*
是同音字	*are homophonous characters*
吃鱼的"**yú**"和年年有 **yú** 的"**yú**"是同音字。	*The "yu" of "吃 yú (吃鱼 eat fish)" and the "yu" of "年年有 yú (年年有余 have surplus every year)" are homophonous characters.*

22	
liáo 天	*chat*
包饺子、**liáo** 天	*wrap dumplings and chat*
家人一起包饺子、**liáo** 天	*family members together wrap dumplings and chat*
年三十，家人一起包饺子、**liáo** 天。	*On the last day of the year, the family members together wrap dumplings and chat.*

23 **biānpào** 放 **biānpào** 到外边去放 **biānpào** 大家都到外边去放 **biānpào** 等到半夜大家都到外边去放 **biānpào** 。	*fireworks* *set off fireworks* *go outside to set off fireworks* *everyone goes outside to set off fireworks* *When it is midnight everyone goes outside to set off fireworks.*
24 热 **nao** 这么热 **nao** 春节这么热 **nao** 中国的春节这么热 **nao** 没想到中国的春节这么热 **nao** 。	*lively* *this lively* *Spring Festival is this lively* *China's Spring Festival is this lively* _____
25 **chuán** 人 龙的 **chuán** 人 他们是龙的 **chuán** 人 中国人说他们是龙的 **chuán** 人	*descendants* *descendants of the dragon* *they are descendants of the dragon* *Chinese people say they are descendants of the dragon.*
26 眼睛 蓝色的眼睛 黄色的头发、蓝色的眼睛 她有黄色的头发、蓝色的眼睛。	*eye* *blue eyes* *blond (yellow) hair, blue eyes* _____
27 龙 **shǔ** 龙 我是 **shǔ** 龙的。	*dragon* *belong to dragon* *My sign is the dragon. (I belong to the dragon sign.)*
28 "龙的 **chuán** 人" 蓝眼睛的 "龙的 **chuán** 人" 黄头发蓝眼睛的 "龙的 **chuán** 人" 我是一个黄头发蓝眼睛的 "龙的 **chuán** 人。"	*"descendant of the dragon"* *blue-eyed descendant of the dragon* *blond-haired blue-eyed descendant of the dragon* *I am a blond-haired blue-eyed "descendant of the dragon."*
29 意思 我的意思 明白我的意思 你明白我的意思吗?	*meaning* *my meaning* *understand my meaning* _____
30 美丽: 新年快乐! 小文: **Gōng** 喜发 **cái** !	*Meili: Happy New Year!* *Xiao Wen: Happy New Year!* *(Congratulations and be prosperous!)*

Language FAQs

同音字 Characters with the same pronunciation

When two characters have identical pronunciation (including their tones), they are called 同音字. 同音字 are commonly used in Chinese puns and riddles and also to convey symbolic significance. In fact, it is sometimes the pronunciation of the syllable alone, and not the character, that conveys the double meaning, and in the dialogue, we learn two instances of this. The first is the character 春 hung upside down (**dào**) to convey the meaning 春到了 *spring has arrived*. The second is the inclusion of a fish (鱼 **yú**) at the New Year's Eve meal every year to suggest the word surplus (余 **yú**) and to convey the meaning *have a surplus every year* (年年有 **yú**). Sometimes pairs of characters that have the same pronunciation in one dialect of Chinese carry symbolic significance even in dialects where they do not have identical pronunciations. This is the case for the number 8 (八 **bā**) and the character for prosperity (发 **fā**). Even in dialects such as Mandarin in which they do not have identical pronunciation, the number 8 is considered a lucky number because of its association with 发 **fā** *prosperity*.

 # Notes on Chinese culture

Referring to the Chinese New Year and New Year greetings

The traditional name for the Chinese New Year holiday is 春节, the Spring Festival. The expression 新年 *New Year* is relatively new in China. It is sometimes used to refer to the Chinese New Year, but it also refers to the New Year on the solar calendar (January 1). The expression 过年 means to observe the rituals associated with the Chinese New Year holiday. **Gōng** 喜 *congratulations* and **Gōng** 喜发 **cái** *congratulations and be prosperous* are traditional Chinese New Year greetings. 新年快乐 *Happy New Year* is a relatively new greeting for the New Year, but it is now widely used in mainland China and in Taiwan during the Chinese New Year holiday.

What is your Chinese zodiac sign?

The Chinese zodiac consists of 12 animal signs, and people born during a particular year are said to have the characteristics associated with their animal sign. The 12-year cycle of the zodiac is paired with a five-year cycle of the elements (earth, metal, water, wood, and fire) so that it takes 60 years to complete the entire cycle of 12 animals and five elements. For this reason, one's 60th birthday is considered very important. The signs of the zodiac are presented below, from *rat* to *pig*. Do a little internet research to find your sign. If you were born in January or February, check the date when the Chinese New Year began in the year you were born, and see if your birthday is before or after that date. The Chinese New Year is based on a lunar cycle and is on a different date in the solar calendar from year to year.

The Twelve Animals of the Chinese Zodiac

鼠 shǔ **rat**	牛 niú **ox**	虎 hǔ **tiger**	兔 tù **rabbit**
龙 lóng **dragon**	蛇 shé **snake**	马 mǎ **horse**	羊 yáng **sheep**
猴 hóu **monkey**	鸡 jī **rooster**	狗 gǒu **dog**	猪 zhū **pig**

Red envelopes

In Chinese culture, red is the color of good luck and happiness, and gifts of money are traditionally presented in 红包 *red envelopes*. Parents, grandparents, uncles, and aunts often give red envelopes to children in their family at the New Year. Wedding gifts are also presented in red envelopes.

Getting a year older at the Chinese New Year

In traditional Chinese culture, you are one year old at birth, and at the Chinese New Year you gain a year, so the New Year is, in effect, everyone's birthday. It has become very common in China for people to celebrate their birthdays on the anniversary of their actual birth date, but China still use the traditional way of calculating age for certain purposes.

Descendants of the dragon

Dragons play an important role in Chinese folk tales and traditions, and Chinese people sometimes call themselves "descendants of the dragon." A song written by singer-songwriter Hou Dejian in the late 1970s further popularized the expression. Find the lyrics to the song on the internet and learn the song.

热 nao and luàn

热 **nao** *lively, bustling* and **luàn** *chaotic, messy* are closely related in meaning and are important concepts in Chinese culture. Places and activities that are

热 **nao** are loud, crowded, bustling with excitement, and fun, and to describe a place or activity as 热 **nao** is high praise. English does not have a single word that entirely captures the qualities associated with the word 热 **nao**. Places and activities that are **luàn** are loud, crowded, and dangerous. They are like 热 **nao**, except that the fun is replaced by danger. The closeness of the concepts is illustrated by how easily a situation that is 热 **nao** can become **luàn**, for example, by a fire breaking out in a crowded indoor gathering, or a balcony crowded with victorious sports fans suddenly collapsing. These kinds of events happen everywhere, of course, but many languages do not have a pair of words that capture the relationship of these concepts the way that Chinese does.

Narrative in English

The Spring Festival is right when students begin winter vacation. This year for winter vacation Gao Meili did not return home, because Ma Xiaowen invited Gao Meili to go home with her to celebrate the Spring Festival. Meili was really happy to be able to go to a Chinese family's home and celebrate the Spring Festival with Chinese people. Xiaowen's home is in Xi'an, pretty far away from Beijing. They took the train there. Because a lot of people throughout China want to return home at this time to see their families, there was an extremely large number of people taking the train. The train was extremely crowded. There were people sitting and people standing. There were people sleeping standing up, and there were people sleeping lying under the seats. They rode for nine hours and finally arrived home.

When they got there, although they were already extremely tired, as soon as they saw Xiaowen's family they didn't feel tired at all. Because it was New Year's Eve, there were a lot of people at Xiaowen's home. Besides her father and mother, there were Xiaowen's grandfather, grandmother, and uncles, and also a few relatives and a few friends. Xiaowen introduced Meili to everyone. Afterwards, they prepared the New Year's Eve dinner with the whole family. Everyone cooked and talked. They talked about the year that had already passed, and they talked about everyone's plans for the New Year.

Dialogue in English

Part A

Meili:	Uncle, Aunt, your New Year's Eve dinner has so much food and it so good. I've eaten until I am too full. I can't eat anything else.
Ma mama:	After we finish, we'll first eat a little fruit, drink a little tea, and then we'll all make dumplings.
Meili:	Why is it that right after we finish eating we begin making dumplings?

Ma mama:	At the Chinese New Year lots of Chinese people eat dumplings. On the last day of the year, that is, on New Year's Eve, before midnight, we make them, and then when it is midnight we eat them.
Xiaowen:	When midnight comes, it is the New Year. Parents give their children red envelopes, and we all also get a year older. Meili, do you know what zodiac animal you are?
Meili:	I know. I am a dragon. I think I am a yellow-haired blue-eyed "descendant of the dragon."
Xiaowen:	Listen, the sound of fireworks outside is getting louder and louder. It's really lively.
Ma baba (to Xiaowen):	Take Meili outside to watch.

Part B

Meili:	Xiaowen, the character "spring" on your door is attached upside down (dào).
Xiaowen:	It isn't that the character "spring" is attached upside down (dào), it is that "spring" has arrived. "Spring" . . . has arrived (dào).
Meili:	I understand. "**dào**" (upside down) and "**dào**" (arrive) have the same pronunciation. To take the character "spring" and hang it upside down is to say that spring has arrived, right?
Xiaowen:	You are right. By the way, was the fish that we just ate good?
Meili:	It was extremely delicious. I've never eaten such a delicious fish before.
Xiaowen:	Do you know, the New Year's Eve dinner must include fish. The fish that we eat and the word **yú** (*surplus*) in the expression "**niánnián yǒu yú**" (*have a surplus every year*) have the same pronunciation. **yú** means to have a surplus, to be unable to use it up. In additional, you are not supposed to finish eating the fish in the New Year's Eve dinner. It signifies that you have a lot, there is left over. The meaning is to let you live even better in the new year and to have an inexhaustible supply of things.
Meili:	I never thought that homophonous characters would play such a big role in Chinese culture.
Xiaowen:	It's 12 o'clock. The New Year has arrived.
Meili:	Happy New Year!
Xiaowen:	Congratulations and be prosperous, and give me red envelopes!

Vocabulary: English to Mandarin pinyin

The lesson number indicates the lesson in which the vocabulary item is introduced. The last two columns of each row show the vocabulary item in Simplified and Traditional characters.

				Simplified	Traditional
A					
abundant	**fēngfù**	adjectival verb	L25	丰富	豐富
activity	**yùndòng**	noun	L22	运动	運動
activity, movement	**huódòng**	noun; verb	L22	活动	活動
advertisement	**guǎnggào**	noun	L23	广告	廣告
after a few days	**guò jǐ tiān**	conversational expression	L17	过几天	過幾天
after all	**dàodǐ**	adverb	L22	到底	到底

agree	**tóngyì**	verb	*L21*	同意	同意
air	**kōngqì**	noun	*L23*	空气	空氣
allow	**ràng**	verb	*L18*	让	讓
amazing, awful; extremely, unbearably	**bùdéliǎo**	adj VP	*L25*	不得了	不得了
American-style	**Měishì**	noun phrase	*L22*	美式	美式
American-style football	**Měishì zúqiú**	noun phrase	*L22*	美式足球	美式足球
and, but, or	**ér**	conjunction	*L22*	而	而
appear, seem to be	**hǎoxiàng**	verb	*L20*	好像	好像
apply	**shēnqǐng**	verb	*L18*	申请	申請
as long as	**zhǐyào**	sentence adverb	*L23*	只要	只要
aspect, perspective, side	**fāngmiàn**	noun	*L18*	方面	方面
attend, participate in	**cānjiā**	verb	*L18*	参加	參加
autumn, fall	**qiūtiān**	noun phrase	*L21*	秋天	秋天
B					
bad, broken	**huài**	adjectival verb	*L18*	坏	壞
ball, sphere, world	**qiú**	noun	*L21*	球	球
bargain back and forth	**tǎo jià-huán jià**	verb phrase	*L24*	讨价还价	討價還價
baseball	**bàngqiú**	noun phrase	*L22*	棒球	棒球
become sick	**shēng bìng**	verb + object	*L20*	生病	生病
become, change into	**biàn**	verb	*L20*	变	變

begin school, school starts	**kāi xué**	verb + object	*L17*	开学	開學
belong to	**shǔ**	verb	*L25*	属	屬
below	**dǐxià**	noun	*L25*	底下	底下
bicycle	**zìxíngchē**	noun	*L22*	自行车	自行車
blow	**guā**	verb	*L21*	刮	刮
body	**shēntǐ**	noun	*L20*	身体	身體
bookcase	**shūjià**	noun	*L19*	书架	書架
bored	**wúliáo**	adjectival verb	*L23*	无聊	無聊
both . . . and; again	**yòu**	adverbial phrase	*L19*	又	又
box	**xiāngzi**	noun	*L23*	箱子	箱子
bring, take	**ná**	verb	*L24*	拿	拿
brown, coffee colored	**kāfēisè**	noun	*L23*	咖啡色	咖啡色
busy doing something	**mángzhe**	adjV + suffix	*L17*	忙着	忙著
but	**bùguò**	conjunction	*L17*	不过	不過
C					
calculate, count	**suàn**	verb	*L24*	算	算
California	**Jiāzhōu**	proper noun	*L21*	加州	加州
card	**kǎ**	noun	*L24*	卡	卡
cardboard box/ paper box	**zhǐ xiāng**	noun phrase	*L23*	纸箱	紙箱
careful	**xiǎoxīn**	adjectival verb	*L20*	小心	小心
cash	**xiànjīn**	noun	*L24*	现金	現金
catch a cold; common cold	**gǎnmào**	noun, verb + object	*L20*	感冒	感冒

celebrate the Chinese New Year	**guò nián**	verb phrase	*L25*	过年	過年
chair	**yǐzi**	noun	*L19*	椅子	椅子
chaotic, disorganized, messy	**luàn**	adjectival phrase	*L19*	乱	亂
characters with identical pronunciations	**tóngyīn zì**	noun phrase	*L25*	同音字	同音字
chat	**liáo tiān**	verb + object	*L25*	聊天	聊天
chemistry	**huàxué**	noun	*L22*	化学	化學
Chinese (lunar) New Year's Eve	**chúxī**	noun	*L25*	除夕	除夕
Chinese (lunar) New Year's Eve	**chúxīyè**	noun	*L25*	除夕夜	除夕夜
class periods classifier	**jié**	classifier	*L17*	节	節
classroom building	**jiàoshì lóu**	noun phrase	*L22*	教室楼	教室樓
clean	**gānjìng**	adjectival phrase	*L19*	干净	乾淨
clear	**qíng**	adjectival verb	*L21*	晴	晴
clear day	**qíngtiān**	noun phrase	*L21*	晴天	晴天
climate	**qìhòu**	noun	*L21*	气候	氣候
climb	**pá**	verb	*L22*	爬	爬
climb a mountain	**pá shān**	verb + object	*L22*	爬山	爬山
clothing	**yīfu**	noun	*L19*	衣服	衣服

cloudy	**duō yún**	adjective phrase	*L21*	多云	多雲
coat, overcoat	**dàyī**	noun	*L24*	大衣	大衣
cold and damp	**shī lěng**	adjectival phrase	*L21*	湿冷	溼冷
collect	**shōu**	verb	*L19*	收	收
collect, gather, put away	**shōuqǐlái**	verb	*L19*	收起来	收起來
come back (to a place), return	**huí lai**	verb	*L17*	回来	回來
come from	**lái zì**	verb + preposition	*L22*	来自	來自
comfortable	**shūfu**	adjectival verb	*L20*	舒服	舒服
compared with*	**bǐ**	verb, preposition	*L21*	比	比
competition	**bǐsài**	noun	*L22*	比赛	比賽
concerned about	**guānxīn**	verb	*L21*	关心	關心
congratulations and be prosperous	**gōngxǐ fācái**	New Year's greeting expression	*L25*	恭喜发财	恭喜發財
connection, relationship	**guānxi**	noun	*L17*	关系	關係
conserve	**jiéyuē**	verb	*L22*	节约	節約
conserve energy	**jiéyuē néngyuán**	verb + object	*L22*	节约能源	節約能源
convene (a meeting), "have" (a party), drive	**kāi**	verb	*L19*	开	開
convenient	**fāngbiàn**	adjectival verb	*L21*	方便	方便

cook, simmer	**shāo**	verb, noun	*L20*	烧	燒
cool (pleasantly cool)	**liángkuai**	adjectival verb	*L21*	凉快	涼快
cough	**késou**	verb, noun	*L20*	咳嗽	咳嗽
credit card	**xìnyòng kǎ**	noun phrase	*L24*	信用卡	信用卡
crowd, squeeze	**jǐ**	verb	*L25*	挤	擠
culture	**wénhuà**	noun	*L17*	文化	文化
customer	**gùkè**	noun	*L23*	顾客	顧客
cute	**kě'ài**	adjectival verb	*L24*	可爱	可愛
D					
debit card	**xiànjīn kǎ**	noun phrase	*L24*	现金卡	現金卡
decide	**juédìng**	verb	*L18*	决定	決定
definitely	**yīdìng**	adverb	*L17*	一定	一定
degree	**dù**	noun	*L21*	度	度
descendant	**chuánrén**	noun	*L25*	传人	傳人
descendant of the dragon	**lóng de chuánrén**	noun phrase	*L25*	龙的传人	龍的傳人
diarrhea, have (literally: "pull the stomach")	**lā dùzi**	verb + object	*L20*	拉肚子	拉肚子
didn't expect that	**méi xiǎngdào**	neg + verb	*L25*	没想到	沒想到
different	**bùtóng**	adjective	*L18*	不同	不同
dining hall, cafeteria	**cāntīng**	noun	*L17*	餐厅	餐廳
dirty	**zāng**	adjectival verb	*L19*	脏	髒
disease enters the body through the mouth	**bìng cóng kǒu rù**	proverb	*L20*	病从口入	病從口入

dizzy	**yūn**	adjectival verb	L20	晕	暈
do you mean to say . . . ?	**nándào**	adverb	L18	难道	難道
doctor	**yīshēng**	noun	L20	医生	醫生
door; classes classifier	**mén**	noun; classifier	L17	门	門
dresser	**guìzi**	noun	L19	柜子	櫃子
dry	**gānzào**	adjectival verb	L21	干燥	乾燥
E					
ear(s)	**ěrduo**	noun	L20	耳朵	耳朵
earmuffs	**ěrzhào**	noun	L24	耳罩	耳罩
earth	**dìqiú**	noun	L22	地球	地球
earth, ground	**dì**	noun	L19	地	地
economics	**jīngjì**	noun	L17	经济	經濟
elevator	**diàntī**	noun	L22	电梯	電梯
energy	**lìqi**	noun	L20	力气	力氣
energy	**néngyuán**	noun	L22	能源	能源
enough	**gòu**	verb	L22	够	夠
enter	**jìn**	verb	L18	进	進
entire body	**quán shēn**	noun phrase	L20	全身	全身
entire*	**quán**	quantifier	L18	全	全
environment	**huánjìng**	noun	L17	环境	環境
environmental management, environmental studies	**huánjìng guǎnlǐ**	noun phrase	L17	环境管理	環境管理

environmental protection	**huánbǎo**	noun phrase abbreviation of huánjìng bǎohù	*L22*	环保	環保
environmental protection	**huánjìng bǎohù**	noun phrase	*L22*	环境保护	環境保護
etcetera	**děngděng**	noun	*L22*	等等	等等
even	**lián**	adverb	*L22*	连	連
even more	**gèng**	intensifier	*L22*	更	更
every field produces a leading expert	**háng háng chū Zhuàngyuán**	proverb	*L18*	行行出状元	行行出狀元
except (for), outside of	**yǐwài**	noun	*L20*	以外	以外
except, besides	**chúle**	preposition	*L20*	除了	除了
exercise	**duànliàn**	verb	*L22*	锻炼	鍛煉
expire	**guòqī**	verb	*L19*	过期	過期
express, indicate, show	**biǎoshì**	verb	*L25*	表示	表示
expression of annoyance or impatience	**āiyā**	interjection	*L21*	哎呀	哎呀
extend	**shēn**	verb	*L22*	伸	伸
extremely	**jíle**	intensifier suffix	*L19*	极了	極了
extremely chaotic, disorganized, messy	**luàn jíle**	adjectival verb phrase	*L19*	乱极了	亂極了
eye(s)	**yǎnjīng**	noun	*L20*	眼睛	眼睛

F

face mask	**kǒuzhào**	noun phrase	*L20*	口罩	口罩

fall asleep	**shuìzháo**	verb + resultative ending	L20	睡着	睡著
family, classifier for restaurants	**jiā**	classifier	L20	家	家
fat	**pàng**	adjectival verb	L23	胖	胖
fear	**pà**	verb	L21	怕	怕
feeling	**gǎnjué**	noun	L24	感觉	感覺
fever, simmer	**shāo**	noun, verb	L20	烧	燒
fever, have	**fā shāo**	verb + object	L20	发烧	發燒
finally	**zuì hòu**	adverb phrase	L17	最后	最後
find	**zhǎodào**	verb	L19	找到	找到
finish, be finished	**wán**	verb	L19	完	完
fireworks	**biānpào**	noun	L25	鞭炮	鞭炮
flow	**liú**	verb	L20	流	流
for example	**bǐfāng shuō**	phrase	L22	比方说	比方說
for the sake of, for the purpose of	**wèile**	preposition	L22	为了	為了
forecast	**yùbào**	noun	L21	预报	預報
four seasons	**sì jì**	noun phrase	L21	四季	四季
full (from eating)	**bǎo**	adjectival verb	L20	饱	飽
future, in the	**jiānglái**	time word	L18	将来	將來

G

global	**quánqiú**	noun, adjective	L21	全球	全球
global warming	**quánqiú nuǎnhuà**	noun phrase	L21	全球暖化	全球暖化

glove	**shǒutào**	noun	*L24*	手套	手套
go out	**chūqu**	verb	*L19*	出去	出去
go to the toilet	**shàng cèsuǒ**	verb + object	*L20*	上厕所	上廁所
gold	**jīn**	adjective, noun	*L23*	金	金
good many times, many times	**hǎojǐcì**	noun phrase	*L20*	好几次	好幾次
good or bad	**hǎo huài**	noun phrase	*L18*	好坏	好壞
grades, academic record	**chéngjì**	noun	*L18*	成绩	成績
grades, points	**fēnshù**	noun	*L18*	分数	分數
graduate	**bìyè**	verb	*L18*	毕业	畢業
grandfather (father's father)	**yéye**	kinship term	*L25*	爷爷	爺爺
grandmother (father's mother)	**nǎinai**	kinship term	*L25*	奶奶	奶奶
gym	**jiànshēn fáng**	noun phrase	*L22*	健身房	健身房
H					
hair	**tóufa**	noun	*L25*	头发	頭髮
Happy New Year	**xīn nián kuàilè**	New Year greeting	*L25*	新年快乐	新年快樂
hard working at studies, diligent	**yònggōng**	adjectival phrase	*L17*	用功	用功
have more than you need every year	**niánnián yǒu yú**	proverb	*L25*	年年有余	年年有餘

head	**tóu**	noun	*L20*	头	頭
headache, have	**tóu téng**	noun + verb	*L20*	头疼	頭疼
healthy	**jiànkāng**	adjectival verb	*L22*	健康	健康
help	**bāngzhù**	noun	*L17*	帮助	幫助
help out, lend a hand	**bāng máng**	verb + object	*L24*	帮忙	幫忙
high school student, senior high school student	**gāozhōng-shēng**	noun phrase	*L18*	高中生	高中生
high school, senior high school	**gāozhōng**	noun	*L18*	高中	高中
hometown	**jiāxiāng**	noun	*L21*	家乡	家鄉
hope	**xīwàng**	verb	*L21*	希望	希望
hospital	**yīyuàn**	noun	*L20*	医院	醫院
hot and humid	**mēn rè**	adjectival phrase	*L21*	闷热	悶熱
hot and spicy	**là**	adjectival phrase	*L20*	辣	辣
humid (in warm weather)	**mēn**	adjectival verb	*L21*	闷	悶
humid (in cold weather)	**shī**	adjectival verb	*L21*	湿	溼

I

ice skating	**huá bīng**	verb + object	*L22*	滑冰	滑冰
illness, sickness, sick	**bìng**	noun	*L20*	病	病
immediately	**mǎshàng**	adverb	*L20*	马上	馬上

important	**zhòngyào**	adjectival verb	*L22*	重要	重要
in addition, besides	**lìngwài**	adverb	*L22*	另外	另外
indoor activities	**shìnèi huódòng**	noun phrase	*L22*	室内活动	室內活動
inflamed	**fā yán**	verb + object	*L20*	发炎	發炎
inflamed	**shàng huǒ**	verb + object	*L20*	上火	上火
interest	**xìngqu**	noun	*L17*	兴趣	興趣
interested in	**yǒu xìngqu**	adjectival phrase	*L17*	有兴趣	有興趣
it is only (that)	**zhǐ shì**	adverb phrase	*L17*	只是	只是
item (classifier for *events and clothing*)	**jiàn**	classifier	*L18*	件	件
J					
just before now	**gāngcái**	adverb	*L25*	刚才	剛才
K					
kick	**tī**	verb	*L22*	踢	踢
L					
lab, experiment	**shíyàn**	noun	*L17*	实验	實驗
last day of the year	**nián sānshí**	noun phrase	*L25*	年三十	年三十
leather shoes	**pí xié**	noun phrase	*L24*	皮鞋	皮鞋
leftover (be leftover), remain	**shèngxia**	verb	*L25*	剩下	剩下
length	**chángduǎn**	noun	*L23*	长短	長短
lie down	**tǎng**	verb	*L25*	躺	躺
life	**shēngmìng**	noun	*L22*	生命	生命

lightheaded, dizzy	**tóu yūn**	noun + adjectival verb	*L20*	头晕	頭暈
like spring all year round	**sì jì rú chūn**	four-character expression	*L21*	四季如春	四季如春
lively	**rènao**	adjectival phrase	*L25*	热闹	熱鬧
long time (literally: *half a day*)	**bàntiān**	idiom	*L19*	半天	半天
low	**dī**	adjectival verb	*L21*	低	低
M					
major (course of study)	**zhuānyè**	adjectival verb	*L18*	专业	專業
make an appointment, arrange to meet	**yuē**	verb	*L22*	约	約
manage	**guǎn**	verb	*L21*	管	管
management	**guǎnlǐ**	noun	*L17*	管理	管理
match	**pèi**	verb, adjectival verb	*L24*	配	配
mathematics	**shùxué**	noun	*L17*	数学	數學
medicine	**yào**	noun	*L20*	药	藥
mention	**tídào**	verb	*L21*	提到	提到
middle of the night	**yèlǐ**	time phrase	*L20*	夜里	夜裡
mistake, mistaken	**cuò**	verb	*L19*	错	錯
more and more	**yuè lái yuè**	intensifier phrase	*L21*	越来越	越來越

moreover, in addition, also	**érqiě**	adverb	*L21*	而且	而且
most	**zuì**	intensifier	*L18*	最	最
mouth	**zuǐba**	noun	*L20*	嘴巴	嘴巴
movement is the essence of life	**shēngmìng zàiyú yùndòng**	conversational expression	*L22*	生命在于运动	生命在於運動
must	**bùdébù**	modal verb	*L23*	不得不	不得不
must V	**fēi VP bù kě**	modal verb – literary expression	*L19*	非 **VP** 不可	非 **VP** 不可
N					
National University Entrance Exam	**gāokǎo**	proper noun	*L18*	高考	高考
nationwide	**quánguó**	noun phrase	*L18*	全国	全國
nature	**dà zìrán**	noun	*L22*	大自然	大自然
nervous, tense	**jǐnzhāng**	adjectival verb	*L18*	紧张	緊張
never before	**cónglái (+ neg)**	adverb + neg	*L25*	从来	從來
New Year	**xīn nián**	noun phrase	*L23*	新年	新年
New Year's Eve family dinner	**niányè fàn**	noun phrase	*L25*	年夜饭	年夜飯
newspaper	**bàozhǐ**	noun	*L19*	报纸	報紙
*night**	**yè**	noun	*L20*	夜	夜
no need to	**bù bì**	modal verb	*L19*	不必	不必
no wonder	**nánguài**	adverb	*L19*	难怪	難怪
not bad	**bù cuò**	neg + verb	*L23*	不错	不錯
not important	**méi guānxi**	verb phrase	*L17*	没关系	沒關係

not only	**bùdàn**	conjunction	L24	不但	不但
O					
oil, petroleum	**shíyóu**	noun	L22	石油	石油
on one side, at the same time	**yībiān**	noun, adverb	L25	一边	一邊
only, it is only that	**jiù shì**	adverbial phrase	L19	就是	就是
open (a door, window)	**dǎkāi**	resultative verb	L19	打开	打開
open	**kāi**	verb	L17	开	開
open (your mouth)	**zhāngkāi**	verb	L20	张开	張開
open (of a business), open the door	**kāi mén**	verb + object	L17	开门	開門
opportunity	**jīhuì**	noun	L18	机会	機會
or	**huòzhě**	conjunction	L20	或者	或者
originally	**běnlái**	adverb	L24	本来	本來
originally	**yuánlái**	adverb	L17	原来	原來
overcast	**yīn tiān**	noun phrase	L21	阴天	陰天
P					
painful, hurt	**téng**	adjectival verb	L20	疼	疼
pair	**shuāng**	classifier	L19	双	雙
pair of, a set of	**fù**	classifier	L24	副	副
pants, trousers, slacks	**kùzi**	noun	L19	裤子	裤子
party (literally: *evening meeting*)	**wǎnhuì**	noun	L19	晚会	晚會

pay	**fù**	verb	*L24*	付	付
physics	**wùlǐ(xué)**	noun	*L17*	物理(学)	物理(學)
ping-pong	**pīngpāng qiú**	noun phrase	*L22*	乒乓球	乒乓球
play baseball	**dǎ bàngqiú**	verb + object	*L22*	打棒球	打棒球
play ping-pong	**dǎ pīngpāng qiú**	verb +object	*L22*	打乒乓球	打乒乓球
play soccer, football	**tī zúqiú**	verb + object	*L22*	踢足球	踢足球
play volleyball	**dǎ páiqiú**	verb + object	*L22*	打排球	打排球
political science	**zhèngzhì xué**	noun phrase	*L17*	政治学	政治學
politics	**zhèngzhì**	noun	*L17*	政治	政治
pollution	**wūrǎn**	noun	*L23*	污染	污染
possibly, possible	**kěnéng**	adverb	*L20*	可能	可能
post, hang up	**tiē**	verb	*L23*	贴	貼
precisely, exactly	**zhèng**	intensifier	*L23*	正	正
price	**jiàqian**	noun	*L24*	价钱	價錢
probably	**dàgài**	adverb	*L20*	大概	大概
protect	**bǎohù**	verb	*L22*	保护	保護
purple	**zǐ**	adjective	*L23*	紫	紫
purple colored	**zǐ sè**	noun	*L23*	紫色	紫色
put	**fàng**	verb	*L19*	放	放
put, place (something somewhere)	**fàng**	verb	*L19*	放	放

Q

QR code	**èrwéi mǎ**	noun phrase	L24	二维码	二維碼

R

rain	**yǔ**	noun	L21	雨	雨
reach the intended goal*	**zháo**	resultative ending	L20	着	著
really, indeed	**díquè**	adverb	L21	的确	的確
receipt	**fāpiào**	noun	L24	发票	發票
recently	**zuì jìn**	adverb	L20	最近	最近
red envelope with money inside given as a gift	**hóngbāo**	noun phrase	L25	红包	紅包
reduce	**jiǎnshǎo**	verb	L23	减少	減少
reduce the price	**jiǎn jià**	verb + object	L23	减价	減價
relatively, comparatively	**bǐjiào**	intensifier	L17	比较	比較
relatives	**qīnqi**	noun	L25	亲戚	親戚
remember	**jìde**	verb	L20	记得	記得
ride a bicycle	**qí zìxíngchē**	verb + object	L22	骑自行车	騎自行車
ride astraddle	**qí**	verb	L22	骑	騎
room	**fángjiān**	noun	L19	房间	房間
room	**wūzi**	noun	L19	屋子	屋子
row	**huá**	verb	L22	划	划
row boats, crew	**huá chuán**	verb + object	L22	划船	划船
run, jog	**pǎo bù**	verb + object	L22	跑步	跑步
runny nose, have	**liú bíshuǐ**	verb + object	L20	流鼻水	流鼻水

S

same sound, homophonous	**tóngyīn**	adjectival phrase	L25	同音	同音
scan a code (cf. sǎo 扫 *sweep, scan*)	**sǎo mǎ**	verb + object	L24	扫码	掃碼
scarf	**wéijīn**	noun	L24	围巾	圍巾
scenery	**fēngjǐng**	noun	L21	风景	風景
school team	**xiàoduì**	noun phrase	L22	校队	校隊
season	**jìjié**	noun	L21	季节	季節
seat	**zuòwèi**	noun	L25	座位	座位
see a doctor	**kàn bìng**	verb + object	L20	看病	看病
select	**xuǎn**	verb	L17	选	選
sell at a discount	**dǎ zhé**	verb + object	L23	打折	打折
semester	**xuéqī**	noun	L17	学期	學期
set off (firecrackers)	**fàng**	verb	L25	放	放
shirt	**chènshān**	noun	L19	衬衫	襯衫
shoes	**xié(zi)**	noun phrase	L19	鞋(子)	鞋(子)
short	**duǎn**	adjectival verb	L21	短	短
Sichuan	**Sìchuān**	Chinese province	L20	四川	四川
similar	**xiāngtóng**	noun	L22	相同	相同
situation, thing (abstract)	**shìqing**	noun	L18	事情	事情
size	**hào**	classifier	L23	号	號
size (abstract)	**dàxiǎo**	noun	L23	大小	大小
skiing	**huá xuě**	verb + object	L22	滑雪	滑雪

skirt	**qúnzi**	noun	*L23*	裙子	裙子
smart, intelligent	**cōngming**	adjectival verb	*L17*	聪明	聰明
smelly, stinky	**chòu**	adjectival phrase	*L19*	臭	臭
sneakers	**yùndòng xié**	noun	*L24*	运动鞋	運動鞋
sneakers, athletic shoes	**qiúxié**	noun	*L19*	球鞋	球鞋
sneeze	**dǎ pēntì**	verb	*L20*	打喷嚏	打噴嚏
snot	**bí shuǐ**	noun phrase	*L20*	鼻水	鼻水
snow	**xuě**	noun	*L21*	雪	雪
soccer, football	**zúqiú**	noun phrase	*L22*	足球	足球
socks	**wàzi**	noun	*L19*	袜子	襪子
sound	**shēngyīn**	noun	*L25*	声音	聲音
speaking of	**shuō dào**	verb	*L21*	说到	說到
speech utterance classifier	**jù**	classifier	*L22*	句	句
spend (time, money); flowers	**huā**	verb; noun	*L19*	花	花
sports activities, exercise	**tǐyù huódòng**	noun phrase	*L22*	体育活动	體育活動
sports, physical training	**tǐyù**	noun	*L22*	体育	體育
spring	**chūntiān**	noun phrase	*L21*	春天	春天
Spring Festival	**chūnjié**	noun phrase	*L23*	春节	春節
staircase, stairs	**lóutī**	noun	*L22*	楼梯	樓梯
stand, station	**zhàn**	verb	*L25*	站	站
stomach	**dùzi**	noun	*L20*	肚子	肚子
store	**shāngdiàn**	noun	*L23*	商店	商店

straighten up	**shōushi**	verb	*L19*	收拾	收拾
street (cf. 路)	**jiē**	noun	*L23*	街	街
strict	**yán**	adjectival verb	*L17*	严	嚴
strict teachers make good students	**yán shī chū gāo tú**	proverb	*L17*	严师出高徒	嚴師出高徒
strong	**qiáng**	adjectival verb	*L18*	强	強
students (plural)	**xuésheng-men**	noun	*L17*	学生们	學生們
stupid	**bèn**	adjectival verb	*L17*	笨	笨
style	**shìyàng**	noun	*L23*	式样	式樣
suitable, appropriate	**héshì**	adjectival verb	*L17*	合适	合適
surplus	**yú**	noun	*L25*	余	餘
sweep	**sǎo**	verb	*L19*	扫	掃
sweep the floor	**sǎo dì**	verb + object	*L19*	扫地	掃地
swimming	**yóu yǒng**	verb + object	*L22*	游泳	游泳
symptom	**zhèng-zhuàng**	noun	*L20*	症状	症狀
T					
table	**zhuōzi**	noun	*L19*	桌子	桌子
tablet, slice	**piàn**	classifier	*L20*	片	片
take *; *classifier for* chairs	**bǎ**	classifier	*L19*	把	把
take care of	**zhàogù**	verb	*L21*	照顾	照顧
take seriously, consider important	**zhòngshì**	verb	*L22*	重视	重視

talk, converse	**tán**	verb	L25	谈	談
taxi	**chūzū qìchē (chūzūchē)**	noun phrase	L24	出租汽车 (出租车)	出租汽車 (出租車)
temperature	**wēndù**	noun	L21	温度	溫度
textbook	**kèběn**	noun	L17	课本	課本
these past few days	**zhè jǐ tiān**	noun phrase	L17	这几天	這幾天
thin	**shòu**	adjectival verb	L23	瘦	瘦
throat	**sǎngzi**	noun	L20	嗓子	嗓子
throw away	**rēng**	verb	L19	扔	扔
time	**cì**	classifier	L20	次	次
tired	**lèi**	adjectival verb	L18	累	累
toilet	**cèsuǒ**	noun	L20	厕所	廁所
tongue	**shétóu**	noun	L20	舌头	舌頭
topic	**huàtí**	noun	L21	话题	話題
try on	**shìchuān**	verb	L23	试穿	試穿
try, test (something) out	**shì**	verb	L23	试	試
turn	**zhuǎn**	verb	L21	转	轉
turning clear	**zhuǎn qíng**	verb phrase	L21	转晴	轉晴
type of	**zhǒng**	classifier	L23	种	種
U					
unable to bear it	**shòubùliǎo**	resultative verb	L21	受不了	受不了
unable to fall asleep	**shuìbúzháo**	potential form of resultative verb	L20	睡不着	睡不著

understand	**míngbai**	verb	*L25*	明白	明白
upside down	**dào**	verb	*L25*	倒	倒
use	**lìyòng**	verb	*L17*	利用	利用
useful	**yǒu yòng**	adjectival phrase	*L17*	有用	有用
usually, typically	**yībān**	adverb	*L18*	一般	一般
V					
visit, stroll through	**guàng**	verb	*L23*	逛	逛
volleyball	**páiqiú**	noun phrase	*L22*	排球	排球
vomit	**tù**	verb	*L20*	吐	吐
W					
warm	**nuǎnhuo**	adjectival verb	*L21*	暖和	暖和
warming	**nuǎnhuà**	verb	*L21*	暖化	暖化
waste	**làngfèi**	verb	*L24*	浪费	浪費
wear	**chuān**	verb	*L19*	穿	穿
wear (on head, neck, hands)	**dài**	verb	*L20*	戴	戴
weather	**tiānqì**	noun	*L20*	天气	天氣
weather forecast	**tiānqì yùbào**	noun phrase	*L21*	天气预报	天氣預報
WeChat	**Wēixìn**	proper noun	*L24*	微信	微信
WeChat Pay	**Wēixìn Zhīfù**	proper noun	*L24*	微信支付	微信支付
weight training	**zhòngliàng xùnliàn**	noun phrase	*L22*	重量训练	重量訓練
what can you do about it?	**zěnme bàn**	question phrase	*L18*	怎么办	怎麼辦

what's the matter?	**zěnme le** ?	conversational expression	*L20*	怎么了	怎麼了
whole night	**yī yè**	noun phrase	*L20*	一夜	一夜
willingly swallowed the bait, willingly got caught	**yuàn zhě shàng gōu**	proverb	*L24*	愿者上钩	願者上鉤
wind	**fēng**	noun	*L21*	风	風
window	**chuānghu**	noun	*L19*	窗户	窗戶
window shopping, strolling along the shopping streets	**guàng jiē**	verb + object	*L23*	逛街	逛街
windy (blow wind)	**guā fēng**	verb + object	*L21*	刮风	刮風
winter	**dōngtiān**	noun phrase	*L21*	冬天	冬天
winter vacation	**hánjià**	noun phrase	*L25*	寒假	寒假
worth	**zhíde**	adverb	*L21*	值得	值得
wrap; classifier for *bags* (see also 红 *bāo*)	**bāo**	verb; classifier	*L25*	包	包
write a prescription	**kāi yào**	verb + object	*L20*	开药	開藥
writing, composition	**xiězuò**	noun	*L17*	写作	寫作

X

Xi'an (city in central northwest China, capital of Shaanxi Province)	**Xī'ān**	proper name	*L25*	西安	西安

Y					
yoga	**yújiā**	noun	*L22*	瑜伽	瑜伽
you are not mistaken; you are correct	**méi cuò**	negation + adjectival verb	*L19*	没错	沒錯
young	**niánqīng**	noun	*L22*	年轻	年輕
young lady, miss	**xiǎojie**	noun	*L24*	小姐	小姐
young people	**niánqīng rén**	noun phrase	*L22*	年轻人	年輕人

Vocabulary: Mandarin pinyin to English

The lesson number indicates the lesson in which the vocabulary item is introduced. The last two columns of each row show the vocabulary item in Simplified and Traditional characters.

				Simplified	Traditional
A					
āiyā	*expression of annoyance or impatience*	interjection	L21	哎呀	哎呀
B					
bǎ	*take**; classifier for *chairs*	classifier	L19	把	把
bàntiān	*a long time* (literally: *half a day*)	idiom	L19	半天	半天

bāng máng	*help out, lend a hand*	verb + object	*L24*	帮忙	幫忙
bàngqiú	*baseball*	noun phrase	*L22*	棒球	棒球
bāngzhù	*help*	noun	*L17*	帮助	幫助
bāo	*wrap*; classifier for *bags* (see also 红 *bāo*)	verb; classifier	*L25*	包	包
bǎo	*full (from eating)*	adjectival verb	*L20*	饱	飽
bǎohù	*protect*	verb	*L22*	保护	保護
bàozhǐ	*newspaper*	noun	*L19*	报纸	報紙
bèn	*stupid*	adjectival verb	*L17*	笨	笨
běnlái	*originally*	adverb	*L24*	本来	本來
bǐ	*compared with**	verb, preposition	*L21*	比	比
bí shuǐ	*snot*	noun phrase	*L20*	鼻水	鼻水
biàn	*become, change into*	verb	*L20*	变	變
biānpào	*fireworks*	noun	*L25*	鞭炮	鞭炮
biǎoshì	*express, indicate, show*	verb	*L25*	表示	表示
bǐfāng shuō	*for example*	phrase	*L22*	比方说	比方說
bǐjiào	*relatively, comparatively*	intensifier	*L17*	比较	比較
bìng	*illness, sickness, sick*	noun	*L20*	病	病
bìng cóng kǒu rù	*disease enters the body through the mouth*	proverb	*L20*	病从口入	病從口入
bǐsài	*competition*	noun	*L22*	比赛	比賽

bìyè	*graduate*	verb	*L18*	毕业	畢業
bù bì	*no need to*	modal verb	*L19*	不必	不必
bù cuò	*not bad*	neg + verb	*L23*	不错	不錯
bùdàn	*not only*	conjunction	*L24*	不但	不但
bùdébù	*must*	modal verb	*L23*	不得不	不得不
bùdéliǎo	*amazing, awful; extremely, unbearably*	adj VP	*L25*	不得了	不得了
bùguò	*but*	conjunction	*L17*	不过	不過
bùtóng	*different*	adjective	*L18*	不同	不同
C					
cānjiā	*attend, participate in*	verb	*L18*	参加	參加
cāntīng	*dining hall, cafeteria*	noun	*L17*	餐厅	餐廳
cèsuǒ	*toilet*	noun	*L20*	厕所	廁所
chángduǎn	*length*	noun	*L23*	长短	長短
chéngjì	*grades, academic record*	noun	*L18*	成绩	成績
chènshān	*shirt*	noun	*L19*	衬衫	襯衫
chòu	*smelly, stinky*	adjectival phrase	*L19*	臭	臭
chuān	*wear*	verb	*L19*	穿	穿
chuānghu	*window*	noun	*L19*	窗户	窗戶
chuánrén	*descendant*	noun	*L25*	传人	傳人
chúle	*except, besides*	preposition	*L20*	除了	除了
chūnjié	*Spring Festival*	noun phrase	*L23*	春节	春節
chūntiān	*spring*	noun phrase	*L21*	春天	春天

chūqu	*go out*	verb	*L19*	出去	出去
chúxī	*Chinese (lunar) New Year's Eve*	noun	*L25*	除夕	除夕
chúxīyè	*Chinese (lunar) New Year's Eve*	noun	*L25*	除夕夜	除夕夜
chūzū qìchē (chūzūchē)	*taxi*	noun phrase	*L24*	出租汽车 (出租车)	出租汽車 (出租車)
cì	*time*	classifier	*L20*	次	次
cónglái (+ neg)	*never before*	adverb + neg	*L25*	从来	從來
cōngming	*smart, intelligent*	adjectival verb	*L17*	聪明	聰明
cuò	*mistake, mistaken*	verb	*L19*	错	錯
D					
dǎ bàngqiú	*play baseball*	verb + object	*L22*	打棒球	打棒球
dǎkāi	*open*	resultative verb	*L19*	打开	打開
dǎ páiqiú	*play volleyball*	verb + object	*L22*	打排球	打排球
dǎ pēntì	*sneeze*	verb	*L20*	打喷嚏	打噴嚏
dǎ pīngpāng qiú	*play ping-pong*	verb +object	*L22*	打乒乓球	打乒乓球
dǎ zhé	*sell at a discount*	verb + object	*L23*	打折	打折
dàgài	*probably*	adverb	*L20*	大概	大概
dàxiǎo	*size* (abstract)	noun	*L23*	大小	大小
dàyī	*coat, overcoat*	noun	*L24*	大衣	大衣
dà zìrán	*nature*	noun	*L22*	大自然	大自然
dài	*wear (on head, neck, hands)*	verb	*L20*	戴	戴

dào	*upside down*	verb	*L25*	倒	倒
dàodǐ	*after all*	adverb	*L22*	到底	到底
děngděng	*etcetera*	noun	*L22*	等等	等等
dī	*low*	adjectival verb	*L21*	低	低
dì	*earth, ground*	noun	*L19*	地	地
diàntī	*elevator*	noun	*L22*	电梯	電梯
díquè	*really, indeed*	adverb	*L21*	的确	的確
dǐxià	*below*	noun	*L25*	底下	底下
dìqiú	*earth*	noun	*L22*	地球	地球
dōngtiān	*winter*	noun phrase	*L21*	冬天	冬天
dù	*degree*	noun	*L21*	度	度
duǎn	*short*	adjectival verb	*L21*	短	短
duànliàn	*exercise*	verb	*L22*	锻炼	鍛煉
duō yún	*cloudy*	adjective phrase	*L21*	多云	多雲
dùzi	*stomach*	noun	*L20*	肚子	肚子
E					
ér	*and, but, or*	conjunction	*L22*	而	而
ěrduo	*ear(s)*	noun	*L20*	耳朵	耳朵
érqiě	*moreover, in addition, also*	adverb	*L21*	而且	而且
èrwéi mǎ	*QR code*	noun phrase	*L24*	二维码	二維碼
ěrzhào	*earmuffs*	noun	*L24*	耳罩	耳罩
F					
fā shāo	*have fever*	verb + object	*L20*	发烧	發燒
fā yán	*be inflamed*	verb + object	*L20*	发炎	發炎

fàng	*put, place (something somewhere); set off (firecrackers)*	verb	*L19* *L25*	放	放
fāngbiàn	*convenient*	adjectival verb	*L21*	方便	方便
fángjiān	*room*	noun	*L19*	房间	房間
fāngmiàn	*aspect, perspective, side*	noun	*L18*	方面	方面
fāpiào	*receipt*	noun	*L24*	发票	發票
fēi VP bù kě	*must V*	modal verb – literary expression	*L19*	非 **VP** 不可	非 **VP** 不可
fēng	*wind*	noun	*L21*	风	風
fēngfù	*abundant*	adjectival verb	*L25*	丰富	豐富
fēngjǐng	*scenery*	noun	*L21*	风景	風景
fēnshù	*grades, points*	noun	*L18*	分数	分數
fù	*pair of, a set of*	classifier	*L24*	副	副
fù	*pay*	verb	*L24*	付	付
G					
gāngcái	*just before now*	adverb	*L25*	刚才	剛才
gānjìng	*clean*	adjectival phrase	*L19*	干净	乾淨
gǎnjué	*feeling*	noun	*L24*	感觉	感覺
gǎnmào	*catch a cold; common cold*	noun, verb + object	*L20*	感冒	感冒
gānzào	*dry*	adjectival verb	*L21*	干燥	乾燥
gāokǎo	*National University Entrance Exam*	proper noun	*L18*	高考	高考

gāozhōng	*high school, senior high school*	noun	*L18*	高中	高中
gāozhōngshēng	*high school student, senior high school student*	noun phrase	*L18*	高中生	高中生
gèng	*even more*	intensifier	*L22*	更	更
gōngxǐ fācái	*congratulations and be prosperous*	New Year's greeting expression	*L25*	恭喜发财	恭喜發財
gòu	*enough*	verb	*L22*	够	夠
guā	*blow*	verb	*L21*	刮	刮
guā fēng	*windy (blow wind)*	verb + object	*L21*	刮风	刮風
guàng	*visit, stroll through*	verb	*L23*	逛	逛
guàng jiē	*window shopping, strolling along the shopping streets*	verb + object	*L23*	逛街	逛街
guǎn	*manage*	verb	*L21*	管	管
guǎnlǐ	*management*	noun	*L17*	管理	管理
guānxi	*connection, relationship*	noun	*L17*	关系	關係
guānxīn	*be concerned about*	verb	*L21*	关心	關心
guǎnggào	*advertisement*	noun	*L23*	广告	廣告
guìzi	*dresser*	noun	*L19*	柜子	櫃子
gùkè	*customer*	noun	*L23*	顾客	顧客
guò jǐ tiān	*after a few days*	conversational expression	*L17*	过几天	過幾天

guò nián	*celebrate the Chinese New Year*	verb phrase	*L25*	过年	過年
guòqī	*expire*	verb	*L19*	过期	過期
H					
háng háng chū Zhuàngyuán	*every field produces a leading expert*	proverb	*L18*	行行出状元	行行出狀元
hánjià	*winter vacation*	noun phrase	*L25*	寒假	寒假
hào	*size*	classifier	*L23*	号	號
hǎo huài	*good or bad*	noun phrase	*L18*	好坏	好壞
hǎojǐcì	*a good many times, many times*	noun phrase	*L20*	好几次	好幾次
hǎoxiàng	*appear, seem to be*	verb	*L20*	好像	好像
héshì	*suitable, appropriate*	adjectival verb	*L17*	合适	合適
hóngbāo	*red envelope with money inside given as a gift*	noun phrase	*L25*	红包	紅包
huā	*spend (time), spend (money); flowers*	verb; noun	*L19*	花	花
huá	*row*	verb	*L22*	划	划
huá bīng	*ice skating*	verb + object	*L22*	滑冰	滑冰
huá chuán	*row boats, crew*	verb + object	*L22*	划船	划船
huá xuě	*skiing*	verb + object	*L22*	滑雪	滑雪
huài	*bad, broken*	adjectival verb	*L18*	坏	壞

huánbǎo	*environmental protection*	noun phrase abbreviation of 环 jìng bǎohù	*L22*	环保	環保
huánjìng	*environment*	noun	*L17*	环境	環境
huánjìng bǎohù	*environmental protection*	noun phrase	*L22*	环境保护	環境保護
huánjìng guǎnlǐ	*environmental management, environmental studies*	noun phrase	*L17*	环境管理	環境管理
huàtí	*topic*	noun	*L21*	话题	話題
huàxué	*chemistry*	noun	*L22*	化学	化學
huí lai	*come back (to a place), return*	verb	*L17*	回来	回來
huódòng	*activity, movement*	noun; verb	*L22*	活动	活動
huòzhě	*or*	conjunction	*L20*	或者	或者
J					
jǐ	*crowd, squeeze*	verb	*L25*	挤	擠
jìde	*remember*	verb	*L20*	记得	記得
jiā	classifier for *restaurants, family*	classifier	*L20*	家	家
jiàn	*item* (classifier for *events and clothing*)	classifier	*L18*	件	件
jiǎn jià	*reduce the price*	verb + object	*L23*	减价	減價
jiānglái	*in the future*	time word	*L18*	将来	將來
jiànkāng	*healthy*	adjectival verb	*L22*	健康	健康
jiǎnshǎo	*reduce*	verb	*L23*	减少	減少

jiànshēn fáng	*gym*	noun phrase	*L22*	健身房	健身房
jiàoshì lóu	*classroom building*	noun phrase	*L22*	教室楼	教室樓
jiàqian	*price*	noun	*L24*	价钱	價錢
jiāxiāng	*hometown*	noun	*L21*	家乡	家鄉
Jiāzhōu	*California*	proper noun	*L21*	加州	加州
jiē	*street* (cf. 路)	noun	*L23*	街	街
jié	*classifier for class periods; festival, holiday*	classifier	*L17* *L23*	节	節
jiéyuē	*conserve*	verb	*L22*	节约	節約
jiéyuē néngyuán	*conserve energy*	verb + object	*L22*	节约能源	節約能源
jīhuì	*opportunity*	noun	*L18*	机会	機會
jìjié	*season*	noun	*L21*	季节	季節
jíle	*extremely*	intensifier suffix	*L19*	极了	極了
jīn	*gold*	adjective, noun	*L23*	金	金
jìn	*enter*	verb	*L18*	进	進
jǐnzhāng	*nervous, tense*	adjectival verb	*L18*	紧张	緊張
jīngjì	*economics*	noun	*L17*	经济	經濟
jiù shì	*only, it is only that*	adverbial phrase	*L19*	就是	就是
jù	*classifier for speech utterances*	classifier	*L22*	句	句
juédìng	*decide*	verb	*L18*	决定	決定
K					
kǎ	*card*	noun	*L24*	卡	卡
kāfēisè	*brown, coffee colored*	noun	*L23*	咖啡色	咖啡色

kāi	*open; convene a meeting, "have" (a party); drive*	verb	*L17* *L19*	开	開
kāi mén	*be open (of a business), open the door*	verb + object	*L17*	开门	開門
kāi xué	*begin school, school starts*	verb + object	*L17*	开学	開學
kāi yào	*write a prescription*	verb + object	*L20*	开药	開藥
kàn bìng	*see a doctor*	verb + object	*L20*	看病	看病
kě'ài	*cute*	adjectival verb	*L24*	可爱	可愛
kèběn	*textbook*	noun	*L17*	课本	課本
kěnéng	*possibly, possible*	adverb	*L20*	可能	可能
késou	*cough*	verb, noun	*L20*	咳嗽	咳嗽
kōngqì	*air*	noun	*L23*	空气	空氣
kǒuzhào	*face mask*	noun phrase	*L20*	口罩	口罩
kùzi	*pants, trousers, slacks*	noun	*L19*	裤子	褲子
L					
là	*hot and spicy*	adjectival phrase	*L20*	辣	辣
lā dùzi	*have diarrhea, (literally: "pull the stomach")*	verb + object	*L20*	拉肚子	拉肚子
lái zì	*come from*	verb + preposition	*L22*	来自	來自
làngfèi	*waste*	verb	*L24*	浪费	浪費
lèi	*tired*	adjectival verb	*L18*	累	累

lián	*even*	adverb	*L22*	连	連
liángkuai	*cool (pleasantly cool)*	adjectival verb	*L21*	凉快	涼快
liáo tiān	*chat*	verb + object	*L25*	聊天	聊天
lìngwài	*in addition, besides*	adverb	*L22*	另外	另外
lìqi	*energy*	noun	*L20*	力气	力氣
liú	*flow*	verb	*L20*	流	流
liú bíshuǐ	*have a runny nose*	verb + object	*L20*	流鼻水	流鼻水
lìyòng	*use*	verb	*L17*	利用	利用
lóng de chuánrén	*descendant of the dragon*	noun phrase	*L25*	龙的传人	龍的傳人
lóutī	*staircase, stairs*	noun	*L22*	楼梯	樓梯
luàn	*chaotic, disorganized, messy*	adjectival phrase	*L19*	乱	亂
luàn jíle	*extremely chaotic, disorganized, messy*	adjectival verb phrase	*L19*	乱极了	亂極了
M					
mángzhe	*busy doing something*	adjV + suffix	*L17*	忙着	忙著
mǎshàng	*immediately*	adverb	*L20*	马上	馬上
méi cuò	*you are not mistaken; you are correct*	negation + adjectival verb	*L19*	没错	沒錯
méi guānxi	*not important*	verb phrase	*L17*	没关系	沒關係
méi xiǎngdào	*didn't expect that*	neg + verb	*L25*	没想到	沒想到

Měishì	*American-style*	noun phrase	L22	美式	美式
Měishì zúqiú	*American-style football*	noun phrase	L22	美式足球	美式足球
mēn	*humid (in warm weather)*	adjectival verb	L21	闷	悶
mén	*classifier for classes; door*	classifier; noun	L17	门	門
mēn rè	*hot and humid*	adjectival phrase	L21	闷热	悶熱
míngbai	*understand*	verb	L25	明白	明白
N					
ná	*bring, take*	verb	L24	拿	拿
nǎinai	*grandmother (father's mother)*	kinship term	L25	奶奶	奶奶
nándào	*do you mean to say . . . ?*	adverb	L18	难道	難道
nánguài	*no wonder*	adverb	L19	难怪	難怪
néngyuán	*energy*	noun	L22	能源	能源
nián sānshí	*the last day of the year*	noun phrase	L25	年三十	年三十
niánnián yǒu yú	*have more than you need every year*	proverb	L25	年年有余	年年有餘
niánqīng	*young*	noun	L22	年轻	年輕
niánqīng rén	*young people*	noun phrase	L22	年轻人	年輕人
niányè fàn	*New Year's Eve family dinner*	noun phrase	L25	年夜饭	年夜飯
nuǎnhuà	*warming*	verb	L21	暖化	暖化
nuǎnhuo	*warm*	adjectival verb	L21	暖和	暖和
P					
pá	*climb*	verb	L22	爬	爬

pà	*fear*	verb	L21	怕	怕
pá shān	*climb a mountain*	verb + object	L22	爬山	爬山
páiqiú	*volleyball*	noun phrase	L22	排球	排球
pàng	*fat*	adjectival verb	L23	胖	胖
pǎo bù	*run, jog*	verb + object	L22	跑步	跑步
pèi	*match*	verb, adjectival verb	L24	配	配
pí xié	*leather shoes*	noun phrase	L24	皮鞋	皮鞋
piàn	*tablet, slice*	classifier	L20	片	片
pīngpāng qiú	*ping-pong*	noun phrase	L22	乒乓球	乒乓球
Q					
qí	*ride astraddle*	verb	L22	骑	騎
qí zìxíngchē	*ride a bicycle*	verb + object	L22	骑自行车	騎自行車
qiáng	*strong*	adjectival verb	L18	强	強
qìhòu	*climate*	noun	L21	气候	氣候
qíng	*clear*	adjectival verb	L21	晴	晴
qíngtiān	*clear day*	noun phrase	L21	晴天	晴天
qīnqi	*relatives*	noun	L25	亲戚	親戚
qiú	*ball, sphere, world*	noun	L21	球	球
qiūtiān	*autumn, fall*	noun phrase	L21	秋天	秋天
qiúxié	*sneakers, athletic shoes*	noun	L19	球鞋	球鞋
quán	*entire**	quantifier	L18	全	全
quán guó	*nationwide*	noun phrase	L18	全国	全國
quán qiú	*global*	noun, adjective	L21	全球	全球

quán shēn	*entire body*	noun phrase	*L20*	全身	全身
quán qiú nuǎnhuà	*global warming*	noun phrase	*L21*	全球暖化	全球暖化
qúnzi	*skirt*	noun	*L23*	裙子	裙子
R					
ràng	*allow*	verb	*L18*	让	讓
rènao	*lively*	adjectival phrase	*L25*	热闹	熱鬧
rēng	*throw away*	verb	*L19*	扔	扔
S					
sǎngzi	*throat*	noun	*L20*	嗓子	嗓子
sǎo	*sweep*	verb	*L19*	扫	掃
sǎo dì	*sweep the floor*	verb + object	*L19*	扫地	掃地
sǎo mǎ	*scan a code* (cf. sǎo 扫 *sweep, scan*)	verb + object	*L24*	扫码	掃碼
shàng cèsuǒ	*go to the toilet*	verb + object	*L20*	上厕所	上廁所
shàng huǒ	*be inflamed*	verb + object	*L20*	上火	上火
shāngdiàn	*store*	noun	*L23*	商店	商店
shāo	*cook, simmer; fever*	verb, noun	*L20*	烧	燒
shétóu	*tongue*	noun	*L20*	舌头	舌頭
shēn	*extend*	verb	*L22*	伸	伸
shēntǐ	*body*	noun	*L20*	身体	身體
shēng bìng	*become sick*	verb + object	*L20*	生病	生病
shēngmìng	*life*	noun	*L22*	生命	生命
shēngmìng zàiyú yùndòng	*movement is the essence of life*	conversational expression	*L22*	生命在于运动	生命在於運動

shèngxia	*leftover (be leftover), remain*	verb	L25	剩下	剩下
shēngyīn	*sound*	noun	L25	声音	聲音
shēnqǐng	*apply*	verb	L18	申请	申請
shī	*humid (in cold weather)*	adjectival verb	L21	湿	溼
shì	*try, test (something) out*	verb	L23	试	試
shìchuān	*try on*	verb	L23	试穿	試穿
shī lěng	*cold and damp*	adjectival phrase	L21	湿冷	溼冷
shìnèi huódòng	*indoor activities*	noun phrase	L22	室内活动	室內活動
shìqing	*situation, thing (abstract)*	noun	L18	事情	事情
shíyàn	*lab, experiment*	noun	L17	实验	實驗
shìyàng	*style*	noun	L23	式样	式樣
shíyóu	*oil, petroleum*	noun	L22	石油	石油
shōu	*collect*	verb	L19	收	收
shòu	*thin*	adjectival verb	L23	瘦	瘦
shòubùliǎo	*unable to bear it*	resultative verb	L21	受不了	受不了
shōuqǐlái	*collect, gather, put away*	verb	L19	收起来	收起來
shōushi	*straighten up*	verb	L19	收拾	收拾
shǒutào	*glove*	noun	L24	手套	手套
shǔ	*belong to*	verb	L25	属	屬
shuō dào	*speaking of*	verb	L21	说到	說到

shuāng	*pair*	classifier	*L19*	双	雙
shūfu	*comfortable*	adjectival verb	*L20*	舒服	舒服
shuìbúzháo	*unable to fall asleep*	potential form of resultative verb	*L20*	睡不着	睡不著
shuìzháo	*fall asleep*	verb + resultative ending	*L20*	睡着	睡著
shūjià	*bookcase*	noun	*L19*	书架	書架
shùxué	*mathematics*	noun	*L17*	数学	數學
sì jì	*four seasons*	noun phrase	*L21*	四季	四季
sì jì rú chūn	*like spring all year round*	four-character expression	*L21*	四季如春	四季如春
Sìchuān	*Sichuan*	Chinese province	*L20*	四川	四川
suàn	*calculate, count*	verb	*L24*	算	算
T					
tán	*talk, converse*	verb	*L25*	谈	談
tǎng	*lie down*	verb	*L25*	躺	躺
tǎo jià-huán jià	*bargain back and forth*	verb phrase	*L24*	讨价还价	討價還價
téng	*painful, hurt*	adjectival verb	*L20*	疼	疼
tī	*kick*	verb	*L22*	踢	踢
tī zúqiú	*play soccer, football*	verb + object	*L22*	踢足球	踢足球
tiānqì	*weather*	noun	*L20*	天气	天氣
tiānqì yùbào	*weather forecast*	noun phrase	*L21*	天气预报	天氣預報
tídào	*mention*	verb	*L21*	提到	提到
tiē	*post, hang up*	verb	*L23*	贴	貼

tǐyù	*sports, physical training*	noun	*L22*	体育	體育
tǐyù huódòng	*sports activities, exercise*	noun phrase	*L22*	体育活动	體育活動
tóngyì	*agree*	verb	*L21*	同意	同意
tóngyīn	*same sound, homophonous*	adjectival phrase	*L25*	同音	同音
tóngyīn zì	*characters with identical pronunciations*	noun phrase	*L25*	同音字	同音字
tóu	*head*	noun	*L20*	头	頭
tóufa	*hair*	noun	*L25*	头发	頭髮
tóu téng	*have a headache*	noun + verb	*L20*	头疼	頭疼
tóu yūn	*lightheaded, dizzy*	noun + adjectival verb	*L20*	头晕	頭暈
tù	*vomit*	verb	*L20*	吐	吐
W					
wán	*finish, be finished*	verb	*L19*	完	完
wǎnhuì	*party* (literally: evening meeting)	noun	*L19*	晚会	晚會
wàzi	*socks*	noun	*L19*	袜子	襪子
wéijīn	*scarf*	noun	*L24*	围巾	圍巾
wèile	*for the sake of, for the purpose of*	preposition	*L22*	为了	為了
Wēixìn	*WeChat*	proper noun	*L24*	微信	微信
Wēixìn Zhīfù	*WeChat Pay*	proper noun	*L24*	微信支付	微信支付
wēndù	*temperature*	noun	*L21*	温度	溫度

wénhuà	*culture*	noun	*L17*	文化	文化
wùlǐ(xué)	*physics*	noun	*L17*	物理(学)	物理(學)
wúliáo	*bored*	adjectival verb	*L23*	无聊	無聊
wūrǎn	*pollution*	noun	*L23*	污染	污染
wūzi	*room*	noun	*L19*	屋子	屋子
X					
Xī'ān	*Xi'an* (city in central northwest China, capital of Shaanxi Province)	proper name	*L25*	西安	西安
xiāngtóng	*similar*	noun	*L22*	相同	相同
xiāngzi	*box*	noun	*L23*	箱子	箱子
xiànjīn	*cash*	noun	*L24*	现金	現金
xiànjīn kǎ	*debit card*	noun phrase	*L24*	现金卡	現金卡
xiàoduì	*school team*	noun phrase	*L22*	校队	校隊
xiǎojie	*young lady, miss*	noun	*L24*	小姐	小姐
xiǎoxīn	*careful*	adjectival verb	*L20*	小心	小心
xié(zi)	*shoes*	noun phrase	*L19*	鞋(子)	鞋(子)
xiězuò	*writing, composition*	noun	*L17*	写作	寫作
xīn nián	*New Year*	noun phrase	*L23*	新年	新年
xīn nián kuàilè	*Happy New Year*	New Year greeting	*L25*	新年快乐	新年快樂
xìngqu	*interest*	noun	*L17*	兴趣	興趣
xìnyòng kǎ	*credit card*	noun phrase	*L24*	信用卡	信用卡
xīwàng	*hope*	verb	*L21*	希望	希望

xuǎn	*select*	verb	*L17*	选	選
xuě	*snow*	noun	*L21*	雪	雪
xuéqī	*semester*	noun	*L17*	学期	學期
xuéshengmen	*students (plural)*	noun	*L17*	学生们	學生們
Y					
yán	*strict*	adjectival verb	*L17*	严	嚴
yán shī chū gāo tú	*strict teachers make good students*	proverb	*L17*	严师出高徒	嚴師出高徒
yǎnjīng	*eye(s)*	noun	*L20*	眼睛	眼睛
yào	*medicine*	noun	*L20*	药	藥
yè	*night**	noun	*L20*	夜	夜
yèlǐ	*middle of the night*	time phrase	*L20*	夜里	夜裡
yéye	*grandfather (father's father)*	kinship term	*L25*	爷爷	爺爺
yī yè	*the whole night*	noun phrase	*L20*	一夜	一夜
yībān	*usually, typically*	adverb	*L18*	一般	一般
yībiān	*on one side, at the same time*	noun, adverb	*L25*	一边	一邊
yīdìng	*definitely*	adverb	*L17*	一定	一定
yīfu	*clothing*	noun	*L19*	衣服	衣服
yīn tiān	*overcast*	noun phrase	*L21*	阴天	陰天
yīshēng	*doctor*	noun	*L20*	医生	醫生
yǐwài	*except (for), outside of*	noun	*L20*	以外	以外

yīyuàn	*hospital*	noun	*L20*	医院	醫院
yǐzi	*chair*	noun	*L19*	椅子	椅子
yònggōng	*hard working at studies, diligent*	adjectival phrase	*L17*	用功	用功
yòu	*both . . . and; again*	adverbial phrase	*L19*	又	又
yǒu xìngqu	*interested in*	adjectival phrase	*L17*	有兴趣	有興趣
yóu yǒng	*swimming*	verb + object	*L22*	游泳	游泳
yǒu yòng	*useful*	adjectival phrase	*L17*	有用	有用
yú	*surplus*	noun	*L25*	余	餘
yǔ	*rain*	noun	*L21*	雨	雨
yuàn zhě shàng gōu	*willingly swallowed the bait, willingly got caught*	proverb	*L24*	愿者上钩	願者上鈎
yuánlái	*originally*	adverb	*L17*	原来	原來
yùbào	*forecast*	noun	*L21*	预报	預報
yuē	*make an appointment, arrange to meet*	verb	*L22*	约	約
yuè lái yuè	*more and more*	intensifier phrase	*L21*	越来越	越來越
yújiā	*yoga*	noun	*L22*	瑜伽	瑜伽
yūn	*dizzy*	adjectival verb	*L20*	晕	暈
yùndòng	*activity*	noun	*L22*	运动	運動
yùndòng xié	*sneakers*	noun	*L24*	运动鞋	運動鞋
Z					
zāng	*dirty*	adjectival verb	*L19*	脏	髒

zěnme bàn	*what can you do about it?*	question phrase	*L18*	怎么办	怎麼辦
zěnme le?	*what's the matter?*	conversational expression	*L20*	怎么了	怎麼了
zhàn	*stand* (cf. *station,* Lesson II)	verb	*L25*	站	站
zhāngkāi	*open*	verb	*L20*	张开	張開
zháo	*reach the intended goal**	resultative ending	*L20*	着	著
zhǎodào	*find*	verb	*L19*	找到	找到
zhàogù	*take care of*	verb	*L21*	照顾	照顧
zhè jǐ tiān	*these past few days*	noun phrase	*L17*	这几天	這幾天
zhèng	*precisely, exactly*	intensifier	*L23*	正	正
zhèngzhì	*politics*	noun	*L17*	政治	政治
zhèngzhì xué	*political science*	noun phrase	*L17*	政治学	政治學
zhèngzhuàng	*symptom*	noun	*L20*	症状	症狀
zhǐ shì	*it is only (that)*	adverb phrase	*L17*	只是	只是
zhǐ xiāng	*cardboard box/ paper box*	noun phrase	*L23*	纸箱	紙箱
zhíde	*worth*	adverb	*L21*	值得	值得
zhǐyào	*as long as*	sentence adverb	*L23*	只要	只要
zhǒng	*type of*	classifier	*L23*	种	種
zhòngliàng xùnliàn	*weight training*	noun phrase	*L22*	重量训练	重量訓練
zhòngshì	*take seriously, consider important*	verb	*L22*	重视	重視

zhòngyào	*important*	adjectival verb	*L22*	重要	重要
zhuǎn	*turn*	verb	*L21*	转	轉
zhuǎn qíng	*turning clear*	verb phrase	*L21*	转晴	轉晴
zhuānyè	*major (course of study)*	adjectival verb	*L18*	专业	專業
zhuōzi	*table*	noun	*L19*	桌子	桌子
zǐ	*purple*	adjective	*L23*	紫	紫
zǐ sè	*purple colored*	noun	*L23*	紫色	紫色
zìxíngchē	*bicycle*	noun	*L22*	自行车	自行車
zuì	*most*	intensifier	*L18*	最	最
zuì hòu	*finally*	adverb phrase	*L17*	最后	最後
zuì jìn	*recently*	adverb	*L20*	最近	最近
zuǐba	*mouth*	noun	*L20*	嘴巴	嘴巴
zuòwèi	*seat*	noun	*L25*	座位	座位
zúqiú	*soccer, football*	noun phrase	*L22*	足球	足球

Chinese characters alphabetically arranged

The lesson number indicates the lesson in which the character is introduced. The last column of each row shows the character in traditional form. * indicates that the character is not an independent word, but is always combined with another character to form a word.

Pinyin	Character	English	Illustrative words	Lesson	T
A					
ài	爱	love	爱好 àihào *hobby, interests*	L18	愛
B					
bǎ	把	take*		L20	把
bái	白	white		L19	白
bǎi	百	hundred	一百块 yī bǎi kuài *one hundred dollars*	L24	百
bāng	帮	help	帮助 bāngzhù *help*	L17	幫

bāo	包	*wrap; classifier for packages*	包饺子 bāo jiǎozi *wrap dumplings,* 红包 hóngbāo *red gift envelope*	L25	包
bǎo	保	*protect**	保护 bǎohù *protect,* 环保 huánbǎo *environmental protection*	L23	保
bǎo	饱	*full (of food)*	吃饱了 chībǎo le *ate until ful*	L25	飽
bèi	备	*prepare**	准备 zhǔnbèi *prepare*	L22	備
bǐ	比	*compare**	比较 bǐjiào *relatively*	L21	比
bì	必	*must*	不必 bù bì *no need to*	L23	必
biān	边	*side, direction*	里边 lǐbian *inside*	L19	邊
biàn	变	*change*		L21	變
biàn	便	*convenient**	方便 fāngbiàn *convenient*	L23	便
bìng	病	*sick*	生病 shēng bìng *become sick*	L21	病

C

cài	菜	*food, dishes of food*	白菜 báicài *cabbage*	L20	菜
cān	参	*participate**	参加 cānjiā *participate*	L22	參
cháng	长	*long*	长短 chángduǎn *length*	L21	長
chèn	衬	*shirt**	衬衫 chènshān *shirt*	L24	襯
chéng	城	*city**	城市 chéngshì *city*	L23	城
chū	出	*produce, exit**	行行出状元 hángháng chū zhuàngyuán *every field produces a leading expert,* 严师出高徒 yánshī chū gāotú *strict teachers produce good students*	L18	出

chú	除	*except, besides*	除了 chúle *except, besides*	L22	除
chuān	穿	*wear*		L20	穿
chuáng	床	*bed*	起床 qǐ chuáng *get out of bed*	L19	床
chūn	春	*spring*	春天 chūntiān *spring,* 春节 Chūnjié *Spring Festival (Chinese New Year)*	L23	春
D					
dài	带	*take*		L20	帶
dài	戴	*wear (on the head, neck, and extremities)*		L24	戴
dān	单	*alone*, odd-numbered**	简单 jiǎndān *simple*	L23	單
dàn	但	*but*	但是 dànshi *but*	L17	但
děng	等	*wait*	等一下 děng yīxià *wait a minute*	L19	等
dìng	定	*set, establish*	一定 yīdìng *certainly,* 决定 juédìng *decide, determine*	L18	定
dōng	冬	*winter*	冬天 dōngtiān *winter*	L22	冬
dòng	动	*move*	运动 yùndòng *movement, exercise*	L23	動
duǎn	短	*short*	长短 chángduǎn *length*	L23	短
duì	队	*team*	校队 xiàoduì *school team*	L22	隊

E

è	饿	*hungry*	饿死了 èsǐle *starving to death*	L24	餓
ér	而	*and, but, or*	而且 érqiě *in addition*	L22	而

F

fā	发	*emit*	发烧 fā shāo *have fever*	L20	發
fán	烦	*annoy*	麻烦 máfan *bother, bothersome*	L18	煩
fāng	方	*side, direction*	地方 dìfang *place*, 方面 fāngmiàn *aspect, side*	L17	方
fáng	房	*room*	房间 fángjiān *room*, 房子 fángzi *house*	L19	房
fàng	放	*put, begin vacation*	放假 fàng jià *begin vacation*	L19	放
fèi	费	*expense, spend, waste*	浪费 làngfèi *waste*, 学费 xuéfèi *tuition*	L24	費
fú	服	*serve, obey, clothing**	shū 服 shūfú *comfortable*, 衣服 yīfu *clothing*	L20	服
fù	复	*resume, renew**	复习 fùxí *review*	L22	復

G

gāi	该	*should, ought to*	应该 yīnggāi *should, ought to*	L21	該
gài	概	*approximate**	大概 dàgài *probably*	L21	概
gān	干	*dry*	干净 gānjìng *clean*	L20	乾
gǎn	感	*feel**	感冒 gǎnmào *a cold*, 感觉 gǎnjué *feeling*	L24	感

gèng	更	*even more*		L23	更
gòng	共	*together**	一共 yīgòng *altogether*	L17	共
guān	关	*close, concern**	关系 guānxi *connection*; 没关系 méi guānxi *not important*	L17	關
guǎn	管	*manage*	管理 guǎnlǐ *management*	L21	管
guàn	惯	*used to**	习惯 xíguàn *be used to, be accustomed to*	L17	惯

H

hái	孩	*child**	孩子 háizi *child*	L25	孩
hǎi	海	*sea, ocean*	海边 hǎibiān *sea shore, sea coast*	L21	海
hé	合	*combine*	合适 héshì *suitable, appropriate*	L18	合
hēi	黑	*black*	黑色 hēisè *black colored*	L24	黑
huā	花	*flower, spend*	花钱 huā qián *spend money*, 花时间 huā shíjiān *spend time, waste time*	L19	花
huà	化	*change, transform*	文化 wénhuà *culture*, 暖化 nuǎnhuà *warming*	L21	化
huà	划	*plan, mark*	计划 jìhuà *plan*	L25	劃
huài	坏	*bad, broken*	好坏 hǎo huài *good (or) bad*	L20	壞
huán	环	*linked-shaped, surround*	环境 huánjìng *environment*	L21	環
huàn	换	*change, exchange*		L18	换

huáng	黄	*yellow*	黄色 huángsè *yellow colored*	L25	黃
huó	活	*live*	生活 shēnghuó *live*	L17	活
huò	或	*or, perhaps*	或者 huòzhě *perhaps*	L22	或
J					
jí	级	*grade, level**	一年级 yī niánjí *first year*	L18	級
jí	极	*extremely**	好极了 hǎojíle *terrific, great*	L24	極
jì	济	*benefit**	经济 jīngjì *economics*	L18	濟
jì	计	*calculate*	计划 jìhuà *plan*	L25	計
jiā	加	*add*	加州 Jiāzhōu *California,* 参加 cānjiā *participate (in)*	L21	加
jià	价	*price*	讨价还价 tǎo jià-huán jià *bargain back and forth,* 价钱 jiàqian *price,* 减价 jiǎn jià *reduce the price*	L24	價
jià	假	*holiday, vacation**	放假 fàng jià *begin vacation,* 暑假 shǔ jià *summer vacation,* 寒假 hán jià *winter vacation*	L25	假
jiǎn	简	*simple**	简单 jiǎndān *simple*	L23	簡
jiàn	件	*classifier for clothing, situations*	一件事qing yī jiàn shìqing *one matter,* 一件衣服 yī jiàn yīfu *one article of clothing*	L19	件
jiāng	将	*about to, will*	将来 jiānglái *in the future*	L21	將

jiāo, jiào	教	*teach*	教室 jiàoshì *classroom*, 家教 jiājiào *tutor*	L22	教
jiǎo	饺	*dumpling**	饺子 jiǎozi *dumpling*	L19	餃
jiào	较	*compare**	比较 bǐjiào *relatively*	L21	較
jiē	街	*street*	逛街 guàng jiē *go window shopping, stroll along the streets*	L24	街
jié	节	*festival*, classifier for classes*	春节 Chūnjié *Spring Festival* (*Chinese New Year*), 一节课 yī jié kè *one class*, 节约 jiéyuē *conserve*	L23	節
jiè	介	*introduce**	介绍 jièshào *introduce*	L25	介
jīn	金	*gold, metal*	金色 jīnsè *gold colored*, 现金 xiànjīn *cash*, 现金卡 xiànjīnkǎ *debit card*	L24	金
jīng	睛	*eyeball**	眼睛 yǎnjing *eye*	L25	睛
jìng	净	*clean**	干净 gānjìng *clean*	L20	淨
jìng	境	*border*	环境 huánjìng *environment*	L21	境
jiǔ	酒	*alcohol, wine*	啤酒 píjiǔ *beer*, 喝酒 hē jiǔ *drink (alcohol)*	L20	酒
jué	决	*decide**	决定 juédìng *decide*	L20	決
K					
kòng	空	*free time*	有空 yǒu kòng *have free time*, 没空 méi kòng *do not have time*	L22	空
kù	裤	*slacks**	裤子 kùzi *slacks*	L24	裤

L

lán	蓝	blue	蓝色 lánsè blue colored	L25	藍
lè	乐	happy*	快乐 kuàilè happy, 可乐 kělè cola, 可口可乐 Kěkǒukělè Coca Cola	L25	樂
lèi	累	tired	累死了 lèisǐle tired to death	L18	累
lěng	冷	cold		L20	冷
lǐ	理	reason, logic	管理 guǎnlǐ management	L21	理
lì	利	advantageous, beneficial*	利用 lìyòng use	L18	利
lián	连	even		L23	連
liàn	练	practice	练习 liànxí practice, 训练 xùnliàn to train	L22	練
liàng	亮	light, shine	漂亮 piàoliang pretty	L21	亮
líng	零	zero	零下 língxià below zero	L21	零
lìng	另	in addition*	另外 lìngwài in addition	L23	另
liú	流	flow	流行 liúxíng fashionable, 流鼻水 liú bíshuǐ have a runny nose	L20	流
lóng	龙	dragon		L25	龍
lóu	楼	building; floor of a building	楼梯 lóutī staircase	L24	樓

M

| má | 麻 | coarse, numb, hemp | 麻烦 máfan bother, bothersome | L18 | 麻 |

mǎ	码	number, symbol, code*	号码 hàomǎ *number (telephone number)*, 扫码 sǎo mǎ *scan a code*	L24	碼
mò	末	end*	周末 zhōumò *weekend*	L19	末
N					
ná	拿	take		L25	拿
nǎi	奶	milk	牛奶 niúnǎi *milk*	L19	奶
nǎo	脑	brain*	电脑 diànnǎo *computer*	L19	腦
néng	能	can, physical ability		L18	能
nuǎn	暖	warm*	暖和 nuǎnhuo *warm*; 暖化 nuǎnhuà *warming*	L22	暖
P					
pá	爬	climb	爬山 pá shān *climb a mountain*	L23	爬
pà	怕	fear		L22	怕
péi	陪	accompany		L17	陪
pián	便	inexpensive*	便宜 piányi *cheap, inexpensive*	L23	便
piàn	片	tablet,	照片 zhàopiàn *photograph*	L20	片
piào	漂	good-looking*	漂亮 piàoliang *pretty*	L21	漂
píng	瓶	bottle	一瓶水 yī píng shuǐ *one bottle of water*	L20	瓶
Q					
qì	气	air, spirit	客气 kèqi *polite*, 天气 tiānqì *weather*, 力气 lìqì *strength, energy*	L20	氣

qì	汽	*steam, gas*	汽车 qìchē *car*, 出 **zū**(汽)车 chūzū (qì) chē *taxi*	L24	汽
qiě	且	*also**	而且 érqiě *moreover*	L23	且
qiú	球	*ball*	球鞋 qiúxié *sneakers, athletic shoes*, 打球 dǎ qiú *play ball*	L19	球
qu	趣	*interest**	兴趣 xìngqu *interest*	L18	趣
quán	全	*entire*	全身 quánshēn *entire body*, 全国 quánguó *national*	L20	全
qún	裙	*skirt**	裙子 qúnzi *skirt*	L24	裙
R					
ràng	让	*let, make*		L20	讓
rè	热	*hot*		L21	熱
S					
sǎo	扫	*sweep, scan*	扫地 sǎo dì *sweep the floor*, 扫码 sǎo mǎ *scan a code*	L24	掃
sè	色	*color**	颜色 yánsè *color*	L19	色
shān	衫	*shirt**	衬衫 chènshān *shirt*	L24	衫
shāng	商	*commerce**	商店 shāngdiàn *(a) shop*	L24	商
shào	绍	*introduce**	介绍 jièshào *introduce*	L25	紹
shè	舍	*house, dwelling**	宿舍 sùshè *dormitory*	L19	舍
shēn	身	*body**	身体 shēntǐ *body*	L22	身
shì	适	*suitable**	合适 héshì *suitable, appropriate*	L18	適
shì	室	*room**	室友 shìyǒu *roommate*, 教室 jiàoshì *classroom*	L19	室

shì	视	*vision**	电视 diànshì *television,* 重视 zhòngshì *value*	*L22*	視
shì	式	*style*	式样 shìyàng *style,* 美式足球 Měishì zúqiú *American football*	*L23*	式
shōu	收	*collect, gather up*	收拾 shōushi *straighten up, clean up*	*L22*	收
shū	叔	*uncle**	叔叔 shūshu *uncle*	*L25*	叔
shù	数	*number**	分数 fēnshù *grade(s),* 数学 shùxué *math*	*L18*	數
shuāng	双	*pair*	一双鞋 yī shuāng xié *a pair of shoes*	*L24*	雙
shuì	睡	*sleep*	睡觉 shuì jiào *sleep,* 睡着 shuìzháo *fall asleep*	*L20*	睡
sǐ	死	*dead*	累死了 lèisǐle *dead tired,* 饿死了 èsǐle *starving to death*	*L24*	死
sòng	送	*send, deliver, give as a present*		*L23*	送
sù	宿	*lodge, stay**	宿舍 sùshè *dormitory*	*L19*	宿
suī	虽	*although**	虽然 suīrán *although*	*L19*	雖
suì	岁	*years of age*		*L21*	歲
suǒ	所	*place**	所以 suǒyǐ *so, therefore*	*L17*	所
T					
tè	特	*special, especially**	特别 tèbié *especially, special*	*L19*	特

tí	题	*topic, subject*	问题 wèntí *problem, question*	*L17*	題
tǐ	体	*body**	身体 shēntǐ *body*	*L22*	體
tiáo	条	classifier for *long, thin objects*	一条裤子 yī tiáo kùzi *a "pair" of slacks*	*L23*	條
tiào	跳	*jump*	跳舞 tiàowǔ *dance*	*L22*	跳
tiē	贴	*paste*		*L25*	貼
tiě	铁	*iron*	地铁 dìtiě *subway*	*L23*	鐵
tóng	同	*same**	同学 tóngxué *classmate,* 同屋 tóngwū *roommate,* 不同 bùtóng *different*	*L18*	同
tóu	头	*head*	钟头 zhōngtóu *hour,* 头疼 tóu téng *headache,* 舌头 shétóu *tongue*	*L20*	頭
W					
wà	袜	*socks**	袜子 wàzi *socks*	*L24*	襪
wàng	忘	*forget*		*L19*	忘
wèi	位	polite classifier for *people*	您是哪位？ nín shì nǎwèi? *Who are you?*	*L24*	位
wū	屋	*room**	屋子 wūzi *room,* 同屋 wūzi *roommate*	*L19*	屋
wǔ	舞	*dance*	跳舞 tiàowǔ *dance*	*L22*	舞
wù	务	*business**	服务员 fúwùyuán *clerk, waiter* (mainland China usage)	*L23*	務
X					
xì	系	*system**	关系 guānxi *connection;* 没关系 méi guānxi *not important*	*L17*	係

xià	夏	summer*	夏天 xiàtiān summer	L21	夏
xiàng	像	resemble	好像 hǎoxiàng appears to be	L20	像
xiào	校	school*	学校 xuéxiào school	L17	校
xié	鞋	shoe	鞋子 xiézi shoe, 运动鞋 yùndòngxié athletic shoes, sneakers, gym shoes, 皮鞋 píxié leather shoes	L24	鞋
xīn	新	new	新年 xīnnián New Year	L23	新
xìn	信	trust	短信 duǎnxìn text message, 信用卡 xìnyòng kǎ credit card, 微信 Wēixìn WeChat	L24	信
xìng	兴	prosper*	兴趣 xìngqu interest, 高兴 gāoxìng happy	L17	興
xuǎn	选	select		L18	選
xuě	雪	snow	下雪 xià xuě to snow, 滑雪 huáxuě skiing	L22	雪
Y					
yán	颜	color*	颜色 yánsè color	L23	顏
yǎn	眼	eye*	眼睛 yǎnjing eye	L25	眼
yè	夜	evening, night	夜里 yèlǐ in the middle of the night, 年夜饭 niányè fàn New Year's Eve family dinner	L25	夜
yī	衣	clothing*	衣服 yīfu clothing	L20	衣
yí	宜	suitable*	便宜 piányi inexpensive, cheap	L23	宜

yīn	因	reason*	因为 yīnwèi because	L17	因
yīn	音	sound	音乐 yīnyuè music	L17	音
yīng	英	hero, English*	英文 Yīngwén English	L17	英
yìng	应	respond*	应该 yīnggāi should, ought to	L21	應
yòng	用	use	利用 lìyòng use, 有用 yǒu yòng useful, 用功 yònggōng hardworking, 用筷子 yòng kuàizi use chopsticks	L17	用
yòu	又	both . . . and; again	又闷又热 yòu mēn yòu rè both humid and hot	L21	又
yú	鱼	fish		L25	魚
yǔ	雨	rain	下雨 xià yǔ (it's) raining	L22	雨
yuán	员	person who performs a job*	服务员 fúwùyuán clerk, waiter (mainland China usage)	L23	員
yuàn	院	courtyard, academy, institute*	电影院 diànyǐng yuàn movie theater, 医院 yīyuàn hospital	L20	院
yuè	越	the more*	越来越 yuèláiyuè more and more	L23	越
yuè; lè	乐	music*; happy*	音乐 yīnyuè music 快乐 kuàilè happy	L17	樂
yùn	运	move, transport	运动 yùndòng movement, exercise	L23	運

Z

| zāng | 脏 | dirty | | L21 | 髒 |

zhào	照	*illuminate; take a photo*	照片 zhàopiàn *photos,* 照照片 zhào zhàopiàn *take photos,* 照顾 zhàogù *take care of*	L21	照
zhé	折	*bend, twist, fold (clothes)*	打折 dǎ zhé *give a discount*	L24	折
zhě	者	*or**	或者 huòzhě *perhaps*	L22	者
zhe; zháo	着	*verb suffix**	忙着 mángzhe *being busy,* 坐着 zuòzhe *sitting;* 睡不着 shuìbuzháo *unable to fall asleep*	L25	著
zhèng	挣	*earn*	挣钱 zhèng qián *earn money*	L17	掙
zhèng	正	*precisely*		L25	正
zhí	直	*straight*	一直 yīzhí *continuously, directly, direct*	L17	直
zhǐ	纸	*paper*	报纸 bàozhǐ *newspaper*	L19	紙
zhōng	钟	*clock, bell**	一点钟 yīdiǎn zhōng *one o'clock* 几点钟? jǐdiǎn zhōng? *what time is it?*	L17	鐘
zhǒng	种	*kind of*	这种衣服 zhè zhǒng yīfu *this kind of clothing*	L24	種
zhòng	重	*heavy, important**	重要 zhòngyào *important*	L18	重
zhōu	周	*week*	周末 zhōumò *weekend*	L19	週
zhǔn	准	*accurate*	准备 zhǔnbèi *prepare*	L22	準
zuì	最	*most*	最后 zuìhòu *finally*	L18	最
zuò	作	*do*	工作 gōngzuò *work (noun)*	L17	作

Chinese characters by lesson

indicates that the character is not an independent word, but is always combined with another character to form a word. The last column of each row shows the character in traditional form.

Pinyin	Character	English	Illustrative words	T
Lesson 17				
bāng	帮	*help*	帮助 bāngzhù *help*	幫
dàn	但	*but*	但是 dànshi *but*	但
fāng	方	*side, direction*	地方 dìfang *place*, 方面 fāngmiàn *aspect, side*	方
gòng	共	*together**	一共 yīgòng *altogether*	共
guān	关	*close, concern**	关系 guānxi *connection*; 没关系 méi guānxi *not important*	關

guàn	惯	used to*	习惯 xíguàn be used to, be accustomed to	慣
huó	活	live	生活 shēnghuó live	活
péi	陪	accompany		陪
suǒ	所	place*	所以 suǒyǐ so, therefore	所
tí	题	topic, subject	问题 wèntí problem, question	題
xì	系	system*	关系 guānxi connection; 没关系 méi guānxi not important	係
xiào	校	school*	学校 xuéxiào school	校
xìng	兴	prosper*	兴趣 xìngqu interest, 高兴 gāoxìng happy	興
yīn	因	reason*	音乐 yīnyuè music	因
yīn	音	sound	因为 yīnwèi because	音
yīng	英	hero, English*	英文 Yīngwén English	英
yòng	用	use	利用 lìyòng use, 有用 yǒu yòng useful, 用功 yònggōng hardworking, 用筷子 yòng kuàizi use chopsticks	用
yuè; lè	乐	music*; happy*	音乐 yīnyuè music 快乐 kuàilè happy	樂
zhèng	挣	earn	挣钱 zhèng qián earn money	掙
zhí	直	straight	一直 yīzhí continuously, directly, direct	直
zhōng	钟	clock, bell*	一点钟 yīdiǎn zhōng one o'clock 几点钟? jǐdiǎn zhōng? what time is it?	鐘

zuò	作	*do*	工作 gōngzuò *work* (noun)	作

Lesson 18

ài	爱	*love*	爱好 àihào *hobby, interests*	爱
chū	出	*produce, exit**	行行出状元 hángháng chū zhuàngyuán *every field produces a leading expert*, 严师出高徒 yánshī chū gāotú *strict teachers produce good students*	出
dìng	定	*set, establish*	一定 yīdìng *certainly*, 决定 juédìng *decide, determine*	定
fán	烦	*annoy*	麻烦 máfan *bother, bothersome*	煩
hé	合	*combine*	合适 héshì *suitable, appropriate*	合
huàn	换	*change, exchange*		換
jí	级	*grade, level**	一年级 yī niánjí *first year*	級
jì	济	*benefit**	经济 jīngjì *economics*	濟
lèi	累	*tired*	累死了 lèisǐle *tired to death*	累
lì	利	*advantageous, beneficial**	利用 lìyòng *use*	利
má	麻	*coarse, numb, hemp*	麻烦 máfan *bother, bothersome*	麻
néng	能	*can, physical ability*		能
qu	趣	*interest**	兴趣 xìng qu *interest*	趣

shì	适	*suitable**	合适 héshì *suitable, appropriate*	適
shù	数	*number**	分数 fēnshù *grade(s)*, 数学 shùxué *math*	數
tóng	同	*same**	同学 tóngxué *classmate*, 同屋 tóngwū *roommate*, 不同 bùtóng *different*	同
xuǎn	选	*select*		選
zhòng	重	*heavy, important**	重要 zhòngyào *important*	重
zuì	最	*most*	最后 zuìhòu *finally*	最

Lesson 19

bái	白	*white*		白
biān	边	*side, direction*	里边 lǐbian *inside*	邊
chuáng	床	*bed*	起床 qǐ chuáng *get out of bed*	床
děng	等	*wait*	等一下 děng yīxià *wait a minute*	等
fáng	房	*room*	房间 fángjiān *room*, 房子 fángzi *house*	房
fàng	放	*put, begin vacation*	放假 fàng jià *begin vacation*	放
huā	花	*flower, spend*	花钱 huā qián *spend money*, 花时间 huā shíjiān *spend time, waste time*	花
jiàn	件	classifier for *clothing, situations*	一件事qing yī jiàn shìqing *one matter*, 一件衣服 yī jiàn yīfu *one article of clothing*	件
jiǎo	饺	*dumpling**	饺子 jiǎozi *dumpling*	餃
mò	末	*end**	周末 zhōumò *weekend*	末

nǎi	奶	milk	牛奶 niúnǎi milk	奶
nǎo	脑	brain*	电脑 diànnǎo computer	腦
qiú	球	ball	球鞋 qiúxié sneakers, athletic shoes, 打球 dǎ qiú play ball	球
sè	色	color*	颜色 yánsè color	色
shè	舍	house, dwelling*	宿舍 sùshè dormitory	舍
shì	室	room*	室友 shìyǒu roommate, 教室 jiàoshì classroom	室
sù	宿	lodge, stay*	宿舍 sùshè dormitory	宿
suī	虽	although*	虽然 suīrán although	雖
tè	特	special, especially*	特别 tèbié especially, special	特
wàng	忘	forget		忘
wū	屋	room*	屋子 wūzi room, 同屋 wūzi roommate	屋
zhǐ	纸	paper	报纸 bàozhǐ newspaper	紙
zhōu	周	week	周末 zhōumò weekend	週

Lesson 20

bǎ	把	take*		把
cài	菜	food, dishes of food	白菜 báicài cabbage	菜
chuān	穿	wear		穿
dài	带	take		帶
fā	发	emit	发烧 fā shāo have fever	發
fú	服	serve, obey, clothing*	舒服 shūfú comfortable, 衣服 yīfu clothing	服
gān	干	dry	干净 gānjìng clean	乾

huài	坏	bad, broken	好坏 hǎo huài good (or) bad	壞
jìng	净	clean*	干净 gānjìng clean	淨
jiǔ	酒	alcohol, wine	啤酒 píjiǔ beer, 喝酒 hē jiǔ drink (alcohol)	酒
jué	决	decide*	决定 juédìng decide	決
lěng	冷	cold		冷
liú	流	flow	流行 liúxíng fashionable, 流鼻水 liú bíshuǐ have a runny nose	流
piàn	片	tablet,	照片 zhàopiàn photograph	片
píng	瓶	bottle	一瓶水 yī píng shuǐ one bottle of water	瓶
qì	气	air, spirit	客气 kèqi polite, 天气 tiānqì weather, 力气 lìqì strength, energy	氣
quán	全	entire	全身 quánshēn entire body, 全国 quánguó national	全
ràng	让	let, make		讓
shuì	睡	sleep	睡觉 shuì jiào sleep, 睡着 shuìzháo fall asleep	睡
tóu	头	head	钟头 zhōngtóu hour, 头疼 tóu téng headache, 舌头 shétóu tongue	頭
xiàng	像	resemble	好像 hǎoxiàng appears to be	像
yī	衣	clothing*	衣服 yīfu clothing	衣
yuàn	院	courtyard, academy, institute*	电影院 diànyǐng yuàn movie theater, 医院 yīyuàn hospital	院

Lesson 21

bǐ	比	compare*	比较 bǐjiào relatively	比
biàn	变	change		變
bìng	病	sick	生病 shēng bìng become sick	病
cháng	长	long	长短 chángduǎn length	長
gāi	该	should, ought to	应该 yīnggāi should, ought to	該
gài	概	approximate*	大概 dàgài probably	概
guǎn	管	manage	管理 guǎnlǐ management	管
hǎi	海	sea, ocean	海边 hǎibiān sea shore, sea coast	海
huà	化	change, transform	文化 wénhuà culture, 暖化 nuǎnhuà warming	化
huán	环	linked-shaped, surround	环境 huánjìng environment	環
jiā	加	add	加州 Jiāzhōu California, 参加 cānjiā participate (in)	加
jiāng	将	about to, will	将来 jiānglái in the future	將
jiào	较	compare*	比较 bǐjiào relatively	較
jìng	境	border	环境 huánjìng environment	境
lǐ	理	reason, logic	管理 guǎnlǐ management	理
liàng	亮	light, shine	漂亮 piàoliang pretty	亮
líng	零	zero	零下 língxià below zero	零
piào	漂	good-looking*	漂亮 piàoliang pretty	漂
rè	热	hot		熱

suì	岁	*years of age*		歲
xià	夏	*summer**	夏天 xiàtiān *summer*	夏
yìng	应	*respond**	应该 yīnggāi *should, ought to*	應
yòu	又	*both . . . and; again*	又闷又热 yòu mēn yòu rè *both humid and hot*	又
zāng	脏	*dirty*		髒
zhào	照	*illuminate; take a photo*	照片 zhàopiàn *photos,* 照照片 zhào zhàopiàn *take photos,* 照顾 zhàogù *take care of*	照

Lesson 22

bèi	备	*prepare**	准备 zhǔnbèi *prepare*	備
cān	参	*participate**	参加 cānjiā *participate*	參
chú	除	*except, besides; remove*	除了 chúle *except, besides*	除
dōng	冬	*winter*	冬天 dōngtiān *winter*	冬
duì	队	*team*	校队 xiàoduì *school team*	隊
ér	而	*and, but, or*	而且 érqiě *in addition*	而
fù	复	*resume, renew**	复习 fùxí *review*	復
huò	或	*or, perhaps*	或者 huòzhě *perhaps*	或
jiāo, jiào	教	*teach*	教室 jiàoshì *classroom,* 家教 jiājiào *tutor*	教
kòng	空	*free time*	有空 yǒu kòng *have free time,* 没空 méi kòng *do not have time*	空
liàn	练	*practice*	练习 liànxí *practice,* 训练 xùnliàn *to train*	練
nuǎn	暖	*warm**	暖和 nuǎnhuo *warm;* 暖化 nuǎnhuà *warming*	暖

pà	怕	*fear*		怕
shēn	身	*body**	身体 shēntǐ *body*	身
shì	视	*vision**	电视 diànshì *television,* 重视 zhòngshì *value*	视
shōu	收	*collect, gather up*	收拾 shōushi *straighten up, clean up*	收
tǐ	体	*body**	身体 shēntǐ *body*	體
tiào	跳	*jump*	跳舞 tiàowǔ *dance*	跳
wǔ	舞	*dance*	跳舞 tiàowǔ *dance*	舞
xuě	雪	*snow*	下雪 xià xuě *to snow,* 滑雪 huáxuě *skiing*	雪
yǔ	雨	*rain*	下雨 xià yǔ *(it's) raining*	雨
zhě	者	*or**	或者 huòzhě *perhaps*	者
zhǔn	准	*accurate*	准备 zhǔnbèi *prepare*	準

Lesson 23

bǎo	保	*protect**	保护 bǎohù *protect,* 环保 huánbǎo *environmental protection*	保
bì	必	*must*	不必 bù bì *no need to*	必
biàn	便	*convenient**	方便 fāngbiàn *convenient*	便
chéng	城	*city**	城市 chéngshì *city*	城
chūn	春	*spring*	春天 chūntiān *spring,* 春节 Chūnjié *Spring Festival (Chinese New Year)*	春
dān	单	*alone**, odd-numbered**	简单 jiǎndān *simple*	單
dòng	动	*move*	运动 yùndòng *movement, exercise*	動
duǎn	短	*short*	长短 chángduǎn *length*	短

gèng	更	*even more*		更
jiǎn	简	*simple**	简单 jiǎndān *simple*	簡
jié	节	*festival**, classifier for classes	春节 Chūnjié Spring Festival (*Chinese New Year*), 一节课 yī jié kè *one class*, 节约 jiéyuē *conserve*	節
lián	连	*even*		連
lìng	另	*in addition**	另外 lìngwài *in addition*	另
pá	爬	*climb*	爬山 pá shān *climb a mountain*	爬
pián	便	*inexpensive**	便宜 piányi *cheap, inexpensive*	便
qiě	且	*also**	而且 érqiě *moreover*	且
shì	式	*style*	式样 shìyàng *style*, 美式足球 Měishì zúqiú *American football*	式
sòng	送	*send, deliver, give as a present*		送
tiáo	条	*classifier for long, thin objects*	一条裤子 yī tiáo kùzi *a "pair" of slacks*	條
tiě	铁	*iron*	地铁 dìtiě *subway*	鐵
wù	务	*business**	服务员 fúwùyuán *clerk, waiter* (mainland China usage)	務
xīn	新	*new*	新年 xīnnián *New Year*	新
yán	颜	*color**	颜色 yánsè *color*	顏
yí	宜	*suitable**	便宜 piányi *inexpensive, cheap*	宜

yuán	员	*person who performs a job**	服务员 fúwùyuán *clerk, waiter* (mainland China usage)	員
yuè	越	*the more**	越来越 yuèláiyuè *more and more*	越
yùn	运	*move, transport*	运动 yùndòng *movement, exercise*	運

Lesson 24

bǎi	百	*hundred*	一百块 yī bǎi kuài *one hundred dollars*	百
chèn	衬	*shirt**	衬衫 chènshān *shirt*	襯
dài	戴	*wear (on the head, neck, and extremities)*		戴
è	饿	*hungry*	饿死了 èsǐle *starving to death*	餓
fèi	费	*expense, spend, waste*	浪费 làngfèi *waste*, 学费 xuéfèi *tuition*	費
gǎn	感	*feel**	感冒 gǎnmào *a cold*, 感觉 gǎnjué *feeling*	感
hēi	黑	*black*	黑色 hēisè *black colored*	黑
jí	极	*extremely**	好极了 hǎojíle *terrific, great*	極
jià	价	*price*	讨价还价 tǎo jià-huán jià *bargain back and forth*, 价钱 jiàqian *price*, 减价 jiǎn jià *reduce the price*	價
jiē	街	*street*	逛街 guàng jiē *go window shopping, stroll along the streets*	街
jīn	金	*gold, metal*	金色 jīnsè *gold colored*, 现金 xiànjīn *cash*, 现金卡 xiànjīnkǎ *debit card*	金

kù	裤	*slacks**	裤子 kùzi *slacks*	褲
lóu	楼	*building; floor of a building*	楼梯 lóutī *staircase*	樓
mǎ	码	*number, symbol, code**	号码 hàomǎ *number (telephone number)*, 扫码 sǎo mǎ *scan a code*	碼
qì	汽	*steam, gas*	汽车 qìchē *car*, 出 **zū**(汽)车 chūzū (qì)chē *taxi*	汽
qún	裙	*skirt**	裙子 qúnzi *skirt*	裙
sǎo	扫	*sweep, scan*	扫地 sǎo dì *sweep the floor*, 扫码 sǎo mǎ *scan a code*	掃
shān	衫	*shirt**	衬衫 chènshān *shirt*	衫
shāng	商	*commerce**	商店 shāngdiàn *(a) shop*	商
shuāng	双	*pair*	一双鞋 yī shuāng xié *a pair of shoes*	雙
sǐ	死	*dead*	累死了 lèisǐle *dead tired*, 饿死了 èsǐle *starving to death*	死
wà	袜	*socks**	袜子 wàzi *socks*	襪
wèi	位	*polite classifier for people*	您是哪位？ nín shì nǎwèi? *Who are you?*	位
xié	鞋	*shoe*	鞋子 xiézi *shoe*, 运动鞋 yùndòngxié *athletic shoes, sneakers, gym shoes*, 皮鞋 píxié *leather shoes*	鞋
xìn	信	*trust*	短信 duǎnxìn *text message*, 信用卡 xìnyòng kǎ *credit card*, 微信 Wēixìn *WeChat*	信

| zhé | 折 | *bend, twist, fold (clothes)* | 打折 dǎ zhé *give a discount* | 折 |
| zhǒng | 种 | *kind of* | 这种衣服 zhè zhǒng yīfu *this kind of clothing* | 種 |

Lesson 25

bāo	包	*wrap; classifier for packages*	包饺子 bāo jiǎozi *wrap dumplings,* 红包 hóngbāo *red gift envelope*	包
bǎo	饱	*full (of food)*	吃饱了 chībǎo le *ate until full*	飽
hái	孩	*child**	孩子 háizi *child*	孩
huà	划	*plan, mark*	计划 jìhuà *plan*	劃
huáng	黄	*yellow*	黄色 huángsè *yellow colored*	黃
jì	计	*calculate*	计划 jìhuà *plan*	計
jià	假	*holiday, vacation**	放假 fàng jià *begin vacation,* 暑假 shǔ jià *summer vacation,* 寒假 hán jià *winter vacation*	假
jiè	介	*introduce**	介绍 jièshào *introduce*	介
jīng	睛	*eyeball**	眼睛 yǎnjing *eye*	睛
lán	蓝	*blue*	蓝色 lánsè *blue colored*	藍
lè	乐	*happy**	快乐 kuàilè *happy,* 可乐 kělè *cola,* 可口可乐 Kěkǒukělè *Coca Cola*	樂
lóng	龙	*dragon*		龍
ná	拿	*take*		拿
shào	绍	*introduce**	介绍 jièshào *introduce*	紹
shū	叔	*uncle**	叔叔 shūshu *uncle*	叔
tiē	贴	*paste*		貼

yǎn	眼	*eye**	眼睛 yǎnjing *eye*	眼
yè	夜	*evening, night*	夜里 yèlǐ *in the middle of the night*, 年夜饭 niányè fàn *New Year's Eve family dinner*	夜
yú	鱼	*fish*		魚
zhe; zháo	着	*verb suffix**	忙着 mángzhe *being busy*, 坐着 zuòzhe *sitting*; 睡不着 shuìbuzháo *unable to fall asleep*	著
zhèng	正	*precisely*		正

Index of radicals for simplified characters

1 stroke

、	一	丨	丿	乙, 乚
1	2	3	4	5

2 strokes

亠	冫	冖	讠	二	十	厂	匚	卜	刂
6	7	8	9	10	11	12	13	14	15
冂	八, 丷	人, 入 亻	勹	儿	几	厶	又	廴	
16	17	18	19	20	21	22	23	24	25
卩, 卪 阝(L)	阝(R)	凵	刀, 𠂊	力					
26	27	28	29	30	31				

3 strokes

氵	忄	宀	丬, 爿	广	门	辶	工	土	士
32	33	34	35	36	37	38	39	40	41

艹	大	卄 (below)	尢	寸	弋	扌	小	口	囗
42	43	44	45	46	47	48	49	50	51
巾	山	彳	彡	夕	攵	犭	忄	彐, 彑	尸
52	53	54	55	56	57	58	59	60	61
己, 巳	弓	屮	女	幺	子	纟, 糸	马	巛	
62	63	64	65	66	67	68	69	70	

4 strokes

灬	斗	文	方	火	心	户	礻, 示	王	书
71	72	74	74	75	76	77	78	79	80
木	犬	歹	车	戈	比	瓦	止	支	日
81	82	83	84	85	86	87	88	89	90
曰	贝	见	父	牛	手	毛	气	攵	片
91	92	93	94	95	96	97	98	99	100
斤	爪, 爫	月	欠	风	殳	聿, 肀	母, 毋	水	
101	102	103	104	105	106	107	108	109	

5 strokes

穴	立	疒	衤	示	石	龙	业	目	田
110	111	112	113	114	115	116	117	118	119
罒	皿	钅	矢	禾	白	瓜	鸟	用	矛
120	121	122	123	124	125	126	127	128	129
疋	皮								
130	131								

6 strokes

衣	羊, 䒑	米	耒	老, 耂	耳	臣	西	页	虍
132	133	134	135	136	137	138	139	140	141

虫	缶	舌	竹, ⺮	白	自	血	舟	羽	艮
142	143	144	145	146	147	148	149	150	151

糸
152

7 strokes

辛	言	麦, 麥	走	赤	豆	酉	辰	豕	卤
153	154	155	156	157	158	159	160	161	162

里	足	豸	谷	釆	身	角
163	164	165	166	167	168	169

8 strokes

青	其	雨	齿	黾, 鼀	金	隹	鱼
170	171	172	173	174	175	176	177

9 strokes

音	革	骨	食	鬼
178	179	180	181	182

10 strokes		11 strokes		12 strokes		14 strokes
鬥	髟	麻	鹿	黑	鼠	鼻
183	184	185	186	187	188	189

Index of radicals for traditional characters

1 stroke

一	丨	丶	丿	乙, ㄥ	亅
1	2	3	4	5	6

2 strokes

二	亠	人, 亻 儿	入	八	冂	冖	冫	几
7	8	9	10	11	12	13	14	15	16
凵	刀, 刂	力	勹	匕	匚	匸	十	卜	卩, 㔾
17	18	19	20	21	22	23	24	25	26
厂	厶	又							
27	28	29							

3 strokes

口	囗	土	士	夂	夊	夕	大	女	子
30	31	32	33	34	35	36	37	38	39

宀	寸	小	尢	尸	屮	山	巛, 川	工	己, 巳, 巳
40	41	42	43	44	45	46	47	48	49
巾	干	幺	广	廴	廾	弋	弓	彐	彡
50	51	52	53	54	55	56	57	58	59
彳									
60									

4 strokes

心, 忄	戈	戶, 户	手, 扌	支	攴, 攵	文	斗	斤	方
61	62	63	64	65	66	67	68	69	70
无	日	曰	月	木	欠	止	歹	殳	毋, 母
71	72	73	74	75	76	77	78	79	80
比	毛	氏	气	水, 氵	火, 灬	爪, 爫	父	爻	爿
81	82	83	84	85	86	87	88	89	90
片	牙	牛	犬, 犭						
91	92	93	94						

5 strokes

玄	玉, 王	瓜	瓦	甘	生	用	田	疋	疒
95	96	97	98	99	100	101	102	103	104
癶	白	皮	皿	目	矛	矢	石	示, 礻	禸
105	106	107	108	109	110	111	112	113	114
禾	穴								
115	116								

6 strokes

立	竹, 竹	米	糸, 糸	缶	网, 罒	羊	羽	老, 耂	而
117	118	119	120	121	122	123	124	125	126
耒	耳	聿	肉, 月	臣	自	至	臼	舌	舛
127	128	129	130	131	132	133	134	135	136

舟	艮	色	艸, 艹	虎	虫	血	行	衣, 衤
137	138	139	140	141	142	143	144	145

7 strokes

西, 襾	見	角	言	谷	豆	豕	豸	貝	赤
146	147	148	149	150	151	152	153	154	155
走	足	身	車	辛	辰	辵, 辶	邑, 阝 (R)	酉	采
156	157	158	159	160	161	162	163	164	165
里									
166									

8 strokes

金	長	門	阜, 阝 (L)	隶	佳	雨	青
167	168	169	170	171	172	173	174

9 strokes

非	面	革	韋	韭	音	頁	風	飛	食
175	176	177	178	179	180	181	182	183	184
首	香								
185	186								

10 strokes

馬	骨	高	髟	鬥	鬯	鬲	鬼
187	188	189	190	191	192	193	194

11 strokes

魚	鳥	鹵	鹿	麥
195	196	197	198	199

12 strokes

麻	黃	黍	黑	黹
200	201	202	203	204

13 strokes

黽, 黾	鼎	鼓	鼠, 鼡
205	206	207	208

## 14 strokes		## 15 strokes	## 16 strokes		## 17 strokes
鼻	齊	齒	龍	龜	龠
209	210	211	212	213	214

Index of structures and functions